CARNIVAL
GLASS

Ellen T. Schroy

©2006 Krause Publications

Published by

kp **krause publications**
An Imprint of F+W Publications

700 East State Street • Iola, WI 54990-0001
715-445-2214 • 888-457-2873

Our toll-free number to place an order or obtain
a free catalog is (800) 258-0929.

Library of Congress Catalog Number: 2006922403

ISBN 13-digit: 978-0-89689-422-8
ISBN 10-digit: 0-89689-422-3

Designed by Stacy Bloch and Kay Sanders
Edited by Kristine Manty

Printed in China

Acknowledgments

I remember personal conversations years ago with Marion Hartung, a pioneer in the glass-researching field, who was eager to impart her wisdom about this beautiful carnival glassware. She stressed how important it was that we consider these pieces as parts of sets, not just water pitchers or tumblers, but *water sets*. She impressed me with how important knowing the base color is to carnival glass. I am fortunate to have known this great lady as well as those who are currently carrying the research forward today.

We appreciate the efforts of auctioneers who regularly catalog and sell the iridescent rainbow of carnival glass all cross the country. They eagerly shared catalogs and photographs with me. A special thank you goes to Kris Remmen of Remmen Auction & Appraisal Service, Portland, OR, for his pricing help and photographs.

Several private collectors also shared their love of carnival glass by lending treasured pieces as well as photographs. Jackie and Randy Poucher, who live in the Tampa Bay area in Florida, graciously invited us into their home, allowing us to photograph one of the finest carnival glass collections in the world. Also deserving of our appreciation are Dick and Sherry Betker, Franklin, WI, and George Pientka, Stevens Point, WI. Without their help and guidance this project would not have been possible. Other private collectors include Susan K. Bargar, Delaware, OH; Miriam Fischer, New York, NY; Susan Howell, Carrollton, TX; Kasi Kirby, Houston, TX; S. Louis Rouse, Niota, TN; Jennifer Smith, Baltimore, OH; Kathryn Smith, San Bernardino, CA; Lynn Tice, Pickens, SC; and Cheryl Webber, Tacoma, WA. A special thank you to photographer Paul Goodwin for his excellent work.

To all of the collectors and auctioneers who helped us, we say thanks. You are as wonderful as the glass you treasure.

Contents

Patterns

Introduction

Warman's Companion: Carnival Glass is a price guide devoted to the magical glass that collectors fondly call mass-produced iridescent glassware. Carnival glass has an interesting history and to many collectors, the majesty of these techniques continue today, allowing them to add more and more examples to their collecting hobby. During the early production years of carnival glass, production was world wide, just as it is today. For the purposes of information gathering, we've chosen to concentrate on the original major American manufacturers.

The term "carnival glass" has evolved through the years as glass collectors have responded to the idea that much of this beautiful glassware was made as give-away glass at local carnivals and fairs. However, more of it was made and sold through the same channels as pattern glass and Depression glass. Some patterns were indeed giveaways, and others were used as advertising premiums, souvenirs, etc. Whatever the origin, the term "carnival glass" today encompasses glassware that is usually pattern molded and treated with metallic salts, creating that unique coloration that is so desirable to collectors.

Early names for iridescent glassware, which early 20th Century consumers believed to have all come from foreign manufacturers, include Pompeian Iridescent, Venetian Art, and Mexican Aurora. Another popular early name was "Nancy Glass" as some patterns were believed to have come from the Daum, Nancy glassmaking area in France. This was at a time when the artistic cameo glass was enjoying great success. While the iridescent glassware being made by such European glassmakers as Loetz influenced the American market place, it was Louis Tiffany's Favrile glass that really caught the eye of glass consumers of the early 1900s. It seems an easy leap to transform Tiffany's shimmering glassware to something that could be mass produced, allowing what we call carnival glass today to become "poor man's Tiffany." However, this seemingly easy leap really took years of experimentation by several of the major glasshouses to develop techniques and formulas that gave the desired results.

To better understand carnival glass, it's necessary to understand some of the basic elements of glass making. Up until the time Deming Jarvis invented and patented glass-making equipment, most glassware was made by blowing hot molten glass into molds or fashioning a piece entirely by hand. Glassware of this period tended to be very expensive and until Jarvis and his associates got the fledging industry running in New England, most glassware was imported to America. However, the industrial advances made using natural materials found in America soon changed that. Quantities of natural materials such as silica, salts, wood, and gas led to the development of glass manufacturers in New England, and after transportation improvements led Americans West, soon another area of glass manufacturing sprang up in the western Pennsylvania region, as well as the Ohio River region.

By using and improving on the techniques developed by Jarvis, molten glass could be taken and put into molds that were pressed into shapes and designs. These designs evolved to reflect the themes that were popular at the time, such as florals, patterns that reflected nature, and fanciful designs. Most of the early glassware production created clear glassware, but some colors were introduced by combining various chemicals into the molten glass. This pressed glass was commonly called "pattern glass" as it became the norm for American consumers to use in their households and commercial enterprises.

Carnival glass is iridized glassware that is created by pressing hot molten glass into molds, just as pattern glass had evolved. Some forms are hand finished, while others are completely formed by molds. After the glassware was made, an iridized coating is added to give the luminescent look we associate with carnival glass today. It was the glass gatherer's skill that allowed him to carefully fill a mold with just the right amount of molten glass. He quickly cut it off with shears, allowing it to gently drop into the mold. A plunger was then usually pressed into the mold and the resulting pressure squeezed the molten mixture to fill the entire mold. After the pressing process was completed, a tool called a "snap" was attached to the collar base, known as the "marie." Any necessary hand finishing would take place at this point. If necessary, the piece was re-heated gently so that the metallic coatings would adhere properly.

Molds used to make carnival glass are similar to those used to make pattern glass and later Depression glass. Some molds were hinged in two to four places to allow for easy removal of the piece. Many patterns had a limited number of molds, such as a bowl and tumbler. During the production process, a bowl could become a plate, a tumbler could become a hat, and a bonbon could become a calling card tray by simple maneuvers of the molds and hand-finishing techniques. Making molds for the glass industry was often the responsibility of the designers at individual glasshouses, but also to specialty companies, such as the Hipkins Novelty Mould Shop in Martin's Ferry, Ohio. Because making molds was so expensive, it should be no surprise that early glassware manufacturers got as much use out of these molds as they could.

Early pattern glass molds were wood and some carnival glass pattern wooden molds are known to exist, but by the time carnival glassware production got into high gear, the molds were constructed of durable metals, such as iron. Because these molds were longer lasting, greater quantities of any particular pattern could be produced; and, if and when a glasshouse failed, the molds could be sold as a valuable asset to another glassmaker. This explains how some patterns traveled from maker to maker. Imperial Glass bought Heisey Glass molds after it closed in 1958. In 1960, Imperial added molds from Cambridge Glass to its inventory. Often the second- or third-generation owner would use the molds to create new colors just as glassmakers are doing today with old molds.

To achieve the marvelous iridescent colors that carnival glass collectors seek, a process was developed where a liquid solution of metallic salts was put onto the still hot glass form after it was unmolded. As the liquid evaporated, a fine metallic surface was left which refracts light into wonderful colors. The name given to the iridescent spray by early glassmakers was "dope." Mixing the chemicals for this metallic mixture usually took place in a separate building at the glass factory, referred to as a "dope house." After the glass was doped, it was sent to annealing lehrs to cool. After the glassware cooled, it was inspected for defects and then often packed in large shipping barrels filled with straw and transported to eager consumers.

Many of the forms created by carnival glass manufacturers were accessories to the china American housewives so loved. Sets to serve berries, numerous types of bowls, and water sets, as well as groupings known as table sets, which included covered butter dishes, creamers, covered sugars, and spooners, were sold with the idea that they would make accent pieces on sideboards and dining room tables. Some pieces were more decorative in nature and meant to help display one's wealth by having it as a centerpiece.

By the early 1900s, consumers could find carnival glassware at such popular stores including F. W. Woolworth or McCrory's. To capitalize on the popular fancy for these colored wares, some other industries bought large quantities of carnival glass and turned them into "packers," a term that reflects the practice where baking powder, mustard, or other household products were packed into a special piece of glass that could take on another life after the original product was used. Lee Manufacturing Co. used iridized carnival glass as premiums for its baking powder and other products, causing some early carnival glass to be known by the generic term "baking powder glass."

Every glasshouse had its own special metallic salts recipe. By experimentation, they discovered that metallic salts applied to very hot glassware turned in a matte or satin-like finish, known as satin. Applying the iridescent materials to slightly cooler glassware created bright shiny surfaces. These shiny finishes are referred to as radium when they have a mirror-like quality. Shades of blue and purple that seem to have an electric quality to their iridescent finish are known as electric. Because the pieces were shaped before being iridized, minute breaks in the iridescent surface can occur. Some manufacturers took this into account when creating interesting designs. Patterns created with three-dimensional characteristics, such as Heavy Grape, took advantage of the fact that the iridized covering would be more colorful on the background than on the plump grapes, making them stand out by contrast. Pieces could be sprayed on both the inside and outsides, while forms such as creamers, pitchers, and tumblers were sprayed only on the outside. Because the "snap" was adhered over the marie, this area is left unsprayed. By observing the color of the marie, collectors know what color the base glass is.

When the glass form was re-heated, some design aspects, often edges, whitened, creating an opalescent quality and colors such as aqua opalescent or peach opalescent. If a piece received a further acid treatment, an icy or frosted effect was created, resulting in some of the pastels, such as ice blue, ice green, and white. Whenever the glassware was reheated, the chances of damage increased, causing the manufacturer to endure more cost in the way of time for the artisan and also in the length of time it took from the first gather of glass to the end product. Just as it is today, "time is money," so pieces created in pastels or opalescent colors were more scarce, their production was limited, and usually their values are higher than ordinary carnival colors.

Today's manufacturing methods are different in that pieces can be sprayed on both sides, eliminating the un-sprayed marie. This can be used as a clue in determining the age of some carnival glass patterns, as well as observing the colors, finding an embossed trademark, etc. Today carnival glass is being made by the great American glasshouse, Fenton Glass. Visitors to the Fenton facilities in Williamstown, WV, can watch as actual pieces of glassware are created right in front of their eyes. Companies in India, Europe, and Egypt are creating other contemporary carnival glass pieces at the present time. How well these pieces will be embraced by the glass collectors remains to be seen.

Classic carnival glass production began in the early 1900s and continued about twenty years, but no one really documented or researched production until the first collecting wave struck in 1960. Today's collectors are much better informed, allowing them to carefully track the new carnival glassware patterns, makers, etc.

Marion T. Hartung was a pioneer in the glass-researching field when she started her project of documenting the myriad carnival glass patterns. By 1967, she had published several books on the topic. Her first series of seven books, published in 1960, include line drawings of the patterns, along with descriptive notes on the patterns and makers. The hobby of collecting antiques in Hartung's day was vastly different than it is today; many of the glasshouses had been destroyed by fires or through bad economics. Since she didn't have the marvelous reference books collectors treasure today, she created them. She researched with original materials and examined as many pieces of iridescent glass as she could, and was responsible for naming many of the patterns that only had factory numbers or codes.

Her book, *Carnival Glass In Color, A Collector's Reference Book*, was the first to include color photographs of this beautiful iridized glassware. In this book,

Hartung carefully discusses the times and fashions that influenced Americans in the early 1900s, noting that fashions were changing rapidly from 1900-1920, the prime time for carnival-glass production. When collectors think about how the styles of carnival glass patterns range from simple to complex geometrics to detailed naturalistic patterns, they can see how the changes in fashion influenced glass designs.

Other advancements that took place during this time period also affected life, allowing more consumers to participate in the free marketplace and seek out their favorite styles and colors. It is important to remember that carnival glasswares were sold in department stores as well as mass merchants, such as F. W. Woolworth, rather than through the general store often associated with a young America. Glassware by this time was mass-produced and sold in large quantities by such enterprising companies as Butler Brothers.

When the economics of the country soured in the 1920s, those interested in purchasing iridized glassware were not spared. Many of the leftover inventories of glasshouses that hoped to sell this mass-produced glassware found their way to wholesalers who in turn sold the wares to those who offered the glittering glass as prizes at carnivals, fairs, circuses, etc. Possibly because this was the last venue people associated the iridized glassware with, it became known as "carnival glass," rather than the exotic names such as Parisian Art, Vineland, Regal, Art Iridescent, Etruscan, or Aurora that the original salesmen of iridized glass probably preferred.

Carnival glass collecting as a hobby is one of the largest areas of the current antique glass marketplace. Part of the reason why is the excellent references today's collectors have in books such as Hartung's, as well as later researchers including Rose Presznick, David Doty, Carl O. Burns, Bill Edwards, Mike Carwile, and Glen and Steve Thistlewood. Add to this the idea that carnival glass collectors love to gather and swap information through club networks, newsletters, and meetings. These gatherings, whether in a small local group or a large convention, allow for the free exchange of information, as well as educational venues and associated auctions.

Organizations such as the American Carnival Glass Association and the International Carnival Glass Association are the largest. Active associations can be found all across America and Canada. The United Kingdom has its own version known as the Carnival Glass Society, Ltd., and collectors Down Under can meet at the Australian Carnival Enthusiasts Association, Inc.

Carnival glass collecting has also gotten a real boost in the formation of two on-line Web sites devoted to carnival glass. Known as www.cga, this for-fee Web site offers collectors a daily Webring, opportunities for on-line chats, plus links to carnival glass related sites, auctions, and educational articles. The on-line world of contemporary carnival glass is represented by Contemporary Carnival Glass Web site, www.carnivalglass.net. Another excellent on-line resource is the Web site of David Doty, www.ddoty.com. Doty includes identification, values, and information about reproductions in this easy-to-use site. (Please see P. 271 for more information about collectors' clubs and Web sites.)

A note about pricing

Collectors of carnival glass will not be surprised to see price ranges in this book. Why? Because the colors of the iridescent finish on a piece of carnival glass can vary from piece to piece and as such, so does the desirability of each piece change. Some carnival glass collectors seek a particular pattern; others specialize in patterns from one particular manufacturer. Other collectors look for particular colors, while others may choose only to collect a specific form. Add to this that the brilliant colors used for the basis of carnival glass can vary from what each set of eyes perceive and one can see how many variables come into play when evaluating the desirability of any given piece.

Sometimes the ranges are vast, representing patterns or forms that offer many differences; other times the ranges are closer, usually reflecting forms that are sold more readily, so more data could be analyzed and numbers calculated. Where only a few pieces are available for the database or prices seem extraordinary high, the term "rare" is used along with a dollar figure. Collectors should assume that lesser priced items might exist for any of the prices listed herein, but also that higher prices may have been averaged into the range formulas. Collectors should always pay what their heart tells them is a fair price, using any price guide as a guide and not an absolute.

Company Histories

Much of vintage American carnival glassware was created in the Ohio Valley, in the glasshouse-rich areas of Pennsylvania, Ohio, and West Virginia. The abundance of natural materials, good transportation, and skilled craftsmen that created the early American pattern glass manufacturing companies allowed many of them to add carnival glass to their production lines. Brief company histories of the major carnival glass manufacturers follow:

Cambridge Glass Company (Cambridge)

Cambridge Glass was a rather minor player in the carnival glass marketplace. Founded in 1901 as a new factory in Cambridge, Ohio, it focused on producing fine crystal tablewares. What carnival glass it did produce was imitation cut-glass patterns.

Colors used by Cambridge include marigold, as well as a few others.

Forms found in carnival glass by Cambridge include tablewares and vases, some with its trademark "Near-Cut."

Fenton Art Glass Company (Fenton)

Frank Leslie Fenton and his brothers, John W. Fenton and Charles H. Fenton, founded this truly American glassmaker in 1905 in Martins Ferry. Frank grew up around glasshouses, and started working at a glasshouse in Indiana, Pa., upon graduating from high school. Within a year, he was foreman at this factory. Three years later, he moved to Jefferson Glass, Steubenville, Ohio, and later to Bastow Glass, Couldersport, Pa. After Bastow Glass burned down, he went to work with Harry Northwood, Wheeling, WV. By 1905, he decided his future would be better if he and his brothers went into the glass business for themselves. Early production was of blanks, which the brothers soon learned to decorate themselves. They moved to a larger factory in Williamstown, WV. Today the Fenton family still makes quality glassware in Williamstown.

By 1907, Fenton was experimenting with iridescent glass, developing patterns and the metallic salt formulas that it became so famous for. Production of carnival glass continued at Fenton until the early 1930s. In 1970, Fenton began to re-issue carnival glass, creating new colors and forms as well as using traditional patterns.

Colors developed by Fenton are numerous. The company developed red and Celeste blue in the 1920s. A translucent pale blue, known as Persian blue, is also one of its more distinctive colors, as is a light yellow-green color known as vaseline. Fenton also produced delicate opalescent colors, including amethyst opalescent and red opalescent.

Forms made by Fenton are numerous. What distinguishes Fenton from other glassmakers is its attention to detail and hand finishing processes. Edges are found scalloped, fluted, tightly crimped, frilled, or pinched into a candy ribbon edge, also referred to as 3-in-1 edge.

Fenton Persian Medallion bowl, blue, candy-ribbon edge, **$85**.

Northwood Glass Company (Northwood)

Englishman Harry Northwood founded the Northwood Glass Company. Like Frank L. Fenton, he, too, was from a glass-making family. His family was well known for making beautiful cameo glass in the Stourbridge area. Also located in that area was the glass-making facility of Thomas Webb, who created "Bronze" and "Iris" glass, both iridescent lines. By the time he immigrated to America in 1881, he was influenced by these glassmakers. He became a glass etcher for Hobbs Brockunier Glass Company, Wheeling, WV. He moved to La Belle Glass Works, Bridgeport, Ohio, then to Phoenix Glass Co. in Pennsylvania, and back to La Belle. In November of 1887, Northwood and other investors bought the old Union Flint Glass factory in Martin's Ferry, Ohio, and renamed it "Northwood Glass Company." By 1892, the factory was moved to Ellwood City, Pa., but it didn't thrive at this location. In 1895, Northwood created the new Northwood Glass Company of Indiana, Pa., by moving into the former factory of Indiana Glass Company. In 1899, this factory was sold to the new glass conglomerate, National Glass Company. Northwood returned to England as its sales representative. He must have missed the American glassmakers as he returned and purchased the old Hobbs Brockunier factory in Wheeling and started the Harry Northwood and Company factory, which continued until 1925. It was at this factory, he developed his glass formulas for carnival glass, naming it "Golden Iris" in 1908. Northwood was one of the pioneers of the glass manufacturers who marked his wares. Marks range from a full script signature to a simple underscored capital N in a circle. However, not all Northwood glassware is marked.

Colors that Northwood created were many. Collectors prefer its pastels, such as ice blue, ice green, and white. It is also known for several stunning blue shades. The one color that Northwood did not develop was red.

Forms of Northwood patterns ranged from typical table sets, bowls, and water sets to whimsical novelties, such as a pattern known as Corn, which realistically depicts an ear of corn.

Millersburg Glass Company (Millersburg)

John W. Fenton started the Millersburg Glass Company in September of 1908. Perhaps it was the factory's more obscure location or the lack of business experience by John Fenton, but the company failed by 1911. The factory was bought by

Northwood Grape and Cable dresser tray, ice blue, **$655.**

Millersburg Zig-Zag ice cream-shaped bowl, green with radium iridescence, **$125.**

Samuel Fair and John Fenton, and renamed the Radium Glass Company, but it lasted only a year.

Colors produced by Millersburg are amethyst, green, and marigold. Shades such as blue and vaseline were added on rare occasions. The company is well known for its bright radium finishes.

Forms produced at Millersburg are mostly bowls and vases. Pattern designers at Millersburg often took one theme and developed several patterns from it. Millersburg often used one pattern for the interior and a different one for the exterior.

Dugan Glass Company (Dugan)

The history of the Dugan Glass Company is closely related to Harry Northwood. Cousin Thomas Dugan came from the same region in England and grew up around the same glass houses as Harry Northwood. He immigrated to America in 1881. The cousins worked together at Hobbs Brockunier, Wheeling, WV, and also at Northwood Glass Co., Martin's Ferry, Ohio. Thomas Dugan became plant manager at the Northwood Glass Co., in Indiana, Pa., in 1895. By 1904, Dugan and his partner W. G. Minnemayer bought the former Northwood factory from the now defunct National Glass conglomerate and opened as the Dugan Glass Company. Dugan brother Alfred joined the company and stayed until the company became

Dugan Double Stem Rose dome-footed bowl with 3-in-1 edge, white and super iridescence, **$60**.

the Diamond Glass Company in 1913. At this time, Thomas Dugan moved to the Cambridge Glass Company, later Duncan and Miller and finally Hocking, Lancaster. Alfred left Diamond Glass, too, but later returned.

Understanding how the Northwood and Dugan families were linked helps collectors to understand the linkage of these three companies. Their productions were similar; molds were swapped, re-tooled, etc.

Colors attributed to Dugan and Diamond include amethyst, marigold, peach opalescent, and white. The company developed deep amethyst shades, some almost black.

Forms made by both Dugan and Diamond mirrored what other glass companies were producing. The significant contribution by Dugan and later Diamond were feet – either ball or spatula shapes; they are also known for deeply crimped edges.

Diamond Glass Company (Diamond)

This company was started as the Dugan brothers departed the carnival glass-making scene in 1913. However, Alfred Dugan returned and became general manager until his death in 1928. After a fire in June 1931, the factory closed.

Imperial Glass Company (Imperial)

Edward Muhleman and a syndicate founded the Imperial Glass Company at Bellaire, Ohio, in 1901, with production beginning in 1904. It started with pressed glass tableware patterns, as well as lighting fixtures. The company's marketing strategy included selling to important retailers of its day, such as F. W. Woolworth and McCrory and Kresge, getting glassware into the hands of American housewives. Imperial also became a major exporter of glassware, including its brilliant carnival patterns. During the Depression, it filed for bankruptcy in 1931, but was able to continue on. By 1962, it was again producing carnival glass patterns. By April 1985, the factory was closed and the molds sold.

Imperial Ripple vase, 12" h, 3-3/8" base, electric purple and electric highlights, **$100**.

Colors made by Imperial include typical carnival colors such as marigold. It added interesting shades of green, known as helios, a pale ginger ale shade known as clambroth, and a brownish smoke shade.

Forms created by Imperial tend to be functional, such as berry sets and table sets. Patterns vary from wonderful imitation cut glass patterns to detailed florals and naturalistic designs.

United States Glass Company (US Glass)

In 1891, a consortium of 15 American glass manufacturers joined together as the United States Glass Company. This company was successful in continuing pattern glass production, as well as developing new glass lines. By 1911, it had begun limited production of carnival glass lines, often using existing pattern glass tableware molds. By the time a tornado destroyed the last of its glass factories in Glassport in 1963, it was no longer producing glassware.

US Glass Palm Beach tri-corner bowl, honey amber, **$125**.

Colors associated with US Glass are marigold, white, and a rich honey amber.

Forms tend to be table sets and functional forms.

Westmoreland Glass Company (Westmoreland)

Started as the Westmoreland Speciality Company, Grapeville, Pa., in 1889, this company originally made novelties, and glass packing containers, such as candy containers. Researchers have identified its patterns being advertised by Butler Brothers as early as 1908. Carnival glass production continued into the 1920s. In the 1970s, Westmoreland, too, began to re-issue carnival glass patterns and novelties. However, this ceased in February of 1996 when the factory burned.

Westmoreland Corinth jack-in-the-pulpit vase, teal, **$50**.

Colors originally used by Westmoreland were typical carnival colors, such as blue and marigold. Forms include tablewares and functional forms, containers, etc.

Time Line

1889 Westmoreland Specialty Glass Company is founded in Grapeville, Pa.

1901 Cambridge Glass is founded in Cambridge, Ohio.

1904 Dugan Glass Company forms. Production also begins at Imperial Glass.

1905 Fenton Glass Company founded in Martins Ferry.

1907 Fenton experiments with metallic salts to create iridescent colors.

1908 Spring—Harry Northwood develops Golden Iris. September—John W. Fenton founds Millersburg Glass Company. September—Butler Brothers first advertise a "Golden Sunset Iridescent Assortment" of glassware made by Fenton, which included its Beaded Star, Diamond Point Columns, and Waterlily and Cattails patterns.

1910 Butler Brothers advertises Westmoreland patterns such as Scales, Louisa, and Smooth Rays as an "Antique Iridescent Novelty Assortment."

1911 Imperial advertises its Imperial Grape line in Amber Flame, Dragon Blue, Helios, and Azure. Butler Brothers advertise Millersburg patterns such as Rose columns, Peacock at Urn, Dolphin, and Cherries.

1911 Millersburg Glass Company files for bankruptcy. Former Millersburg factory buys and renames Radium Glass Company. US Glass starts production of carnival glass.

1912 Radium Glass Company goes out of business. Butler Brothers advertises US Glass patterns including Palm Beach and Cosmos and Cane.

1913 Dugan Glass Company closes. Diamond Glass Company forms.

1915 Imperial advertises patterns such as Lustre Rose, Imperial Grape, Pansy, Double Dutch, Ripple, and Windmill. Diamond advertises patterns such as Stork and Rushes, Vining Twigs, Beaded Basket, Maple Leaf, Persian Garden, Leaf Rays, and Wildflower.

1919 Harry Northwood dies.

1920s Fenton introduces red and celeste blue. Late—Westmoreland discontinues carnival glass production.

1925 Harry Northwood and Company goes out of business.

1930s Fenton switches its focus from carnival glass to other glasswares.

1931 Diamond Glass Company closes.

1948 Frank L. Fenton dies.

1950s Imperial buys out Cambridge Glass.

1962 Imperial begins to re-make carnival glass.

1963 US Glass closes.

1970 Fenton re-issues carnival glass.

1970s Westmoreland re-issues carnival glass.

1985 Imperial Glass closes.

1996 Westmoreland closes.

Colors of Carnival Glass

Think of "color, color, color" just as realtors go about shouting "location, location, location." Color is certainly what carnival glass is all about. There are two types of colors that carnival glass collectors need to know. The first is the base color. To determine the base color of carnival glass, you need to find the marie (non-iridized base). The next step is to hold the piece up to check the color. Having a strong light source is crucial to determining the base color. Knowing the base color will help you determine the value of your carnival glass. While still holding the piece near that strong light source, examine the iridescent coloration to determine the color of that as well as the base color. Knowing the pattern is the third most important element in determining value.

Carnival glass collectors now recognize more than 60 colors of glassware. It is important to remember that every glass manufacturer had its own recipes for batch colors and also secret combinations of the metallic salts that created the iridescent effect. Add to that the thought that every one of us perceives color slightly different, and you can easily see how variations exist and that no two pieces of carnival glass are the same. Embracing these variations helps collectors find the treasured pieces of carnival glass and enjoy them for years.

Listed here are brief explanations of the most often seen colors and examples to illustrate them.

Amber and honey amber

Amber is a yellow to brown tinted base glass, which usually shows off multicolored iridescence well. Honey amber is a brownish-marigold iridescence on a clear base. This color is usually restricted to US Glass pieces.

Amberina

Amberina is a blend of red glass shading to a yellowish color. Putting selenium into the molten batch causes the red coloration. When the mixture is reheated, the colors blend into amberina.

Amber, Omnibus, US Glass, tumbler, 4-1/4" h, **$150-$250 (scarce).**

Amberina, Double Scroll, Imperial, candlesticks, red to amberina, **$600.**

Amethyst, Lavender and Purple

The terms amethyst, lavender, and purple were used inter-changeable for many years of carnival glass collecting. Today, collectors prefer to identify pieces as amethyst when the base color of a piece is a medium to light shade of purple; lavender pieces as the lightest shade of purple; and purple when they resemble deep purple grape juice.

Amethyst, Hobnail, Millersburg, tumbler, one rough hob, **$600.**

Amethyst, Holly, Fenton, flat plate, 9-1/2" d, **$700-$1,000.**

Lavender, Grape and Cable, Northwood, tumbler, 4" h, **$100-$150.**

Purple, Heavy Grape, Imperial, chop plate, 11" d, **$400-$800.**

Purple, Greek Key, Northwood, tumbler, 4-1/4" h, **$125-$200.**

Aqua and aqua opalescent

Aqua carnival glass is a pretty shade of light blue with a hint of green. Some collectors call pieces "teal" when the blue is more predominate. **Aqua opalescent** is very popular with carnival glass collectors as it combines the vibrancy of aqua with the allure of milky white opalescence and marigold carnival iridescence. Northwood perfected the color and created most of the known aqua opalescent pieces. **Butterscotch** refers to the color created when marigold iridescence is found on an aqua opalescent base.

Aqua opalescent, Dragon and Lotus, Fenton, ruffled bowl, 9" d, **$2,200.**

Above: Aqua opalescent, Dandelion, Northwood, mug, 3-1/2" h, **$450-$600.** Left: Aqua, Holly, Fenton, 3-in-1 bowl, 8-1/2" d, **$200-$350 (rare).**

Black amethyst

Black amethyst is such a dense color that it appears almost opaque. It is the name used to describe a very deep amethyst.

Black amethyst, Persian Medallion, Fenton, flat plate, 6-1/4" d, **$250-$400.**

Blues: blue, celeste, ice, Persian, powder, Renninger and sapphire

Generally when blue is used to describe the base color of a piece, it is cobalt blue, but there are many colors and variations, from pale blue to aqua and violet. **Celeste blue** is created when pastel iridescence is used over a blue base. **Ice blue** is a base color that is a very pale blue; Northwood introduced its ice blue in 1912. **Persian blue** is a light blue base with a pastel iridescent finish. Most pieces in this color exhibit a cloudy appearance. **Powder blue** is a medium blue opaque, often called slag glass by collectors. **Renninger blue** is created when a dark marigold iridescence is used over a dark blue to purple base, with some turquoise influence. The name Renninger blue was coined after so many examples of this shade of blue were found at Renninger's Flea Markets. **Sapphire blue** is created when marigold iridescence is used over a blue base.

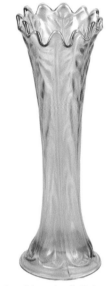

Ice blue, Leaf Columns, Northwood, vase, **$450.**

Celeste blue, Lustre Rose, Imperial, tumbler, **$200.**

Blue, Good Luck, Northwood, eight-ruffled bowl, 8-1/2" d, **$300-$550.**

Sapphire, Leaf Columns, Northwood, squatty vase, 7" h, **$850-$1,000 (rare).**

Clambroth

Clambroth is a color that is determined by the iridescence. The coloration is a light marigold over a slightly tinted base. Some collectors call pieces with a weak iridescence on a clear base clambroth. Imperial was responsible for most of the lightly tinted bases associated with this color. One of its most popular colors is known as "Ginger Ale" because of the close similarity to beverage color.

Emerald green, Imperial Grape, Imperial, carafe, 9" h, **$2,000-$3,000;** outstanding example, **$4,300.**

Greens: Green, emerald green, helios, ice green, lime green, lime green opalescent, olive green and russet green

As with many carnival colors, every manufacturer's recipe for green was slightly different. Fenton's green tends to be intense, while Millersburg is lighter. **Emerald green** carnival glass is a deep rich green; both Imperial and Northwood made emerald green. **Helios** is Imperial's original name for its interesting shade of green that is found with a pale golden iridescence. **Ice green** is a pale green base color covered with a frosty-looking pastel iridescence; Northwood introduced its ice green in 1912. **Lime green** is a bright almost neon green; it can be found with marigold iridescence. **Lime green opalescent** is a lime green base with pastel iridescence. **Olive green** is a deep brownish green, usually found with a marigold iridescent finish. **Russet green** is an olive- to brown-toned green.

Green, Peacocks, Northwood, bowl, pie-crust edge, 8-1/2" d, **$900-$1,400.**

Ice green, Oriental Poppy, Northwood, water pitcher and one tumbler, **$6,800.**

Lime green opalescent, Rustic, Fenton, vase, 9-1/4" h, **$1,250.**

Horehound

Horehound is a smoky gray base color, usually with blue or green highlights. It can also be a brownish tone.

Marigold, marigold over milk glass, pastel marigold, and pumpkin marigold

The most predominate color in carnival glass is marigold. It is the only color that takes its coloration from the iridescent treatment because it is usually on a clear glass body. If one thinks of the marigold flowers that bloom in the garden, this color will be easy to remember, as it is often a vibrant orange-toned hue. **Marigold over milk glass** is a combination that blends a bright marigold iridescence with a slightly translucent white milk glass base. Sometimes this is also called Moonstone. **Pastel marigold** is marigold iridescence over a clear glass body, but the iridescent finish is reheated into a satin finish, creating a soft color, often more of a yellow tone than the brighter orange associated with marigold. **Pumpkin marigold** is a collector's name for a deep dark marigold shade, more reminiscent of pumpkins than a marigold blossom.

Marigold, Corn, Northwood, vase, plain base, 6-1/2" h, **$900-$1,500** (scarce).

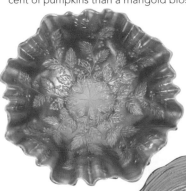

Marigold over milk glass, Holly, Fenton, bowl, 3-in-1 edge, **$2,000.**

Pastel marigold, Rose Show, Northwood, plate, 9" d, **$1,200-$1,800.**

Marigold, Diamond and Rib, Fenton, funeral vase, plunger base 21-1/2" h, **$1,100.**

Peach opalescent

Peach opalescent is a color that varies with each piece as the opalescence was created by reheating. Bone ash is added to the glass to create this milky white effect as the piece cooled. Dugan perfected the process and made the greatest quantity of this color. The pieces will also usually have a marigold iridescence.

Above: Peach opalescent, Fisherman's Mug, Dugan, mug, 4" h, **$1,000-$1,200 (rare)**. Right: Peach opalescent, Heavy Iris, Dugan, water pitcher, tankard, **$2,000**.

Red

Red is one of the most sought after carnival base colors. The red coloration is caused by putting selenium into the molten batch. Fenton and Imperial both created strong reds.

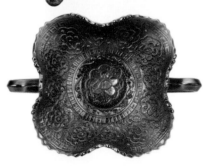

Left: Red, Lustre Rose, Imperial, bowl, footed, large, **$2,500**. Below: Red, Holly, Fenton, ruffled bowl, 9" d, **$1,200**. Below left: Red, Persian Medallion, Fenton, bonbon, two handles, **$700**.

Reverse amberina

Reverse amberina occurs when a piece shades from a red base to a yellow rim. The red coloration is caused by putting selenium into the molten batch. When the mixture is reheated, the colors blend into amberina.

Smoke

Smoke is a light gray base with iridescence that usually includes an iridescent cast of colors such as blue, green, amber, or brown. Both Imperial and Northwood made smoke colored pieces.

Left. Smoke, Morning Glory, Imperial, squatty vase, 5" h, **$165.**

Vaseline

The base color for vaseline is a light green-yellow. Because of uranium oxide added to create this color, it will glow if subjected to black light.

White

White is another color that is found on a clear base. The coloration is derived from a pastel iridescent finish. Dugan, Fenton, Millersburg, and Northwood all made white forms, each one differing slightly in hue. Northwood introduced its icy white in 1912.

Vaseline, Morning Glory, Imperial, miniature vase, 5" h, **$600-$800 (very rare).**

White, Drapery, Northwood, tumbler, **$3,100.**

White, Heavy Iris, Dugan, tumbler, 4" h, **$200-$300.**

Wisteria

Wisteria is a delicate light amethyst base color.

Acanthus

Made by Imperial.

Colors known: aqua, blue, clambroth, emerald green, green, helios, marigold, purple, and smoke.

Forms: bowls and chop plates.

Identifying characteristics: Design consists of swirling acanthus leaves. Carnival glass clubs have used this pattern for souvenirs with Fenton using original Imperial molds to make these limited-edition novelties. This pattern was first advertised in 1911.

Also known as: Imperial's #465; Parrot Tulip Swirl.

Reproductions: Fenton made a celeste blue bowl as a souvenir for the International Carnival Glass Association's Dallas 1995 convention.

Acanthus, Imperial, bowl, purple, electric iridescence, **$150.**

Acorn

Made by Fenton.

Colors known: amber opalescent, amethyst, aqua, blue, green, ice blue, lime green, marigold, marigold over milk glass, peach opalescent, powder blue, red, and vaseline.

Forms: bowls; rarely found in plates.

Identifying characteristics: Look for clusters of two raised acorns among swirling leaves. Made from 1915 to 1925.

Also known as: Fenton's #835; Grape Leaves and Acorns.

Made by Millersburg or US Glass.

Colors known: amethyst, green, marigold, and vaseline.

Forms: compotes.

Identifying characteristics: Pattern identified by large oak leaves that meet in the center and extend to outer edge with acorns interspersed between the leaves.

Acorn, Fenton, bowl, dark red, ruffled 6-1/2" d, **$400.**

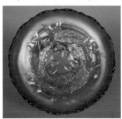

Acorn, Fenton, bowl, dark aqua, ice cream shape, **$20.**

Acorn, maybe US Glass or possibly Millersburg, vase, green, one of two known, **$9,000.**

Acorn, maybe US Glass or possibly Millersburg, vase, vaseline, only one known in this color, **$11,000.**

Acorn Burrs, Northwood, punch cup, blue, 2-1/2" h, **$150-$250 (rare).**

Acorn Burrs

Made by Northwood.

Colors known: amethyst, blue, green, ice blue, ice green, marigold, pastel, purple, and white.

Forms: bowls, punch sets, table sets, and water sets.

Identifying characteristics: This very three-dimensional pattern shows detailed leaves and large chestnut-type acorns. Production began in 1911.

Also known as: Acorn Burrs and Bark.

Acorn Burrs, Northwood, punch bowl, base, five cups, ice blue, **$1,150.**

Acorn Burrs, Northwood, punch bowl, base, six cups, ice green, very few known, **$23,000.**

Acorn Burrs, Northwood, punch bowl, base, six cups, white, **$6,500.**

Advertising

Several manufacturers made interesting plates and bowls that were used as promotional give-away pieces by advertisers. Today these advertising pieces command high prices.

Colors known: amethyst, blue, green, and marigold.

Forms: bonbons, bowls, hats, mugs, and plates.

Identifying characteristics: Names of advertisers are the predominate characteristic. Many advertisers chose popular patterns of the day to add their names to, such as Heart and Vine or Grape and Cable. Many of these premiums were made in limited quantities. The listing below is a sampling of the current market.

Advertising card tray, Fenton, amethyst, "Utah Liquor Co.," 6" l, **$800-$1,000.**

Advertising plate, Northwood, amethyst, "Fern Brand Chocolates," 6" d, **$1,300-$1,800.**

Advertising plate, Fenton, amethyst, "Seasons Greetings, Eat Paradise Sodas," 6" d, **$500-$800.**

Advertising plate, Northwood, amethyst, "Dreibus Parfait Sweets," 6" d, **$900-$1,300.**

Apple Blossom Twigs

Made by Dugan.

  Colors known: amethyst, blue, lavender, lavender slag, marigold, peach opalescent, purple, and white.

  Forms: banana boats, bowls, and plates.

   Identifying characteristics: This pattern features four branches with leaves that frame a central flower. Plates can have a serrated edge or smooth edge. The pattern was first made in 1912.

Above: Apple Blossom Twigs, Dugan, 3 in 1 bowl, purple, 10 ruffles, 9" d, **$200 to $300;** outstanding example, **$800.**
Right: Apple Blossom Twigs, Dugan, ice cream shaped bowl, purple, 8-1/2" d, **$200 to $300.**

April Showers

Made by Fenton.

Colors known: amethyst, amethyst opalescent, blue, green, marigold, red, vaseline, and white.

Forms: vases.

Identifying characteristics: This pattern looks as though there are three-dimensional raindrops sliding down the exterior walls. Because these vases are made using the "swung" method, heights range from 5 to 15 inches and variations exist in the scallops at the top. The bases are plain. The pattern was first made in 1911.

Also known as: Fenton #412.

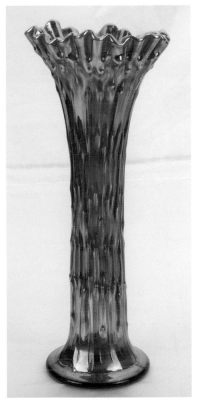

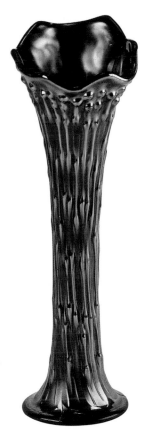

April Showers, Fenton, vase, amethyst opal, 11-1/4" h, **$1,450.**

April Showers, Fenton, vase, black amethyst, 12" h, **$80 to $150.**

Beaded Bullseye

Made by Imperial.

Colors known: amber, cobalt blue, green, helios, lime green, marigold, purple, smoke, and teal.

Forms: vases.

Identifying characteristics: The pattern consists of large circles edged by beads, further separated by fine ribbing. The base is a 20-point star. Production began in 1912.

Also known as: Beaded Medallion and Teardrop.

Beaded Bullseye, Imperial, squat vase, purple, 7" h, **$250-$350 (scarce).**

Beaded Bullseye, Imperial, vase, marigold, 10" h, **$60-$100.**

Beaded Bullseye, Imperial, vase, amber, 8 1/2" h, **$300-$400 (scarce).**

Beaded Shell

Made by Dugan-Diamond.

Colors known: amethyst, blue, green, marigold, pastel opalescent, purple, red, and white.

Forms: bowls, mugs, table sets, water sets, and whimsies.

Identifying characteristics: This pattern with a naturalistic-looking shell motif was first made as pattern glass. Also found in custard and opalescent glass.

Also known as: New York; Shell.

Reproductions.

Beaded Shell, Dugan, set of water pitcher and six tumblers, marigold, **$1,400.**

Beaded Spears

Made by Jain.

Colors known: amethyst, blue, and marigold.

Forms: water sets.

Identifying characteristics: Tumblers are known in several different sizes and may be flared or straight at the top. Jain Glass Works is in Firozabad, India.

Beaded Spears, Jain, set of water pitcher and five tumblers (one shown), marigold, **$1,000.**

Big Basketweave

Made by Dugan-Diamond.

Colors known: amethyst, blue, celeste blue, horehound, ice blue, marigold, peach opalescent, purple, and white.

Forms: baskets, bowls, and vases.

Identifying characteristics: The pattern is found on the exterior of the forms as they resemble woven wicker items. Produced 1911-1913.

Also known as: Wicker Weave.

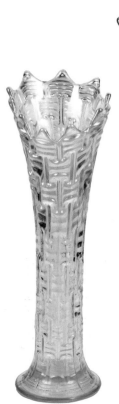

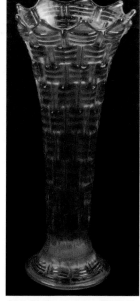

Big Basketweave, Dugan, vase, ice blue, 11-1/4'' h, **$600.**

Big Basketweave, Dugan, vase, horehound, 9-1/2" h, **$350.**

Big Basketweave, Dugan, vase, white, 10'' h, **$500.**

Big Fish

Made by Millersburg.

Colors known: amethyst, green, marigold, and vaseline.

Forms: bowls.

Identifying characteristics: A large center trout graces this pattern and is further enhanced by water lilies. The pattern was introduced in 1911.

Big Fish, Millersburg, bowl, marigold, square, **$900-$1,100.**

Big Fish, Millersburg, rose bowl, purple, only one known, 6" w, 3" d, rare.

Birds and Cherries

Made by Fenton.

Colors known: amethyst, blue, green, marigold, pastel marigold, vaseline, and white.

Forms: bonbons, bowls, card trays, compotes, and plates.

Identifying characteristics: The pattern features birds on cherry tree branches, complete with blossoms, leaves, and cherries. The pattern was introduced in 1911.

Also known as: Fenton's #1075

Bird and Cherries, Fenton, bowl, blue, candy ribbon edge, **$750.**

Blackberry

Made by Fenton.

Colors known: amethyst, blue, green, marigold, purple, and white.

Forms: compotes and plates.

Identifying characteristics: This pattern features blackberries and leaves. The miniature compotes are found in several styles, including ruffled and tricorn. Production was from 1911 to 1913.

Blackberry, Fenton, ruffled bowl, green, **$75.**

Blackberry Block

Made by Fenton.

Colors known: amethyst, blue, green, marigold, and white.

Forms: water sets.

Identifying characteristics: This is an all-over squares pattern with vining berries and leaves. The tankard-shaped water pitcher has a scalloped rim and applied handle.

Blackberry Block, Fenton, ruffled-top tankard, blue, 11" h, **$1,500-$1,800.**

Blackberry Block, Fenton, water pitcher, one tumbler, green, **$4,000.**

Blackberry Open Edge

Made by Fenton.

Colors known: amethyst, blue, celeste blue, green, marigold, powder blue, red, and white.

Forms: baskets, bowls, and whimsies.

Identifying characteristics: This blackberry pattern is often found with a basket-weave exterior. The pattern was introduced in 1911.

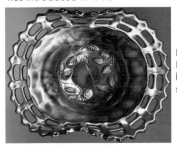

Blackberry Open Edge, Fenton, basket, red, two sides up, 7", **$250.**

Blackberry Open Edge, Fenton, Two Row, vase, blue, whimsy, 7" h, **$2,000.**

Blackberry Spray

Made by Fenton.

Colors known: amber, amberina, amethyst, aqua, aqua opalescent, blue, green, lime green, marigold, red, reverse amberina opalescent, vaseline, and white.

Forms: hats.

Identifying characteristics: This blackberry pattern features sprays of berries that encircle the interior edge. The exteriors are plain. The pattern was introduced in 1911.

Also known as: Fenton's #1216.

Blackberry Spray, Fenton, hat, sapphire opal, jack in the pulpit, **$1,700.**

Blackberry Spray, Fenton, ruffled hat, red opal, **$650.**

Blackberry Wreath

Made by Millersburg.

Colors known: amethyst, blue, clambroth, green, marigold, and vaseline.

Forms: bowls.

Identifying characteristics: This pattern features a plump berry in the center with three leaves. The wreath-like border includes more berries, leaves, and tendrils. The pattern was introduced in 1911.

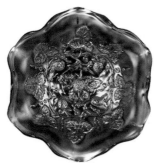

Blackberry Wreath, Fenton spittoon, marigold, whimsey, **$700.**

Blackberry Wreath, Millersburg, large bowl, purple, ruffled, **$40.**

Blossomtime

Made by Northwood

Colors known: amethyst, green, marigold, and purple.

Forms: compotes.

Identifying characteristics: A circle of flowers and leaves are the major design element of this pattern. Some pieces also feature a Wildflower pattern exterior.

Top view of the green compote.

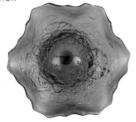

Blossomtime, Northwood, compote, green, 5", **$400-$700.**

Blueberry

Made by Fenton.

Colors known: blue, marigold, and white.

Forms: water sets.

Identifying characteristics: This pattern has life-like blueberries. The tops of the water pitchers are scalloped and flared out, with handles always applied. Production began in 1912.

Also known as: #1562.

Blueberry, Fenton, ruffled-top tankard, blue, 10" h, **$1,000-$1,400;** outstanding example, **$4,500.**

Blueberry, Fenton, set of water pitcher and three tumblers (one shown), white, **$1,450.**

Bouquet

Made by Fenton.

Colors known: blue and marigold.

Forms: water sets.

Identifying characteristics: As the name implies, this design features flowers, but also incorporates a cable. The water pitchers have crimped tops and applied handles. The pattern was introduced in 1913.

Also known as: Spring Flowers.

Bouquet, Fenton, set of water pitcher and six tumblers (one shown), marigold, **$265.**

Broken Arches

Made by Imperial.

Colors known: marigold and purple.

Forms: punch sets.

Identifying characteristics: The name correctly describes this intricate pattern. The arches are broken in a keystone-type arrangement. The pattern was first advertised in 1911.

Also known as: Imperial's Snap-14.

Broken Arches, Imperial, punch bowl and base, purple, 13" d, **$1,000-$1,300;** outstanding example, **$2,000.**

Broken Arches, Imperial, ruffled punch bowl and base, purple, 13" d, **$1,500-$2,000 (very rare).**

Broken Arches, Imperial, punch cup, purple, 2-1/4" h, **$40-$70.**

Bullseye and Beads

Made by Fenton.

Colors known: amber, blue, and marigold.

Forms: vases.

Identifying characteristics: This pattern features rows of stretched bull's eyes. Beads are found under the scalloped rim and at the base.

Bullseye and Beads, Fenton, vase, blue, 11-1/4" h, **$350.**

Bushel Basket

Novelty pattern made by Northwood.

Colors known: amethyst, amethyst slag, aqua opalescent, blue, green, ice blue, ice green, lavender, marigold, purple, sapphire blue, smoke, and white.

Forms: only two basket forms known – with either a round or octagon-shaped base.

Identifying characteristics: As the name implies, this pattern looks like a woven wicker basket, complete with two handles and small feet. Handles are commonly ribbed, but variations with smooth handles and more flare to the top exist. The pattern was made from 1910 to 1921.

Bushel Basket, Northwood, pastel marigold, **$50.**

Bushel Basket, Northwood, eight-sided, amethyst, **$50.**

Butterfly

Made by Northwood.

Colors known: amethyst, blue, green, horehound, ice blue, marigold, purple, and smoke.

Forms: bonbons.

Identifying characteristics: Look for a single center butterfly in this pattern that looks like it will fly right over the rays that border it. This pattern was produced from 1910 to 1913.

Butterfly, US Glass, tumbler, one of four known, green, **$10,000.**

Butterfly, Fenton, ornament, marigold, 3" w, **$1,200-$1,500.**

Butterfly and Berry

Made by Fenton.

Colors known: amethyst, blue, green, marigold, red, and white.

Former made: bowls, hatpin holders, table set, vases, water sets, and whimsies.

Identifying characteristics: This pattern is found in a paneled form with alternating butterflies and leaves in one panel, blackberries and leaves in other panels. This popular pattern was also used as an exterior pattern on Fenton bowls in Hearts and Trees, Fantail, and Panther patterns. It was produced from 1911-1926.

Also known as: Butterfly and Grape.

Reproductions: The large bowl has been reproduced in purple and white. Tumblers have been reproduced in amethyst.

Butterfly and Berry, Fenton, vase, amethyst, 7" h, **$150.**

Butterfly and Berry, Fenton, vase, red, 8-1/2" h, **$1,200-$1,500.**

Butterfly and Berry, Fenton, water pitcher, amethyst, **$3,000.**

Butterfly and Fern

Made by Fenton.

Colors known: amethyst, blue, green, and marigold.

Forms: water sets.

Identifying characteristics: The central motif is a butterfly with leaves. Water pitcher tops are crimped, and handles are applied.

Also known as: Fenton's #910; Butterfly and Plume.

Butterfly and Fern, Fenton, set of water pitcher and six tumblers, amethyst, **$1,050.**

Butterfly and Tulip

Made by Dugan.

Colors: amethyst, marigold, peach opalescent, and purple.

Forms: bowls,

Identifying characteristics: A large central butterfly appears ready to fly to the well-designed tulips and leaves that extend to the edges of this design. Feather Scroll is commonly used as the exterior pattern. This pattern was introduced in 1910.

Also known as: Flower Pot.

Butterfly and Tulip, Dugan, square-ruffled bowl, purple, footed, 11" d, **$2,000-$3,500.**

Butterfly and Tulip, Dugan, bowl, purple, **$2,000-$3,500.**

Captive Rose

Made by Fenton.

Colors known: amethyst, blue, green, and marigold.

Forms: bonbons, bowls, calling card trays, compotes, and plates.

Identifying characteristics: This pattern has a lacy embroidered motif. Look for the rose in the center as well as the garland of roses. Production began in 1910.

Also known as: Battenburg Lace #2B.

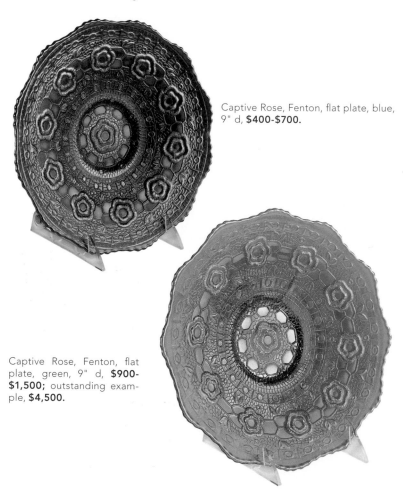

Captive Rose, Fenton, flat plate, blue, 9" d, **$400-$700.**

Captive Rose, Fenton, flat plate, green, 9" d, **$900-$1,500;** outstanding example, **$4,500.**

Chatelaine

Made by Imperial.

Color known: purple.

Forms: water sets.

Identifying characteristics: This pattern is a very detailed design with fans, hobstars, and volutes. A clear example is shown in a 1909 Imperial catalog. The first carnival example was advertised in a 1913 *Butlers Brothers Wholesale* catalog.

Chatelaine, Imperial, water pitcher, purple, 8-1/2" h, **$2,400-$3,000 (rare).**

Chatelaine, Imperial, tumbler, purple, 4-1/4" h, **$200-$350 (rare).**

Checkerboard

Made by Westmoreland.

Colors known: amethyst and marigold.

Forms: goblets, punch cups and water sets.

Identifying characteristics: This pattern consists of raised blocks, criss-cross diagonals, and fans.

Also known as: Old Quilt.

Reproductions: Water pitchers and tumblers have been reproduced by L. G. Wright using old molds. Westmoreland also reissued the water set in honey, lime green, and ice blue.

Checkerboard, Westmoreland, water pitcher and six tumblers, amethyst, **$4,100.**

Cherries

Made by Dugan-Diamond.

Colors known: amethyst, electric blue, marigold, peach opalescent, and purple.

Forms: banana boat, bowls, and plates.

Identifying characteristics: This pattern features clusters of stemmed cherries on leaves and branches. It was made from 1909 until 1914.

Also known as: Cherry.

Reproductions: A round bowl has been made.

Cherries, Dugan, eight-ruffled bowl, purple, 9" d, **$350-$450.**

Cherries, Dugan, tri-fold bowl, purple, 9" d, **$200-$350.**

Cherries, Dugan, ruffled plate, purple, candy-ribbon edge, 6-1/2" d, **$200-$350.**

Cherry Chain

Made by Fenton.

Colors known: amethyst, blue, clambroth, electric blue, marigold, red, vaseline, and white.

Forms: bowls and plates.

Identifying characteristics: This cherry pattern features clusters of three plump cherries within a circle, surrounded by foliage and other elements. Another cluster of cherries is in the center. The Orange Tree pattern was used as the exterior design for this busy pattern. A pattern known as Cherry Chain Variant has clusters with five cherries each.

Reproductions: Fenton reissued this pattern in a number of shapes, such as the round bowl, ruffled bowl, chop plates, and rose bowls.

Cherry Chain, Fenton, chop plate, dark electric marigold, 10-3/4'' d, **$1,400.**

Cherry Chain, Fenton, bonbon, red, large, **$5,000.**

Cherry Chain, Fenton, bowl, green, 3 in 1 Edge, large, **$200.**

Chrysanthemum

Made by Fenton.

Colors known: amethyst, blue, green, lime green, marigold, red, vaseline, and white.

Forms: bowls.

Identifying characteristics: This pattern features large full-blossomed chrysanthemums, leaves, and windmills. Production began in 1914.

Also known as: Chrysanthemum and Windmills.

Chrysanthemum, Fenton, bowl, electric blue, large, footed, **$250.**

Circle Scroll

Made by Dugan.

Colors known: amethyst and marigold.

Forms: bowls, hats, table sets, vases, and water sets.

Identifying characteristics: The design motif includes a swirling vine within a circle. This pattern was also made in opalescent glass.

Circle Scroll, Dugan, set of water pitcher and six tumblers (one shown), marigold, SSCGA, **$1,100.**

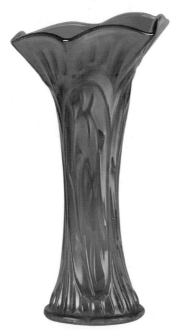

Circle Scroll, Dugan, vase, marigold, 7-1/2" h, **$100-$200 (scarce).**

Circle Scroll, Dugan, vase, purple, 7-1/4" h, **$200-$400;** outstanding example, **$750.**

Colonial Lady

Made by Imperial.

Colors known: marigold and purple.

Forms: vases.

Identifying characteristics: This pattern is a series of panels with a very distinctive rib between each.

Colonial Lady, Imperial, vase, purple, 6" h, **$1,400.**

Colonial Lady, Imperial, vase, purple, 5-1/2" h, **$600-$1,000;** outstanding example, **$2,300.**

Colonial Lady, Imperial, vase, marigold, rare and beautiful, **$525.**

Concave Flute

Made by Westmoreland.

Colors known: amethyst, marigold, marigold with moonstone, and teal.

Forms: banana dish, rose bowls, and vases.

Identifying characteristics: This paneled pattern consists of nine flutes that radiate from a sharp arch.

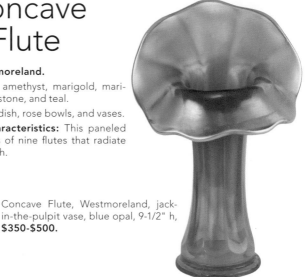

Concave Flute, Westmoreland, jack-in-the-pulpit vase, blue opal, 9-1/2" h, **$350-$500.**

Concord

Made by Fenton.

Colors known: amethyst, blue, green, marigold, and pumpkin marigold.

Forms: bowls and plates.

Identifying characteristics: This pattern features clusters of grapes, vines, and leaves, while the whole background resembles a net.

Concord, Fenton, blue ruffled bowl, has some loss of iridescence on grapes, **$75.**

Concord, Fenton, flat plate, purple, 9" d, **$2,000-$3,000.**

Concord, Fenton, six-ruffled bowl, emerald green, 8-1/2" d, **$300-$500;** outstanding, **$850.**

Constellation

Made by Dugan.

Colors known: amethyst, lavender, marigold, peach opalescent, and white.

Forms: compotes.

Identifying characteristics: This pattern features a large center star with bubble dots and rays stretching towards the rim. The exterior is S-Repeat pattern.

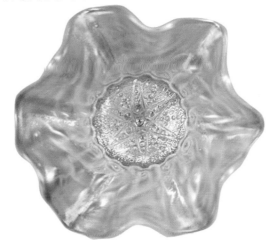

Constellation, Dugan, compote, white, **$45.**

Coral

Made by Fenton.

Colors known: blue, green, ice green, and marigold.

Forms: bowls, plates.

Identifying characteristics: This interesting pattern is one of only a few that has two bands. Abstract nautical motifs complete the design.

Coral, Fenton, plate, marigold, **$1,100.**

Corinth

Made by Westmoreland.

Colors known: amber, amethyst, marigold, marigold on milk glass, olive green, peach opalescent, teal, and white.

Forms: banana boats, bowls, and vases.

Identifying characteristics: This pattern features 12 heavy ribs. Vases have plain bases. Produced from 1904 to 1910. Dugan-Diamond made a similar pattern, which is valued the same.

Also known as: Westmoreland's #252.

Corinth, Westmoreland, jack-in-the-pulpit vase, blue opal, 9-1/2" h, **$300-$400.**

Corinth, Dugan, jack-in-the-pulpit vase, blue opal, 8-3/4" h, **$175.**

Corinth, Dugan, jack-in-the-pulpit vase, peach opal, 10" h, **$150.**

Corn

Made by Northwood.

Colors known: amethyst, aqua opalescent, blue, green, ice blue, ice green, lime green, marigold, purple, teal, and white.

Forms: vases.

Identifying characteristics: This pattern looks like its name implies, an ear of corn, with the husk forming the base.

Corn, Northwood, vase, aqua, stalk base, 6-1/2" h, **$2,200-$3,000 (rare).**

Corn, Northwood, vase, ice green, stalk base, 6-1/2" h, **$400-$700.**

Corn, Northwood, vase, green, stalk base, 6-1/2" h, **$700-$1,100.**

Cosmos and Cane

Made by US Glass.

Colors known: amethyst, honey amber, marigold, and white.

Forms: baskets, berry sets, chop plates, compotes, rose bowls, spittoons, table sets, trays, and water sets.

Identifying characteristics: As the name implies, there is a panel of cane design and pretty cosmos flowers on this pattern. Produced from 1914 until 1917.

Also known as: Diamond Point and Daisy.

Cosmos and Cane, US Glass, square bowl, honey amber, **$70.**

Cosmos and Cane, US Glass, set of water pitcher and six tumblers, white, **$4,500.**

Curved Star

Attributed to US Glass, Brockwitz of Germany, Karhula-Iittala, Finland.

Colors known: blue and marigold.

Forms: bowls, chalices, cheese dishes, compotes, epergnes, flower holders, fruit bowls, and table sets.

Identifying characteristics: This imitation cutglass pattern features an elongated six-point star in each of the curved panels. The pattern has been documented in the 1938 catalog of *Karhula-Iittala.*

Also known as: Cathedral.

Curved Star, Brockwitz, cylinder vase, marigold, 7-1/2" h, **$350-$500.**

Curved Star Brockwitz, cylinder vase, blue, 7-1/2" h, **$350-$500.**

Curved Star, Brockwitz, small bowl, blue, 4-1/2" d x 1-1/2" h, **$80-$150.**

Dahlia

Made by Dugan.

Colors known: amethyst, marigold, and purple.

Forms: berry sets, table sets, and water sets.

Identifying characteristics: The intricate dahlia flower is raised in this pattern. Production began in 1912.

Reproductions: L. G. Wright created reproduction water pitchers in 1977 using original Westmoreland molds in amethyst and white. Tumblers have also been reproduced, possibly by Mosser, but are easier to identify, as they do not include the many-rayed star in the base.

Dahlia, Dugan, set of water pitcher and six tumblers, marigold, **$1,750.**

Daisy and Drape

Made by Northwood.

Colors known: amethyst, aqua, aqua opalescent, blue, green, ice blue, ice marigold, and white.

Forms: vases.

Identifying characteristics: This pattern features a drape-like body with a ring of daisies around the top. Production began in 1912.

Also known as: Daisy Band and Drape.

Daisy and Drape, Northwood, vase, flared top, aqua opalescent, **$500.**

Daisy and Drape, Northwood, vase, turned in, ice green, **$4,000.**

Daisy and Plume

Made by Northwood and also Dugan.

Colors known: amethyst, aqua, blue, green, horehound, marigold, peach opalescent, purple, and white.

Forms: bowls, candy dishes, compotes, and rose bowls.

Identifying characteristics: A large plume separates the stippled fields that hold a single daisy blossom in this pattern. Production was from 1909 until 1912.

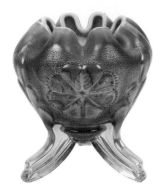

Daisy and Plume, Northwood, rose bowl, butterscotch opalescent, footed, one of three known, **$7,000.**

Daisy Wreath

Made by Westmoreland.

Colors known: amethyst, aqua opal, blue opal, marigold, marigold on milk glass, and peach opalescent.

Forms: bowls, plates, and vases.

Identifying characteristics: This pattern features a central daisy surrounded by a wreath border. Production began in 1910.

Also known as: Daisy Bowl.

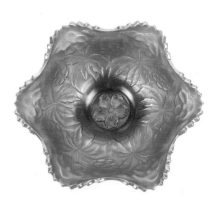

Daisy Wreath, Westmoreland, bowl, marigold over moonstone, **$200.**

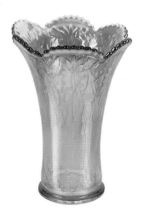

Daisy Wreath, Westmoreland, vase, marigold, whimsey from bowl, 5" h, **$2,100.**

Dandelion

Made by Northwood.

Colors known: amethyst, aqua opalescent, blue, blue opalescent, green, ice blue, ice green, marigold, purple, and white.

Forms: mugs, vases, and water sets

Identifying characteristics: This pattern features a large multi-petaled flower blossom and leaves. Mugs in this pattern are available with a Knights Templer decoration.

Dandelion, Northwood, tumbler, smoky lavender streaks, **$425.**

Dandelion, Northwood, tankard, purple, 14" h, **$600-$1,000;** outstanding example, **$2,200.**

Dandelion, Northwood, tumbler, 4-1/4", purple, **$50-$150.**

Dandelion, Northwood, water pitcher and six tumblers, marigold, **$1,700.**

Diamond and Rib

Made by Fenton.

Colors known: amethyst, blue, green, marigold, and white.

Forms: jardinières and vases.

Identifying characteristics: This pattern features elongated ovals with ribbing in each one. Production began in 1911.

Also known as: Fenton's #504; Melon and Fan.

Reproductions: Fenton has re-issued vases, but most are marked.

Diamond and Rib, Fenton, jardinière, marigold, 6-1/2" h, **$1,800-$2,500.**

Diamond and Rib, Fenton, vase, green, pinched in, whimsy, **$2,800-$3,200.**

Diamond and Rib, Fenton, funeral vase, green, 19" h, 9" mouth, **$1,600-$2,500.**

Diamond and Rib, Fenton, jardinière vase, amethyst, **$2,500-$4,000.**

Diamond and Rib, Fenton, funeral vase, amethyst, 18" h, 5-1/4", **$2,800-$3,200.**

Diamond Lace

Made by Imperial.

Colors known: green, marigold, and purple.

Forms: berry sets, rose bowls, and water sets.

Identifying characteristics: This imitation cut-glass pattern was first made in crystal. It features hobstars, files, fans, etc. Production began in 1909.

Also known as: Imperial's #434-1/2.

Reproductions.

Diamond Lace, Imperial, water pitcher, purple, 8-1/2" h, **$325-$525.**

Diamond Lace, Imperial, tumbler, purple, 4-1/4" h, **$50-$80.**

Diamond Points

Made by Northwood.

Colors known: amethyst, aqua opalescent, blue, green, horehound, ice blue, ice green, marigold, sapphire blue, and white.

Forms: baskets, rose bowls, and vases.

Identifying characteristics: This pattern features squares set on the diagonal, each filled with further criss-cross diamond elements. Production was between 1912 and 1916.

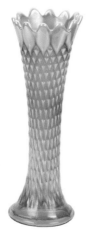

Diamond Points, Northwood, vase, aqua opal, pastel, 10-1/2" h, **$1,200.**

Diamond Points, Northwood, vase, ice blue, 12" h, **$450.**

Diamond Points, Northwood, vase, teal blue, 11-1/2" h, **$1,150.**

Diamond Points, Northwood, vase, blue, 9-1/2" h, **$300-$400 (scarce).**

Diamond Points, Northwood, vase, sapphire, 10-1/2" h, **$700-$1,100 (rare).**

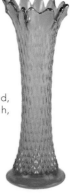

Diamonds

Made by Millersburg.

Colors known: amethyst, aqua, green, and marigold.

Forms: punch bowls and water sets.

Identifying characteristics: This bold diamond pattern features a row of beading inside each diamond. An odd form was made in this pattern When a water pitcher form was created with a handle, but no pouring spout. Production was from 1910 to 1911.

Diamonds, Millersburg, tumbler, amethyst, 4" h, **$70-$110.**

Diamonds, Millersburg, set of water pitcher and six tumblers (one shown), green, **$850.**

Diamonds, Millersburg, set of water pitcher and four tumblers (one shown), amethyst, **$850.**

Dogwood Sprays

Made by Dugan.

Colors known: amethyst, blue, blue opalescent, marigold, peach opalescent, and purple.

Forms: bowls and compotes.

Identifying characteristics: Two large floral sprays, leaves and tendrils are the basis of this pattern. The center is a single four-petaled blossom with five leaves. Production was between 1910 and 1912.

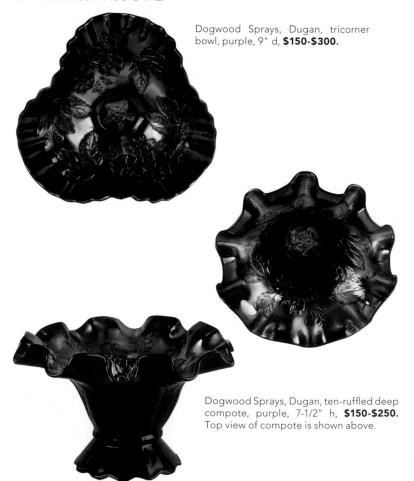

Dogwood Sprays, Dugan, tricorner bowl, purple, 9" d, **$150-$300.**

Dogwood Sprays, Dugan, ten-ruffled deep compote, purple, 7-1/2" h, **$150-$250.** Top view of compote is shown above.

Double Star

Made by Cambridge.

Colors known: amethyst, green, and marigold.

Forms: bowls, water sets, and whimsies.

Identifying characteristics: This pattern features a large central buzz star over an interesting fan shape. Production began in 1913 and continued until 1915.

Also known as: Cambridge's #2699; Buzzstar; Hobstar and Torch.

Double Star, Cambridge, water pitcher, amethyst, **$850.**

Double Star, Cambridge, set of water pitcher and six tumblers (one shown), green, **$1,400.**

Dozen Roses

Attributed to Imperial.

Colors known: amethyst, green, marigold, and purple.

Forms: bowls.

Identifying characteristics: This pattern is the same on the interior as it is on the exterior—twelve shaped frames that each have a incised and raised rose blossom.

Dozen Roses, possibly Imperial, bowl, amethyst, **$850.**

Dragon and Lotus

Made by Fenton.

Colors known: amber, amethyst, aqua opalescent, blue, cobalt blue, dark blue, green, marigold, marigold on milk glass, peach opalescent, red, reverse amberina, and vaseline opalescent.

Forms: bowls and plates.

Identifying characteristics: This popular pattern shows ovals with a whimsical flying dragon alternating with rose type flowers. A busy inner band is found between the dragons and the lotus flowers in the center. Production started in 1915 and continued until 1920.

Dragon and Lotus, Fenton, eight-ruffled bowl, red, 9" d, **$1,500-$2,500;** outstanding example, **$5,000.**

Dragon and Lotus, Fenton, bowl, dark red, ruffled collar, 8-1/2" d, **$1,800.**

Dragon and Lotus, Fenton, bowl, marigold over moonstone, ice cream shape, **$1,000.**

Dragon and Strawberry

Made by Fenton.

Colors known: amethyst, blue, green, and marigold.

Forms: bowls.

Identifying characteristics: This pattern was a contemporary of Dragon and Lotus. It is less detailed than Dragon and Lotus, and shows plump berries in addition to the dragon. Made in 1915.

Also known as: Dragon and Berry.

Dragon and Strawberry, Fenton, bowl, blue, 8-3/4" d, **$650.**

Drapery

Made by Northwood.

Colors known: amethyst, aqua opalescent, blue, electric blue, green, ice blue, ice green, lavender, lime green, marigold, purple, Renninger blue, and white.

Forms: candy dishes, rose bowls and vases.

Identifying characteristics: Think of heavy folded drapes with sturdy ribs when envisioning this popular pattern. Production began in 1914 and continued until 1916.

Also known as: Northwood's Drapery.

Reproductions: Fenton has made rose bowls in contemporary colors, which are generally marked.

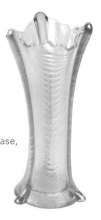

Drapery, Northwood, vase, ice blue, 7-1/4" h, **$200.**

Drapery, Northwood, vase, ice green, 8" h, **$250.**

Drapery Variant

Attributed to Fenton and Northwood.

Colors known: blue, marigold, purple, and sapphire blue.

Forms: bowls, vases.

Identifying characteristics: The folds found in this variant are less defined than those of the original Drapery pattern.

Drapery, Variant, Northwood, vase, amethyst, electric at base, 8-1/2" h, **$150.**

Embroidered Mums

Made by Northwood.

Colors known: amethyst, aqua opalescent, blue, electric blue, green, ice blue, ice green, lavender, lime green opalescent, marigold, peach opalescent, purple, sapphire blue, and white.

Forms: bonbons, bowls, and plates.

Identifying characteristics: This elegant pattern features a Greek key ring with interspersed chrysanthemums and leaves. An embroidered-type star flower is in the center. Production was from 1911 to 1912.

Also known as: Mums and Greek Key.

Embroidered Mums, Northwood, bowl, electric blue, 8-1/2" d, **$500.**

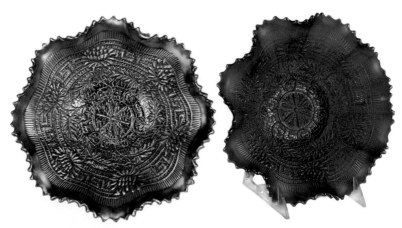

Embroidered Mums, Northwood, bowl, purple, electric highlights, **$250.**

Embroidered Mums, Northwood, eight-ruffled bowl, blue, 8-1/2" d, **$550-$850.**

Enameled patterns

Various manufacturers.

Colors known: amethyst, blue, green, marigold, purple, and white.

Forms: goblets, plates, vases, and water sets.

Identifying characteristics: Many patterns of carnival glass are found which have been further enhanced by enamel decoration. Some collectors specialize in these interesting patterns. Most are limited in forms and productions. This edition contains a sampling of what is available in the carnival glass market, but be aware more color patterns await those searching for these gems.

Enameled Grape, Northwood, water pitcher and six tumblers, blue, **$875**.

Estate

Made by Westmoreland and Dugan.

Colors known: aqua, aqua opalescent, marigold, and smoke.

Forms: mugs, perfumes, and pin dishes.

Identifying characteristics: This pattern features an almost Celtic-like band.

Also known as: Capital.

Estate, Dugan, vase, purple, 6" h, **$25**.

Estate, Westmoreland, vase, smoke, 5" h, **$100**.

Fanciful

Fanciful, Dugan, low 10-ruffled bowl, purple, 9" d, **$300-$600;** outstanding example, **$1,300.**

Made by Dugan.

Colors known: amethyst, blue, electric blue, electric purple, lavender, marigold, peach opalescent, purple, root beer, and white.

Forms: bowls and plates.

Identifying characteristics: A design that looks like quilted strawberries dance around an inner border with scrolls.

Also known as: Battenburg Lace #3C.

Fantail

Fantail, Fenton, ice cream-shaped bowl, blue, 9" d, **$250-$350.**

Made by Fenton.

Colors known: blue, green, marigold, and white.

Forms: bowls and chop plates.

Identifying characteristics: This pattern is a whimsical depiction of six swirling peacock tails, which come together in the center. Butterfly and Berry is often used as the exterior pattern. Production began in 1911.

Also known as: Peacock Tail and Daisy.

Reproductions: 9" bowls with the Butterfly and Berry exterior are known in blue and red, complete with the original Fenton logo.

Farmyard

Farmyard, Dugan, ruffled bowl, purple, **$5,500.**

Made by Dugan.

Colors known: green, peach opalescent, and purple.

Forms: bowls.

Identifying characteristics: This pattern is found on the interior of bowls and features a rooster and chickens. The exterior pattern used is Jeweled Heart.

Also known as: Busy Chickens.

Reproductions: Reproductions of bowls and chop plates are known in contemporary colors.

Fashion

Made by Imperial.

Colors known: clambroth, emerald green, helios, horehound, marigold, purple, and smoke.

Forms: bowls, breakfast sets, compotes, punch cups, rose bowls, and water sets.

Identifying characteristics: Fashion is one of Imperial's imitation cut-glass patterns. It's not quite as detailed as most, but includes a hobstar and zippered band, as well as fans and diamonds. Production began in 1910.

Also known as: Imperial's #402-1/2.

Reproductions: This pattern never was made in a toothpick holder, but those creating reproductions made one, often found in blue, purple, or red.

Fashion, Imperial, tumbler, 4-1/4", purple, **$300-$500;** outstanding example, **$800 (rare).**

Fashion, Imperial, pitcher, 8-1/2", purple, **$900-$1,500;** outstanding example, **$2,500 (rare).**

Fashion, Imperial, rose bowl, purple, 6-1/2" w, **$1,200-$1,600;** outstanding example, **$2,400.**

Fashion, Imperial, compote, smoke, **$900.**

Feather and Heart

Made by Millersburg.

Colors known: amethyst, green, and marigold.

Forms: water sets and whimsies.

Identifying characteristics: This pattern features well-defined feathers over arcs containing hobstars, diamonds, and fans. Produced from 1910 until 1912.

Also known as: Heart Band and Herringbone.

Feather and Heart, Millersburg, water pitcher and six tumblers, dark marigold, **$875.**

Feathered Serpent

Made by Fenton.

Colors known: amethyst, blue, green, and marigold.

Forms: bowls.

Identifying characteristics: This pattern is a series of feathered swirls with four swirled feathers in the center. Production began in 1910.

Also known as: Feathered Scroll.

Feathered Serpent, Fenton, lady's spittoon, green, 3-3/4" w, 2-1/4" h, **$7,500.**

Feathered Serpent, Fenton, bowl, amethyst, candy-ribbon edge, **$150.**

Fentonia

Made by Fenton.

Colors known: blue and marigold.

Forms: berry sets, table sets, and water sets.

Identifying characteristic: Fentonia is one of Fenton's all-over patterns of diamonds filled with scales and embroidery stitches.

Also known as: Diamond and Cable.

Fentonia, Fenton, set of water pitcher and two tumblers (one shown), blue, **$875.**

Field Flower

Made by Imperial.

Colors known: amber, aqua, clambroth, cobalt blue, helios, marigold, olive, purple, red, smoke, and violet.

Forms: milk pitchers and water sets.

Identifying characteristics: The design is a flower framed by two strands of wheat, all on a stippled background, double arches border the stippling and serve as panels. Production began in 1912.

Also known as: Imperial's #494; Sunflower and Wheat.

Reproductions: Water sets have been re-issued in contemporary colors.

Field Flower, Imperial, water pitcher, purple, 9" h, **$400-$700;** outstanding example, **$1,200.**

Field Flower, Imperial, tumbler, purple, 4" h, **$90-$150.**

Field Flower, Fenton, water pitcher and six tumblers, marigold, **$450.**

Field Thistle

Made by US Glass and Jenkins.

Colors known: green, ice blue, and marigold.

Forms: berry sets, breakfast sets, compotes, plates, table sets, and water sets.

Identifying characteristics: A motif of thistles and open-petaled flowers swirl from a flower center.

Field Thistle, Jenkins, vase, light marigold, **$325.**

File

Made by Imperial.

Colors known: marigold and purple.

Forms: bowls, compotes, table sets, and water pitchers.

Identifying characteristics: As the name implies, this pattern looks like a series of two rows of small files standing upright.

Also known as: Imperial's #256.

File, Imperial, water pitcher and six tumblers, marigold, **$600.**

File, Imperial, ruffled bowl, electric purple, **$55.**

Fine Rib

Made by Fenton.

Colors known: amberina, amethyst, aqua, aqua opalescent, blue, celeste blue, green, lime green opalescent, marigold, marigold over milk glass, peach opalescent, powder blue, red, sapphire blue, teal, smoke, and vaseline.

Forms: bowls, vases, and plates.

Identifying characteristics: This pattern is divided into six sections, each having six ribs when the base is large. Smaller bases have five ribs. Base diameters of the standard size vases range from 2-1/4 inches to 2-3/4 inches, with the large standard size vase having a diameter of 3 inches. Heights of vases range from 8 inches to 17 inches. Look for a banded top edge on Fenton's Fine Rib vases, which helps distinguish it from the plain top edge on Northwood's Fine Rib. Production began in 1911.

Also known as: Fenton's #1126.

Fine Rib, Fenton, vase, red with red streaks, 9-1/2" h, **$450.**

Fine Rib, Fenton, vase, red, 10" h, **$300-$500.**

Fine Rib, Fenton, vase, red opalescent, **$600.**

Fine Rib

Made by Northwood.

Colors known: amethyst/purple, blue, green, ice blue, ice green, marigold, sapphire, and white.

Forms: vases.

Identifying characteristics: This finely ribbed pattern has ribs that are of equal size. The top edge is plain. The base should measure 3-1/2" d. Some are marked with the Northwood trademark "N."

Fine Rib, Northwood, standard vase, aqua opalescent, 11" h, **$1,200-$1,900 (very rare).**

Fine Rib, Northwood, vase, ice green, **$450.**

Fisherman's Mug

Made by Dugan/Diamond.

Colors known: amethyst, blue, custard, horehound, lavender, marigold, and peach opalescent.

Forms: mug.

Identifying characteristics: This mug must have been designed with a fisherman in mind as it shows a fish, water lilies, and cattails. The design is found only on one side, the other side is blank. Butler Brothers included this pattern in its 1911 catalog. Production continued from 1911 until 1914.

Also known as: Cattails and Fish.

Reproductions by L. G. Wright.

Fisherman's, Dugan, mug, marigold, 4" h, **$200-$300;** outstanding example, **$600.**

Fisherman's, Dugan, mug, purple, 4" h, **$100-$250.**

Fisherman's, Dugan, mug, blue, 4" h, **$1,000-$1,200 (rare).**

Fisherman's, Dugan, mug, amethyst, 4" h, **$100-$250.**

Fishscale and Beads

Made by Dugan.

Colors known: amber, amethyst/purple, aqua, marigold, pastels, peach opalescent, and white.

Forms. bowls and plates.

Identifying characteristics: This pattern was named Fishscale and Beads by carnival researcher Marion T. Hartung. It does look like fish scales with its honeycomb design on the interior, while a garland of beads is on the exterior.

Also known as: Honeycomb Collar; Honeycomb Variant.

Fishscale and Beads, Dugan, small plate, purple, 6" d, **$200-$300;** outstanding example, **$600.**

Fleur De Lis

Made by Millersburg.

Colors known: amethyst, green, marigold, and vaseline.

Forms: bowls.

Identifying characteristics: This detailed pattern has a more formal look about it with numerous fleur-de-lis shapes. It is often found with a Hobstar and Feather or Country Kitchen exterior. Production began in 1910.

Fleur De Lis, Millersburg, ruffled radium bowl, green, **$275-$425.**

Fleur De Lis, Millersburg, bowl, square pedestal base, vaseline, 8" w, 4-1/2" h, **$5,000.**

Floral and Grape

Made by Dugan.

Floral and Grape Variant

Made by Fenton.

Colors known: amethyst/purple, blue, horehound, marigold, and purple.

Forms: water sets, whimsies.

Identifying characteristics: The designs used by both Fenton and Dugan are remarkably similar. Water pitchers produced by Dugan have ribs in the bands that lean to the left, while the Fenton pitchers have the same element leaning to the right. A raised cable on either side of the ribs distinguishes a tumbler as Dugan rather than Fenton, whose tumblers do not have a cable at all. Production was from 1910 to 1911.

Also known as: Floral and Grapevine.

Floral and Grape Variant, Fenton, tumbler, blue, 4" h, **$60-$120.**

Floral and Grape Variant, Fenton, tankard, blue, candy-ribbon edge, 9-1/2" h, **$300-$500;** outstanding example, **$900.**

Floral and Grape, Fenton, pitcher, white, has internal fracture in handle, **$75.**

Floral and Optic

Made by Imperial.

Colors known: clambroth, marigold, marigold on milk glass, purple, red, smoke, teal, and white.

Forms: bowls, cake plates, and rose bowls.

Identifying characteristics: This common paneled pattern features a border band with vines, flowers, and leaves. Production began in 1914.

Floral and Optic, Imperial, bowl, red, footed, **$150.**

Floral and Optic, Imperial, rose bowl, marigold over milk glass, footed, **$250.**

Flowers and Frames

Made by Dugan.

Colors known: peach opalescent and purple.

Forms: bowls.

Identifying characteristics: This pattern has six loops that form frames which each contain one stemmed flower with leaves. Fleur-de-lis shapes protrude from each of the Vs formed by the loops. Production began in 1910.

Flowers and Frames, Dugan, tricorner bowl, purple, 9" d, **$400-$600;** outstanding example, **$900.**

Flowers and Frames, Dugan, 10-ruffled bowl, 9" d, purple, **$300-$450.**

Fluffy Peacock

Made by Fenton.

Colors known: amethyst, cobalt blue, green, and marigold.

Forms: water sets.

Identifying characteristics: One of the peacock patterns, Fenton used a rather stylized peacock for this design with a large feather being used as a divider between panels.

Fluffy Peacock, Fenton, water pitcher and six tumblers, amethyst, **$1,050.**

Flute

Made by Imperial.

Colors known: aqua, blue, clambroth, emerald green, helios, lime green, marigold, purple, red, smoke, and vaseline.

Forms: berry sets, bowls, breakfast sets, cruets, cups, punch sets, table sets, toothpicks, vases, and water sets.

Identifying characteristics: Imperial used a simple side paneled loop to create this popular pattern. Production began in 1909.

Also known as: Imperial's #700.

Flute, Imperial, vase, smokey blue, squatty, damage, **$150.**

Flute, Imperial, celery, purple, #700, 5-1/2" h, **$600.**

Flute, Imperial, water pitcher and six tumblers, purple, #700, **$1,650.**

Flute, Imperial, toothpick holder, green, 2-1/4" h, **$60-$90.**

Flute, Imperial, toothpick holder, purple, 2-1/4" h, **$70-$90.**

Flute, Imperial, toothpick holder, blue, 2-1/4" h, **$700-$1,000 (rare).**

Flute, Imperial, sugar bowl, purple, 3-1/4" h, **$80-$100.**

Flute

Made by Northwood.

Colors known: amethyst, aqua opalescent, blue, green, marigold, sapphire blue, vaseline, white.

Forms: berry sets, breakfast sets, nut cups, plates, salts, sherbets, table sets, vases, water sets.

Identifying characteristics: Northwood used twelve wide panels as their flutes.

Also known as: Northwood's #21.

Flute, Northwood, funeral vase, mid-size, purple, 15-3/4" h, 4-3/4" base, **$1,200.**

Flute and Cane

Made by Imperial.
Colors known: marigold.
Forms: bowls, compotes, milk pitchers, stemware, and water sets.
Identifying characteristics: This pattern has narrower flutes which top a band of cane pattern. Production began in 1909.
Also known as: Cane.

Flute and Cane, Imperial, tumbler, marigold, **$450.**

Flute and Cane, Imperial, milk pitcher, small, marigold, **$150.**

Formal

Made by Dugan.
Colors known: black amethyst, marigold, and purple.
Forms: hatpin holders and vases.
Identifying characteristics: This pattern features vertical rows of mirrored dots separated by a band of random threading.

Formal, Dugan, jack-in-the-pulpit vase, black amethyst, 7" h, **$600-$900;** outstanding example, **$1,300.**

Four Flowers

Made by Dugan, Diamond, and possibly Riihimaki.

Colors known: amethyst, green, marigold, peach opalescent, powder blue, and smoke.

Forms: bowls and plates.

Identifying characteristics: Four Flowers is a bold pattern with four open flowers alternating with a pointed oval. The design forms a striking geometric design.

Also known as: Posy and Pods; Pods and Posies; Stippled Posy and Pods.

Four Flowers, Dugan, eight-ruffled bowl, purple, 10" d, **$300-$500;** outstanding example, **$1,700.**

Four Flowers Variant

Attributed to Dugan and Eda Glassworks, Sweden.

Colors known: Dugan: amber, amethyst/purple, black amethyst, green, marigold, peach opalescent, teal, vaseline; Eda: lavender, and teal.

Forms: bowls and plates.

Identifying characteristics: This variation shows pointed ovals that are a little broader, allowing room for a flower bud in each. The alternating flowers are also less full blossomed.

Four Pillars

Made by Northwood, Dugan, Diamond.

Colors known: amber, amethyst, aqua opalescent, green, ice blue, ice green, lime green, marigold, olive green, peach opalescent, and white.

Forms: vases.

Identifying characteristics: This pattern features sturdy looking ribs with graceful ribs between each corner. Forms with advertising on the base are known. Some pieces are marked with the Diamond D mark.

Four Seventy Four

Made by Imperial.

Colors known: aqua, cobalt blue, emerald green, helios, lavender, lime green, marigold, olive green, purple, red, teal, and violet.

Forms: bowls, compotes, punch bowls, stemware, vases, and water sets.

Identifying characteristics: This pattern features an open cut-type flower with petals, stem, leaves with bands of cane like elements. This pattern was popular in crystal, as well as carnival glass. Production began in 1911.

Also known as: Imperial's #474; Mayflower.

Reproductions: New colors and forms were made in the 1960s-70s as compotes, covered boxes, mugs, salt and pepper shakers, sugar shakers, vases, and water sets.

Four Seventy Four, Imperial, vase, marigold, 10" h, **$450-$650;** outstanding example, **$1,500.**

Four Seventy Four, Imperial, punch bowl, base and six cups, marigold, **$150-$250.**

Frolicking Bears

Made by US Glass.

Colors known: gunmetal luster over olive green.

Forms: water sets.

Identifying characteristics: This oddity has bears enjoying their natural habitat, with mountains in the background, and grapes on a grapevine twist around the top. Even the handle has a twig-like quality to its design. This is an extremely rare pattern.

Also known as: Bears Tumbler.

Reproductions: The International Carnival Glass Association commissioned this pattern in several new forms to be used as its convention souvenirs. These are becoming quite collectible, too.

Frolicking Bears, US Glass, water pitcher and one tumbler, green, one of three known, **$42,000.**

Fruits and Flowers

Made by Northwood.

Colors known: amethyst/purple, amethyst opalescent, aqua opalescent, blue, electric blue, green, ice blue, ice blue opalescent, ice green, lavender, marigold, Renninger blue, sapphire blue, teal, violet, and white.

Forms: berry sets, bonbons, and plates.

Identifying characteristics: This pattern features realistic cherries, apples, and pears, plus flower blossoms. The centers are plain. Backgrounds can be plain or stippled. Production began in 1911.

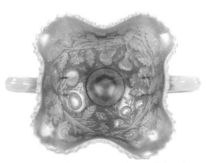

Fruits and Flowers, Northwood, bonbon, aqua opalescent, two handles, **$450.**

Reproductions: Bonbons were made by Fenton in the 1970s in purple. L. G. Wright made 14" chop plates and bowls. The chop plates include a fake Northwood "N" logo.

Garden Path
Garden Path Variant

Made by Dugan.

Colors known: amethyst/purple, marigold, peach opalescent, and white.

Forms: bowls, chop plates, and rose bowls.

Identifying characteristics: These two patterns are very similar. Garden Path features a busy field of hearts, fleur-de-lis, and arches. Garden Path Variant has an additional six winged hearts. Values for each pattern are the same.

Garden Path Variant, Dugan, chop plate, purple, 11" d, **$3,000-$6,000;** outstanding example (scarce), **$13,500.**

Garden Path Variant, Dugan, small plate, purple, 7" d, **$900-$1,200 (rare).**

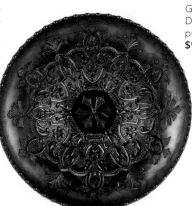

Garden Path Variant, Dugan, bowl, ice-cream shape, purple, 9-1/2" d, **$1,100-$1,400.**

Gay Nineties

Made by Millersburg.

Colors known: amethyst, green, and marigold.

Forms: water sets.

Identifying characteristics: This is a rare pattern that features stripes of leaf veining alternating with a smooth ray that has a stippled petal at the base.

Gay Nineties, Millersburg, water pitcher and one tumbler, green. Only one perfect known, second known pitcher, second known tumbler, **$24,000.**

God and Home

Made by Dugan, later by Diamond.

Colors known: cobalt blue.

Forms: water sets.

Identifying Characteristics: The pattern features a laurel wreath and shield, a rising sun with long rays. One side is lettered "In God We Trust," the other side reads "God Bless Our Home." Production began in 1912.

Also known as: Constitution.

Reproductions: Reproductions have been by L. G. Wright in amethyst, cobalt blue, green, ice green, and red. They contain the Westmoreland "W" in circle trademark. Ice blue production was made in 1976 for Levay.

God and Home, Diamond, water pitcher and six tumblers, blue. First set ever sold at auction, **$2,250.**

Good Luck

Made by Northwood.

Colors known: amethyst/purple, aqua, aqua opalescent, blue, green, horehound, ice blue, ice blue opalescent, ice green, lavender, lime green, marigold, peach opalescent, Renninger blue, sapphire blue, teal, and white.

Forms: bowls and plates.

Identifying characteristics: Look for the traditional good luck sign, a horseshoe and the words "Good Luck" in the center of this design. A riding crop crosses the center of the horseshoe while floral sprays dance around the rest of the design. Bowls and plates may have basket weave, ribbed, or stippled features, and values are fairly similar. Production began in 1911.

Reproductions: Ruffled bowls have been reproduced by Fenton in light amethyst and contain a modern Fenton logo. Ruffled bowls also are known in blue, green, and marigold, and they exhibit a harsh metallic iridescence.

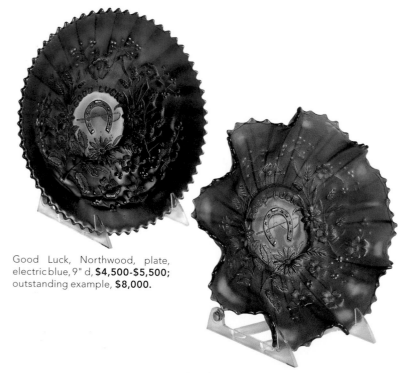

Good Luck, Northwood, plate, electric blue, 9" d, **$4,500-$5,500;** outstanding example, **$8,000.**

Good Luck, Northwood, eight-ruffled bowl, sapphire, 8-1/2" d, **$1,600-$2,300.**

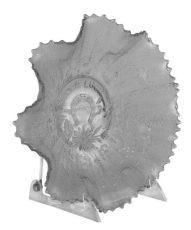

Good Luck, Northwood, eight-ruffled bowl, ice blue, 8-1/2" d, **$3,500-$4,500.**

Good Luck, Northwood, bowl, ruffled, ribbed back, ice blue, 8-1/2" d, **$4,000.**

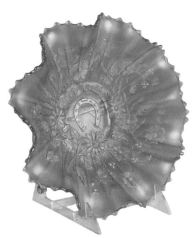

Good Luck, Northwood, eight-ruffled bowl, marigold, 8-1/2" d, **$175-$300;** outstanding example, **$950.**

Good Luck, Northwood, bowl, blue, enameled; only one known, **$800.**

Good Luck, Northwood, bowl, ribbed exterior, ruffled, sapphire, **$2,100.**

Gothic Arches

Made by Imperial.

Colors known: marigold and smoke.

Forms: vases.

Identifying Characteristics: This interesting pattern has large graceful arched loops that start at the flared top and gently flow to the round base.

Reproductions: Reproduction vases have been made by Imperial in ice blue and pale yellow.

Gothic Arches, Imperial, vase, smoke, 11" h, mouth 7-1/2" d, **$1,100-$1,500;** outstanding example, **$2,500.**

Gothic Arches, Imperial, vase, marigold, 11" h, mouth 8" d, **$1,200.**

Grape and Cable

Made by Fenton.

Colors known: amberina, amethyst, blue, celeste blue, green, lime green, marigold, marigold over milk glass, moonstone, powder blue, red, vaseline, and violet blue.

Formal bowls and plates.

Identifying characteristics: Fenton's Grape and Cable is bolder than the Northwood design. Expect to find large oval-shaped grapes and large leaves as well as the cable design. Orange bowls in this pattern sometimes are found with a Persian Medallion interior pattern. Production began in 1920 and continued until 1925. Scroll feet forms usually are Fenton, as are scalloped and fluted edges.

Grape and Cable, Fenton, bowl, ice-cream shaped, red-slag, 6" d, **$225.**

Also known as: Fenton Grape.

Reproductions: Ruffled bowls and spittoons, made from an original humidor mold, are known. Fenton produced a punch set in light amethyst and called it Paneled Grape. Noted carnival glass researcher Rose Presznick had Fenton make amethyst humidors in 1969. However, these are marked with Fenton's logo and information about Presznick's museum.

Grape and Cable

Made by Northwood.

Colors known: amethyst, aqua, aqua opalescent, black amethyst, blue, electric blue, emerald green, green, horehound, ice blue, ice green, lavender, lime green, marigold, pastels, peach opalescent, pearl (custard), purple, sapphire blue, smoke, teal, and white.

Forms: an extensive pattern, with more than 30 forms known.

Identifying characteristics: Grape and Cable represents the largest number of pieces of any carnival glass pattern. Look for delicate grapes, detailed leaves, and tendrils, along with a detailed cable running through each form. Both Northwood and Fenton

Grape and Cable, Northwood, fernery with crystal inset, amethyst, damage, **$400.**

made forms with spatula-shaped feet and collar bases. Bowls with pie crust edges are Northwood. Northwood began to produce this ever-popular pattern in 1910.

Reproductions: Reproductions include a butter dish made by Mosser in amber, cobalt blue, and ice blue. Fenton is making a variety of shapes and finishes using original Northwood molds for the descendents of the Northwood family. Hatpin holders have also been reproduced.

Grape and Cable, Northwood, hatpin holder, green, 7" h, **$250-$400.**

Grape and Cable, Northwood, hatpin holder, purple, 7" h, **$250-$400.**

Grape and Cable, Northwood, hatpin holder, aqua opalescent, **$20,000.**

Grape and Cable, Northwood, cologne, purple, 9" h, **$250-$350.**

Grape and Cable, Northwood, bowl, pie-crust edge/rib, aqua opalescent pastel, **$3,500-$5,000.**

Grape and Gothic Arches

Made by Northwood.

Colors known: blue, electric blue, marigold, pearl (custard), and smoke.

Forms: berry sets, table sets, vases, and water sets.

Identifying characteristics: Arches reminiscent of Grandmother's grape arbor form a border over the full grapes of this pattern. Also made in crystal, and crystal with gold decoration. Pattern made from 1910 until 1916.

Grape and Gothic Arches, Northwood, water pitcher and two tumblers, emerald green, **$4,250.**

Grape and Gothic Arches, Northwood, tumbler, blue, 4" h, **$50-$125.**

Grape Arbor

Made by Northwood.

Colors known: amethyst/purple, blue, ice blue, ice green, iridized custard, marigold, and white.

Forms: hats and water sets.

Identifying characteristics: This three-dimensional pattern features large life-like grapes and leaves, with a lattice design around the bases of the tumblers and water sets. Northwood also made this pattern in custard glass. Dugan made a similar pattern, which was less three-dimensional than Northwood's.

Grape Arbor, Northwood, tumbler, pearlized custard, **$800.**

Grape Arbor Northwood, tankard, purple, 11-1/2", **$600-$900.**

Grape Arbor, Northwood, tumbler, electric blue, 4-1/4" h, **$400-$550.**

Grape Arbor, Northwood, tumbler, lavender, 4-1/4" h, **$150-$250.**

Grape Arbor, Northwood, water pitcher, electric blue, **$14,000.**

Grape Arbor, Northwood, water pitcher and one tumbler, ice green, one of three known, **$10,000.**

Grape Delight

Made by Dugan/Diamond.

Colors known: amethyst, black amethyst, blue, electric purple, horehound, marigold, peach opalescent, and white.

Forms: nut bowls and rose bowls.

Identifying characteristics: This pattern features round, plump grapes and full, well-defined leaves.

Reproductions: Highly reproduced, some with a fake Northwood mark. Reproductions are known in amethyst, blue, ice blue, ice green, and white.

Grape Delight, Dugan, rose bowl, footed, electric purple, **$80**.

Grape Leaves

Made by Northwood.

Colors known: amber, amethyst, black amethyst, blue, ice blue, green, lavender, and marigold.

Forms: bowls.

Identifying characteristics: This grape pattern features a cluster of four grape stems and leaves and four bunches of grapes that cluster in the center and radiate toward the edges. The exterior pattern often found with this pattern is Blossom and Palm. Production was from 1900 until 1912.

Also known as: Wild Grapes.

Grape Leaves, Northwood, ruffled bowl, marigold, **$10**.

Grape Leaves, Northwood, ruffled bowl, lavender, **$50**.

Grapevine Lattice

Made by Dugan/Diamond.

Colors known: amethyst, marigold, and white.

Forms: bowls, hats, plates, and water sets.

Identifying characteristics: This pattern features detailed crisscrossed twigs. It is similar to Apple Blossom and Twigs, but has no flowers. Production began in 1912 and continued into the 1920s.

Also known as: Grapevine Diamonds.

Reproductions: L. G. Wright has made reproduction water sets.

Grapevine Lattice, Dugan, water pitcher and two tumblers (one shown), white, **$1,000.**

Grapevine Lattice, Dugan, plate, flat, purple, 7-1/2" d, **$250-$400.**

Grapevine and Lattice, Dugan, ruffled bowl, white, 7" d, **$30.**

Greek Key

Made by Northwood.

Colors known: amethyst/purple, blue, green, ice green, and marigold.

Forms: bowls, plates, and water sets.

Identifying characteristics: A band of a traditional Greek Key design flows through this pattern. This pattern began production in 1909 and found such favor with buyers that it was expanded to other forms in 1911 and production continued until 1913.

Greek Key, Northwood, bowl, pie-crust edge, electric blue, 9" d, **$700.**

Greek Key, Northwood, tankard, purple, 11-1/2" h, **$700-$1,100.**

Greek Key, Northwood, tumbler, green, 4-1/4" h, **$100-$150.**

Greek Key, Northwood, water pitcher and six tumblers (one shown), amethyst, **$2,000.**

Hanging Cherries

Made by Millersburg.

Colors known: amethyst, blue, green, and marigold.

Forms: bowls, chop plates, compotes, table sets, and water sets.

Identifying characteristics: Clusters of hanging cherries dominate this popular pattern.

Also known as: Millersburg Cherries.

Reproductions: Fenton made a very similar pattern in 1974. Production was limited to amethyst creamer and sugars.

Hanging Cherries, Millersburg, water pitcher and six tumblers (one shown), green, **$3,200.**

Hattie

Made by Imperial.

Colors known: amber, clambroth, helios, marigold, purple, and smoke.

Forms: bowls, chop plates, and rose bowls.

Identifying characteristics: This detailed pattern features arched lines and floral elements and is the only carnival glass pattern used on both the interior and exterior. Production began in 1911.

Also known as: Imperial's #496; Busy Lizzie.

Reproductions: Reproduction bowls are known in green, pink, smoke, and white. Bowls are all marked with the IG trademark.

Hattie, Imperial, chop plate, purple, 10" d, **$1,600-$2,000.**

Hearts and Flowers

Made by Northwood.

Colors known: amethyst, aqua opalescent, blue, blue opalescent, clambroth, electric blue, green, ice blue, ice green, lavender, marigold, pearl (custard), purple, and white.

Forms: bowls, compotes, and plates.

Identifying characteristics: This intricate pattern features a circular band of heart shapes. Production began in 1912.

Also known as: Battenburg Lace #1.

Reproductions: Domed 11-inch ruffled bowls are known in amberina, amethyst, and red and usually have the Fenton logo.

Hearts and Flowers, Northwood, compote, electric blue, 6", **$400-$600;** outstanding example, **$900.**

Hearts and Flowers, Northwood, compote (top view), purple, 6", **$400-$700.**

Hearts and Flowers, Northwood, compote, green, 6", **$1,500-$2,000 (scarce).**

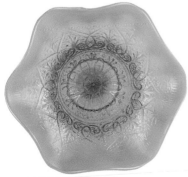

Hearts and Flowers, Northwood, compote (top view), aqua opalescent, 6", **$600-$1,000.**

Heavy Grape

Made by Imperial.

Colors known: amber, purple, aqua, cobalt blue, helios, ice green, light blue with marigold overlay, marigold, olive green, purple, smoke, and white.

Forms: bowls, chop plates, nappy, plates, and punch sets.

Identifying characteristics: This member of the carnival grape pattern family is enhanced by a diamond-quilted effect around the edge and a simple fluted back. Production began in 1910.

Also known as: Imperial's #700; Imperial's Heavy Grape.

Reproductions: Fenton has reproduced this pattern using original Imperial molds, but included the Fenton logo. The 7-1/2-inch wide ruffled bowl was made in aqua opalescent as a convention souvenir for the Southern California Carnival Glass Club in 1996.

Heavy Grape, Imperial, plate, purple, 8" d, **$100-$200.**

Heavy Grape, Imperial, deep round bowl, blue, 6-1/2" d, **$600-$1,000 (rare).**

Heavy Iris

Made by Dugan.

Colors known: amber, amethyst, ice blue, horehound, lavender, marigold, pastel marigold, peach opalescent, purple, and white.

Forms: water sets.

Identifying characteristics: This pattern was very sculpted, giving it a realistic three-dimensional quality.

Also known as: Iris.

Reproductions: L. G. Wright reproduced this pattern in 1978. Reproductions can be identified because they have a plain band around the top between the pattern and the ruffled top. Tumblers have been made in aqua opalescent, cobalt blue, and vaseline opalescent.

Heavy Iris, Dugan, tumbler, purple, **$150.**

Heavy Iris, Dugan, tumbler, purple, 4" h, **$75-$150;** outstanding example, **$400.**

Heavy Iris, Dugan, water pitcher, tankard, and one tumbler, white, **$1,600.**

Heron

Made by Dugan.

Colors known: amethyst, black amethyst, marigold, and purple.

Forms: mugs.

Identifying characteristics: A lonely heron, facing to the left, stands among cattails and rushes. A companion pattern is Dugan's Stork and Rushes, which has four birds.

Heron, Dugan, mug, black amethyst, 4" h, **$250-$350.**

Hobnail

Made by Millersburg.

Colors known: amethyst, blue, green, marigold, and purple.

Forms: spittoons, rose bowls, table sets, vases, and water sets.

Identifying characteristics: As the name implies, this design features pointy hobnails arranged in alternating rows. Most pieces of this interesting pattern have a brilliant radium finish. Production began in 1910 and continued until 1912.

Also known as: Stippled Dots.

Hobnail, Millersburg, water pitcher, blue, **$4,100.**

Hobnail, Millersburg, tumbler, blue, **$1,800.**

Hobnail, Millersburg, spittoon, amethyst, 5" d, **$800-$1,000.**

Hobnail, Millersburg, tumbler, green, one of four known, **$2,700.**

Hobstar

Made by Imperial.

Colors known: emerald green, helios, marigold, purple.

Forms: bowls, bride's baskets, covered jars, pickle castors, punch sets, table sets.

Identifying characteristics: This typically geometric pattern from Imperial features a large hobstar surrounded by circle arches of diamond borders, fans, and other typical imitation cut-glass elements. Carnival production began in 1912, production of crystal began before that time.

Also known as: Imperial's #282.

Reproductions: Green cracker jars, complete with the IG logo, are known. Punch sets were also reissued by Imperial.

Hobstar, Imperial, creamer, purple, **$100-$180.**

Hobstar, Imperial, covered butter dish, purple, **$200-$300.**

Hobstar and Feather

Made by Millersburg.

Colors: amethyst, clear, frosted, green, marigold, and white.

Forms: bowls, compotes, punch sets, rose bowls, table sets, water sets, and whimsies.

Identifying characteristics: large feathered leafed stems dominate this large-scale pattern with large hobstars filling the space between each leaf. Production began in 1910.

Also known as: Intaglio Mazie.

Reproductions: Reproduced tumblers are reported.

Hobstar and Feather, Millersburg, punch bowl, base, eight cups, master, marigold, **$2,750.**

Hobstar Flower

Made by Imperial.

Colors known: emerald green, helios, lavender, marigold, purple, and smoke.

Forms: compotes.

Identifying characteristics: This geometric pattern features a large hobstar along with the popular imitation cut glass motifs that Imperial designers so often used. Production began in 1909.

Also known as: Imperial's #302 and #302-1/2.

Hobstar Flower, Imperial, compote, purple, 5" h, **$100-$200.**

Holly

Made by Fenton.

Colors known: amethyst, aqua opalescent, blue, blue opalescent, celeste blue, green, lime green, lime green opalescent, marigold, marigold on milk glass, moonstone, powder blue, red, vaseline, and white.

Forms: bowls, compotes, goblets, hat, plates, rose bowls, and vases.

Identifying characteristics: Fenton's popular Holly pattern features sprigs of holly berries and leaves that converge in the center and radiate to the edges of the pattern. Production began in 1911.

Also known as: Carnival Holly.

Reproductions: Ruffled bowls have been reproduced in aqua opalescent and amethyst.

Holly, Fenton, flat plate, green, 9-1/2" d, **$700-$900.**

Holly, Fenton, flat plate, blue, 9-1/2" d, **$300-$500.**

Holly, Fenton, flat plate, marigold, 9-1/2" d, **$200-$300.**

Holly and Berry

Made by Dugan.

Colors known: black amethyst, blue, marigold, peach opalescent, and purple.

Forms: bowls and nappies.

Identifying characteristics: This holly pattern features springs of holly and large berries that surround the center motif of more leaves and berries. Production began in 1909 and continued until 1912.

Holly and Berry, Dugan, six-ruffled bowl, purple, 7-1/2" d, **$100-$200.**

Holly and Berry, Dugan, tricorner nappy, purple, 7" d, **$100-$200.**

Holly and Berry, Dugan, seven-ruffled nappy, purple, 7" d, **$100-$200.**

Holly Sprig

Made by Millersburg.

Colors known: amethyst, clambroth, green, lavender, marigold, and vaseline.

Forms: bonbons, bowls, calling card trays, and nappies

Identifying characteristics: Millersburg's Holly Sprig has a wreath of holly leaves and small berries, with four leaves that point to the blank center. This interior pattern is often paired Near Cut Wreath of Flute on the exterior. Production began in 1910.

Also known as: Holly; Holly Spray; Millersburg Holly.

Holly Sprig, Millersburg, bowl, purple with radium iridescence, **$100.**

Homestead

Made by Imperial.

Colors known: amber, cobalt blue, electric purple, emerald green, forest green, helios, marigold, purple, smoke, and white.

Forms: chop plates, with some marked "Nu-Art."

Identifying characteristics: Original chop plates have a ribbed back and smooth base. Production began in 1911.

Also known as: Imperial's #525; Nu-Art Homestead; and Nu-Art Currier and Ives.

Reproductions: Imperial reissued this chop plate in ice blue, marigold, pink, smoke, and white. Reproduction chop plates have a plain back and stippled base. Another

Homestead, Imperial, chop plate, electric purple, signed Nu-Art, **$3,200.**

reproduction by Summit Art Glass Company is known in vaseline.

Imperial Grape

Made by Imperial.

Colors known: amber, aqua, clambroth, cobalt blue, emerald green, helios, horehound, lavender, light blue with marigold overlay, marigold, marigold over milk glass, olive green, purple, smoke, and violet.

Forms: bowls, compotes, cups and saucers, plates, water sets, and wine sets.

Identifying characteristics: This extensive pattern is found with lush round grapes attached to meandering grapevines, realistic leaves, plus an arched border trim. The molded handles are textured to resemble the bark found on grapevines. Production began in 1912.

Also known as: Imperial's #473; Grape.

Imperial Grape, Imperial, water pitcher, emerald green, **$2,800-$4,000.**

Reproductions: Imperial reissued this pattern in the 1960s. Forms it issued include a small bowl, pedestal creamer and sugar, cruet, goblet, footed juice glasses, salt and pepper shakers, water carafe, wine set, and other forms. Colors of new Imperial forms include amber, aurora jewels, helios, marigold, smoke, and other colors. The Imperial molds have been sold to other glass companies, such as Wetzel Glass and Summit Art Glass. Colors produced by these companies include electric blue, iridized custard, red, vaseline, and possibly other colors.

Imperial Grape, Imperial, water pitcher, purple, 10-1/2" h, **$250-$400;** outstanding example, **$800.**

Imperial Grape, Imperial, low ruffled bowl, purple, 9" d, **$200-$300.**

Imperial Grape, Imperial, flat plate, purple, 6-1/2" d, **$250-$350.**

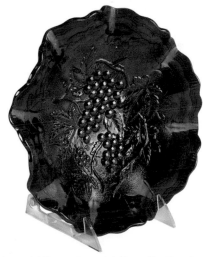

Imperial Grape, Imperial, tumbler, purple, 4" h, **$60-$100.**

Imperial Grape, Imperial, low ruffled bowl, blue, 9" d, **$10,000 (very rare, only one known).**

Imperial Grape, Imperial, wine decanter, marigold, 12" h, **$70-$125.**

Imperial Grape, Imperial, stemmed wine, marigold, 4" h, **$20-$35.**

Imperial Grape, Imperial, punch bowl, base, seven cups, electric purple, **$1,700-$2,200.**

Inverted Feather

Made by Cambridge.

Colors known: amethyst, green, and marigold.

Forms: compotes, cracker jars, milk pitchers, punch sets, stemware, table sets, and water sets.

Identifying characteristics: This geometric pattern includes a row of hobstars over upright feathers over another row of hobstars. Production began in 1915 and continued to 1917.

Also known as: Cambridge's #2651; Feather and Hobstar.

Inverted Feather, Cambridge, water pitcher and tankard, marigold, **$8,100.**

Inverted Feather, cracker jar, green, **$175.**

Inverted Strawberry

Made by Cambridge.

Colors known: amethyst, blue, green, and marigold.

Forms: berry sets, candlesticks, celery vases, compotes, milk pitchers, powder jars, spittoons, table sets, and water sets.

Identifying characteristics: Cambridge made several exquisite intaglio patterns, including Inverted Strawberry and Inverted Thistle. The strawberries on this pattern are very detailed and are highlighted by strawberry blossoms and leaves. Many, but not all, pieces are marked with the trademark "Near Cut."

Reproductions: Both the tumblers and water pitchers have been reproduced. A miniature punch bowl has been created. The American Carnival Glass Association commissioned a pedestaled creamer in purple slag as its convention souvenir in 1996. Other table set forms and a spittoon were made for other ACGA conventions.

Inverted Strawberry, Cambridge, water pitcher and tankard, green, **$2,800.**

Inverted Thistle

Made by Cambridge.

Colors known: amethyst, blue, green, and marigold.

Forms: berry sets, chop plates, nut bowls, table sets, and water sets.

Identifying characteristics: Like Inverted Strawberry, this is an intaglio pattern with very detailed thistle blossoms and leaves.

Inverted Thistle, Cambridge, water pitcher and six tumblers, amethyst, **$1,500.**

Jeweled Heart

Made by Dugan.

Colors known: amethyst, marigold, peach opalescent, and white.

Forms: bowls, plates, water sets, and whimsies.

Identifying characteristics: This pattern takes its name from the oval "jewel" included in the stylized heart that predominates the design. Carnival production began in 1910.

Also known as: Victor when found in opalescent glass.

Jeweled Heart, Dugan, water pitcher and six tumblers, pedestal, marigold, **$1,600.**

Kittens

Made by Fenton.

Colors known: amethyst, aqua, blue, green, marigold, pastel powder blue, teal, and topaz (vaseline).

Forms: banana boats, bowls, cups and saucers, plates, and vases.

Identifying characteristics: This pattern is one of the very few that was geared toward children and is often considered as children's toy dishes. The first ads for Fenton's Kittens appeared in 1918.

Also known as: Fenton's #299.

Kittens, Fenton, bowl, peach opalescent, ruffled, **$150.**

Kittens, Fenton, cup and saucer, marigold, **$200.**

Knotted Beads

Made by Fenton.

Colors known: amber, aqua, blue, marigold, red, and vaseline.

Forms: vases.

Identifying characteristics: This pattern can be identified by its four rows of six ovals, each filled with connected beading. Production began in 1915.

Also known as: Fenton's #509; Variegated Vase.

Knotted Beads, Fenton, vase, marigold, candy-ribbon edge, high shelf, 7-1/2" h, **$75.**

Knotted Beads, Fenton, vase, sapphire, **$450.**

Lattice and Daisy

Made by Dugan/Diamond.

Colors known: amethyst, blue, marigold, and white.

Forms: bowls, hats, and water sets.

Identifying characteristics: This elegant-looking pattern features bands of lattice-work along with delicate daisies and leaves. Production began in 1915 and continued until 1920.

Also known as: Daisy and Lattice Band.

Lattice and Daisy, Dugan, water pitcher and six tumblers, tankard, marigold, **$175.**

Lattice and Grape

Made by Fenton.

Colors known: blue, marigold, and white.

Forms: water sets.

Identifying characteristics: This design has a zigzag dotted border over a cluster of grapes which are suspended over a lattice border, again with dots in the center of each diamond shaped block.

Also known as: Lattice and Grapevine.

Lattice and Grape, Fenton, tankard, marigold, **$100.**

Lattice and Grape, Fenton, six tumblers, marigold, **$60.**

Lattice and Points

Made by Dugan.

Colors known: amethyst, blue, marigold, peach opalescent, and white.

Forms: bowls and vases.

Identifying characteristics: This pattern has intersecting lines of lattice that form distinctive points. The center is a daisy.

Also known as: Vining Twigs.

Lattice and Points, Dugan, low bowl, purple, eight ruffles, 7" d, **$50-$100**; outstanding example, **$300.**

Lattice and Points, Dugan, vase, purple, 8" h, **$150-$250.**

Lattice and Points, Dugan, vase, peach opalescent, eight-ruffled hat shape, 5-1/2" h, **$75-$150.**

Laurel Band

Maker unknown.

Colors known: marigold.

Forms: water sets.

Identifying characteristics: A delicate laurel-type flower highlights the band at the top of this ribbed pattern.

Laurel Band, unknown, set of water pitcher and four tumblers (one shown), pedestal, electric marigold, **$285.**

Leaf and Beads

Made by Northwood.

Colors known: amethyst, aqua, aqua opalescent, blue, green, ice blue, ice green, lavender, marigold, peach opalescent, purple, Renninger blue, teal, and white.

Forms: bowls, candy dishes, nut bowls, plates, and rose bowls.

Identifying characteristics: Rows of vertical beads cascade toward the well defined leaves found at the base or center of this design. Northwood clearly used the same mold to create the rose bowl, and then widened it to create the candy dish and nut bowl forms. The interiors of the rose bowls can be plain, rayed, or have a sunflower design.

Also known as: Stippled Leaf and Beads.

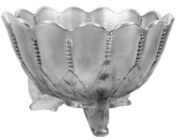

Leaf and Beads, Northwood, nut bowl, aqua opalescent, footed, flared, **$1,500.**

Leaf Chain

Made by Fenton.

Colors known: amberina, amethyst, aqua, aqua opalescent, blue, celeste blue, clambroth, green, ice blue, ice green, lavender, marigold, red, teal, vaseline, and white.

Forms: bowls and plates.

Identifying characteristics: This busy pattern features a ring of open flowers surrounded by stars, scale background between each flower, and a looped edge. The center shows a ring of stars, scale, and an open flower. Production began in 1921.

Also known as: Leaf Medallion.

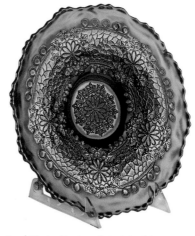

Leaf Chain, Fenton, flat plate, blue, 9" d, **$700-$1,200;** outstanding example, **$3,100.**

Leaf Columns

Made by Northwood.

Colors known: amethyst, green, horehound, ice blue, ice green, marigold, purple, sapphire blue, teal, and white.

Forms: vases.

Identifying characteristics: This pattern features an upright form of leaves radiating off a center stem. The bases are a standard 3-1/2 inch diameter, while the height can range from 6 inches to a slender 12 inches.

Leaf Columns, Northwood, squatty vase, white, 7" h, **$350-$600.**

Leaf Columns, Northwood, squatty vase, green, 6-1/2" h, **$250-$350.**

Leaf Tiers

Made by Fenton.

Colors known: marigold.

Forms: berry sets, table sets, and water sets.

Identifying characteristics: This pattern features rows of detailed vertical leaves, which are staggered so they completely cover the forms.

Also known as: Stippled Leaf.

Leaf Tiers, Fenton, water pitcher, second one known in blue, glued on foot, **$1,150.**

Leaf Tiers, Fenton, footed tumbler, marigold, one of the best examples, **$70.**

Leaf Tiers, Fenton, covered sugar and creamer, marigold, **$200.**

Lined Lattice

Made by Dugan.

Colors known: amethyst, marigold, peach opalescent, purple, smoky lavender, and white.

Forms: vases.

Identifying characteristics: This is one of the most popular swung vase designs. The pattern includes a delicate lattice motif with each diamond the lattice creates filled in with lines. The sizes range from 5 inches to 15 inches high.

Lined Lattice, Dugan, squatty vase, purple, 5-1/2" h, **$250-$400 (scarce).**

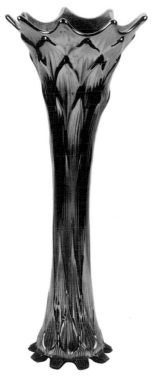

Lined Lattice, Dugan, vase, amethyst, feet, 15" h, **$250-$400.**

Lined Lattice, Dugan, vase, peach opalescent, squatty, flared, 5-1/4" h, **$265.**

Little Fishes

Made by Fenton.

Colors known: amethyst, aqua, blue, green, and marigold.

Forms: bowls.

Identifying characteristics: A band of fish swim among decorative borders. Bases can be three ball-shaped feet or collar.

Also known as: Sea Lanes.

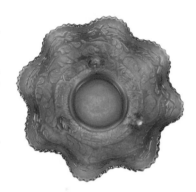

Little Fishes, Fenton, bowl, marigold, ruffle, 10" d, **$165.**

Little Flowers

Made by Fenton.

Colors known: amberina, amethyst, aqua, blue, green, marigold, powder blue, red, and vaseline.

Forms: bowls and plates.

Identifying characteristics: Rows of large petal flowers with stems that extend to form arches are interspersed with smaller daisy-like flowers, completed by a wheel-type device center. Production began in 1910.

Also known as: Stippled Diamond and Flower.

Little Flowers, Fenton, bowl, red/amberina, ruffled, 9-1/2" h, **$2,000.**

Little Flowers, Fenton, bowl, blue, 8" d, **$150.**

Little Stars

Made by Millersburg.

Colors known: amethyst, blue, clam-broth, green, marigold, and pastel marigold.

Forms: bowls and plates.

Identifying characteristics: This pattern has elongated loops each containing a stemmed flower, small six-pointed stars alternate with the loops and stippled ground. Production began in 1910.

Also known as: Stippled Clematis.

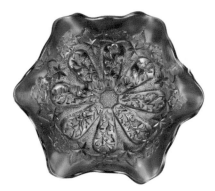

Little Stars, Millersburg, bowl, blue, ruffled, 10" d, **$550.**

Loganberry

Made by Imperial.

Colors known: amber, emerald green, helios, marigold, purple, and smoke.

Forms: vases.

Identifying characteristics: This pattern was made only in baluster-shaped vases, using a life-like three-dimensional effect for the berries that cluster around the middle to the base. Production began in 1912.

Also known as: Imperial's #477.

Reproductions: Ruffled vases in green, ice green, and pink are known. Old vases have a plain or starred base, new ones have a stippled ground, often with the LIG or IG mark.

Loganberry, Imperial, vase, purple, 10" h, **$1,500-$2,800.**

Long Thumbprint

Made by Fenton.

Colors known: amethyst, aqua, blue, green, marigold, and olive green.

Forms: vases.

Identifying characteristics: It is easy to see how this pattern probably got its name. Oval thumbprint-type devices vary in length as they descend to the base of these vase forms. Production was between 1911 and 1915.

Long Thumbprint, Dugan, jack-in-the-pulpit vase, green, 6-1/2" h, **$280.**

Long Thumbprint Variant, Dugan, vase, amethyst, 5-1/4" h, **$1,200.**

Lotus and Grape

Made by Fenton.

Colors known: amethyst, aqua, blue, green, lime, marigold, Persian blue, purple, red, red slag, teal, and vaseline.

Forms: bonbons, bowls, and plates.

Identifying characteristics: This pattern shows alternating grape clusters and full blossomed lotus flowers and leaves, with two opposing lotus flowers in the center. Production of this pattern began in 1911 and continued until 1915.

Also known as: Ruffled Magnolia and Grape.

Lotus and Grape, Fenton, ice-cream shaped bowl, Persian blue, **$575.**

Lustre Rose

Made by Imperial.

Colors known: amber, amberina, aqua, clambroth, cobalt blue, emerald green, helios, lavender, light blue with marigold overlay, lime green, marigold, marigold on milk glass, purple, olive, red, smoke, teal, vaseline, and white.

Forms: berry sets, bowls, plates, table sets, vases, and water sets.

Identifying characteristics: Modern researchers have agreed that the patterns known as Lustre Rose and Open Rose are actually the same pattern. The pattern can be identified by the three-dimensional open rose and foliage

Lustre Rose, Imperial, tumbler, whimsey, powder blue/marigold, 5" mouth, **$500.**

that dominates each form. The backgrounds have a pebbly or stippled effect. This pattern was made from 1911 until 1914.

Also known as: Imperial's #489; Imperial Rose; Open Rose.

Reproductions: Bowls, plates, table sets, and water sets have been reproduced in amber, helios, meadow green, marigold, pink, purple, red, smoke, and white. These reproductions were made by Imperial and those who succeeded them. Imperial reproductions are marked with IG, LIG, or ALIG logos.

Lustre Rose, Imperial, water pitcher and six tumblers, electric purple, **$2,200.**

Many Fruits

Made by Dugan.

Colors known: blue, green, marigold, purple, and white.

Forms: punch sets.

Identifying characteristics: The fruits found in this pattern are full and well defined, as are the leaves that compliment each fruit. Production began in 1911.

Many Fruits, Dugan, punch bowl with ruffled rim and ruffled base, white, sold as set with five cups, **$1,800.**

Many Fruits, Dugan, punch bowl, ruffled base, purple, **$1,200-$1,500.**

Many Stars

Made by Millersburg.

Colors known: amethyst, blue, green, and marigold.

Forms: bowls and chop plates.

Identifying characteristics: This pattern may remind collectors of starry nights with its rows of stippled stars and a bright stippled star center, which can be either a five-point or six-point star. Production began in 1910.

Many Stars, Millersburg, 3-in-1 bowl, amethyst, 9" d, **$650.**

Many Stars, Millersburg, ruffled bowl, has radium iridescence, amethyst, **$450.**

Many Stars, Millersburg, bowl, green radium, ice-cream shape, **$375.**

Maple Leaf

Made by Dugan/Diamond.

Colors known: amethyst, blue, green, marigold, and purple.

Forms: berry sets, table sets, and water sets.

Identifying characteristics: This exterior pattern shows a detailed maple leaf against a stippled veined background. Berry sets may have Peacock Tail as their interior pattern. Production began in 1912 and continued until 1928.

Reproductions: Westmoreland reproduced table sets and water sets for L. G. Wright. Reproduction toothpick holders and tumblers are also reported.

Maple Leaf, Dugan, water pitcher and one tumbler, blue, **$550.**

Maple Leaf, Dugan, spooner, pumpkin marigold, **$125.**

Mary Ann

Made by Dugan/Diamond.

Colors known: amethyst, lavender, marigold, pink, and purple.

Forms: loving cups and vases.

Identifying characteristics: This pattern with a well defined open flower and leaves was named for Fanny Mary Ann Dugan, sister of Thomas E. and Alfred Dugan. It can be found in crystal, satin glass, and also opalescent glass. Production began about 1915 and continued until 1918.

Also known as: Cordelia.

Reproductions.

Mary Ann, Dugan, three-handled vase, amethyst, **$800.**

Memphis

Made by Northwood.

Colors known: amethyst, blue, ice blue, ice green, marigold, purple, and white.

Forms: berry sets, fruit bowls, and punch sets.

Identifying characteristics: Memphis is an ornate pattern with a checkerboard motif between the caned arcs and hobstar designs. This pattern is unique in that it comes with a stand that fits both the fruit bowl and the punch bowl. To determine which bowl is which, collectors need to study the collar base of the bowl: the punch bowl has a collar base that fits into the stand while the fruit bowl has a large octagonal collar that fits over the top of the stand.

Also known as: Northwood's #19.

Memphis, Northwood, punch bowl, base, six cups, green, **$3,200.**

Memphis, Northwood, punch bowl, base, six cups, electric marigold, **$600.**

Memphis, Northwood, punch bowl, base, six cups, white, **$4,000.**

Morning Glory

Made by Imperial.

Colors known: amber, clambroth, cobalt blue, emerald green, helios, lavender, light blue with marigold overlay, marigold, olive green, purple, red, smoke, and white.

Forms: vases.

Identifying characteristics: As the name implies, the pattern reflects on the beauty of a morning glory with slight ribs that extend to the base. Vases range from 4 inches to 22 inches high. The pattern was first advertised 1910 and continued until 1917.

Morning Glory, Imperial, vase, purple, 12-1/2" h, **$800-$1,200.**

Morning Glory, Imperial, vase, marigold, 12-1/2" h, **$200-$350.**

Morning Glory, Imperial, miniature vase, smoke, 4-3/4" h, **$100-$180.**

Morning Glory, Imperial, miniature vase, marigold, 3-1/2" h, shortest to be known, **$150-$250**.

Morning Glory, Imperial, funeral vase, purple, 14-1/2" h, 8-1/2 " mouth, **$700**.

Multi-Fruits and Flowers

Made by Millersburg.

Colors known: amethyst, green, and marigold.

Forms: compotes, punch sets, and water sets.

Identifying characteristics: Millersburg designers added as many fruits to this pattern as they could fit—cherries, peaches, pears, and grape clusters are surrounded by leaves and flowers.

Also known as: Multi-Fruits.

Multi-Fruits and Flowers, Millersburg, tumbler, amethyst, small chip, **$375**.

Multi-Fruits and Flowers, Millersburg, water pitcher, green, **$15,000**.

Nautilus

Made by Dugan and also Northwood.

Colors known: marigold, peach opalescent, and purple.

Forms: table sets and vases.

Identifying characteristics: This pattern is modeled after a seashell and includes marine motifs on the base. The original molds were made for Northwood's custard glass production and later used by Dugan.

Also known as: Argonaut Shell when found in custard or opalescent glass.

Reproductions: Toothpick holders, never originally made by Dugan or Northwood, are now being made.

Nautilus, Dugan, vase, purple, 9-1/2" h, **$300-$500.**

Nesting Swan

Made by Millersburg.

Colors known: amethyst, blue, green, and marigold.

Forms: bowls.

Identifying characteristics: A graceful swan dominates the center of this design, which is further enhanced by a bed of reeds, leaves, blossoms, and cattails. The exteriors are Diamond and Fan. Production began in 1911.

Nesting Swan, Millersburg, bowl, green with satin iridescence, **$250-$400.**

Nippon

Made by Northwood.

Colors known: amethyst, aqua, blue, green, ice blue, ice green, lime green, lime green opalescent, marigold, teal, and white.

Forms: bowls and plates.

Identifying characteristics: This design is based on graceful peacock feathers, each radiating from the center flower design. The pattern was first advertised in 1912.

Nippon, Northwood, ruffled bowl with basket-weave exterior, purple with near-electric iridescence, **$475.**

Octagon

Made by Imperial.

Colors known: amber, aqua, clambroth, helios, ice blue, light blue with marigold overlay, marigold, olive green, purple, smoke, teal, and white.

Forms: berry sets, nappies, stemware, toothpicks, table sets, water sets, and wine sets.

Identifying characteristics: Imperial designers included many cut-glass type motifs in this pattern which has a vertical feel to it with its upright bands of hobstars, buttons, and diamonds. Production began in 1911.

Also known as: Imperial's #505; Princess Lace.

Reproductions: Imperial has issued an 8-inch vase in red which contemporary carnival glass collectors call "Imperial Lace." Other shapes reissued include large bowls, butter dishes, small compotes, and toothpick holders. Reissues are found in blue or green.

Octagon, Imperial, wine decanter, purple, 10-1/2" h, **$1,300-$1,600 (rare).**

Octagon, Imperial, stemmed wine, purple, 4" h, **$100-$200;** outstanding example, **$400 (rare).**

Octagon, Imperial, small-sized pitcher, purple, 8" h, **$1,900-$2,300 (rare).**

Ohio Star

Made by Millersburg.

Colors known: amethyst, clambroth, crystal, green, marigold, and white.

Forms: compotes, relishes, and vases.

Identifying characteristics: The design includes a circled six-pointed star over another and another with graceful caned arches between each vertical row. This pattern was first made by Millersburg in crystal in 1909.

Ohio Star, Millersburg, vase, green, 10" h, **$4,400.**

Open Edge

Made by Fenton.

Colors known: amber, amberina, aqua, black amethyst, celeste blue, green, ice blue, ice green, lime green, marigold, olive green, powder blue, red, and white.

Forms: bowls, baskets, and hats.

Identifying characteristics: This pattern uses a design that resembles the weaving found in reeded baskets.

Also known as: Basketweave Open Edge; Open Edge Basketweave.

Reproductions: Fenton reissued this pattern in 1970-73 in amethyst and in marigold in 1976-77. The Canadian Carnival Collectors Association commissioned red baskets for their convention in 1990.

Open Edge, Fenton, basket, marigold, with "Miller's Furniture" advertising, **$25.**

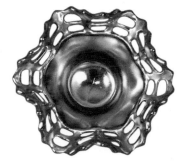

Open Edge, Fenton, basket, amberina, **$75.**

Orange Tree

Made by Fenton.

Colors known: amber, amberina, amethyst, aqua, aqua opalescent, blue, chocolate, green, lime green, marigold, marigold on milk glass, peach opalescent, Persian blue, powder blue, red, vaseline, and white.

Forms: bowls, breakfast sets, hatpin holders, mugs, plates, punch bowls, shaving mugs, table sets, and water sets.

Identifying characteristics: This pattern is one of the most popular Fenton created. The number of items available is extensive as well as the colors available, making it easy to collect and enjoy. The motif is reflected in the name with well-designed orange trees, ripe with fruit. Production began in 1911.

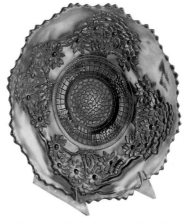

Orange Tree, Fenton, flat plate, blue, 9" d, **$300-$600;** outstanding example, **$1,500.**

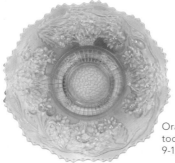

Orange Tree, Fenton, water pitcher and six tumblers, blue, **$750.**

Orange Tree, Fenton, bowl, ice-cream edge, marigold over moonstone, **$1,500.**

Orange Tree, Fenton, sawtooth plate, dark marigold, 9-1/4" d, **$350.**

Oriental Poppy

Made by Northwood.

Colors known: blue, green, ice blue, ice green, lime green, marigold, purple, and white.

Forms: water sets.

Identifying characteristics: Northwood used a tankard-style pitcher to show off this design of an opened poppy flower and delicate foliage. Production began in 1911.

Oriental Poppy, Northwood, tumbler, blue, 4-1/4" h, **$250-$400 (rare)**.

Oriental Poppy, Northwood, tankard, blue, 14" h, **$7,000-$10,000 (rare)**.

Oriental Poppy, Northwood, water pitcher and four tumblers, ice blue, **$2,500**.

Oriental Poppy, Northwood, tumbler, purple, 4-1/4" h, **$50-$100;** outstanding example, **$250**.

Palm Beach

Made by US Glass.

Colors known: amethyst, honey amber, lime green, marigold, and white.

Forms: berry sets, bowls, plates, rose bowls, table sets, vases, and whimsies.

Identifying characteristics: This pattern started as a crystal pattern by the conglomerate known as US Glass. It features clusters of rounded grapes and foliage on a vine that curves from the top to the base. Pieces in this pattern are often found with gold or silver trim. Some have additional amethyst flashing in the interior.

Palm Beach, US Glass, whimsey rose bowl, smoke, **$600.**

Palm Beach, US Glass, vase, white, **$250.**

Palm Beach, US Glass, vase, whimsey, marigold, 6-1/2" h, 3-1/2" base, **$800.**

Paneled Dandelion

Made by Fenton.

Colors known: amethyst, blue, green, and marigold.

Forms: water sets.

Identifying characteristics: Fenton used a tankard-style water pitcher to show off this whimsical pattern that reminds one of all those dandelion puffs that pop up every year and get blown off into the wind. Production began in 1910.

Paneled Dandelion, Fenton, vase, blue, made as a whimsey using a water pitcher mold, never had a handle attached, rare, **$16,000.**

Pansy

Made by Imperial.

Colors known: amber, aqua, clambroth, cobalt blue, helios, lavender, marigold, purple, and smoke.

Forms: bowls, breakfast sets, dresser trays, nappies, pickle dishes, and table sets.

Identifying characteristics: A cluster of spring pansies and leaves awaits the viewer of this pretty pattern. Production began in 1910.

Also known as: Imperial's #478.

Reproductions: Creamers, nappies, pickle dishes, and sugars have been reissued by Imperial.

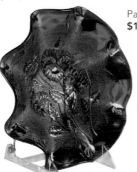

Pansy, Imperial, bowl, purple, eight ruffles, 9" d, **$150-$250;** outstanding example, **$500.**

Pansy, Imperial, nappy, blue, 5-1/2" d, **$800-$1,100 (rare).**

Panther

Made Fenton.

Colors known: amberina, amethyst, aqua, blue, clambroth, ginger ale, green, lavender, marigold, nile green, olive green, and red.

Forms: berry sets.

Identifying characteristics: This interior pattern features two large stalking panthers accented by scrolling foliage. The exterior pattern used is Butterfly and Berry. Production began in 1914.

Panther, Fenton, bowl, red, six ruffles, footed, 6" d, **$800-$1,200.**

Peach

Made by Northwood.

Colors known: blue, marigold, and white.

Forms: berry sets, table sets, and water sets.

Identifying characteristics: This pattern features two rounded peaches and foliage, which appear to be hanging from the cable border. Production was from 1911 to 1912.

Also known as: Northwood Peach.

Peach, Northwood, water pitcher, powder blue slag, only one known, **$1,000.**

Peacock

Made by Millersburg.

Colors known: amethyst, blue, green, and marigold.

Forms: berry sets, bowls, plates, and rose bowls.

Identifying characteristics: This pattern features a large well-defined standing peacock with an urn in the background. It is identified by the lack of a bee and no beading on the urn. Production began in 1910.

Also known as: The Fluffy Bird.

Peacock, Millersburg, large berry bowl, amethyst, 9-1/2" d, **$400-$550.**

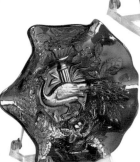

Peacock, Millersburg, sauce, marigold, six ruffles, 6" d, **$175-$300;** outstanding example, **$700.**

Peacock, Millersburg, sauce, amethyst, six ruffles, 6" d, **$150-$250.**

Peacock, Millersburg, master berry bowl, amethyst, six small, variant, no bee, deep flared, **$1,100.**

Peacock and Grape

Made by Fenton.

Colors known: amethyst, aqua, blue, green, lime green opalescent, marigold, peach opalescent, pumpkin marigold, and red.

Forms: bowls and plates.

Identifying characteristics: This pattern is similar to Peacock and Dahlia, but instead of a dahlia, there is a cluster of grapes and leaves. The top of the wedges has a flat border rather than a scallop. Production began in 1911.

Also known as: Fenton's #1646.

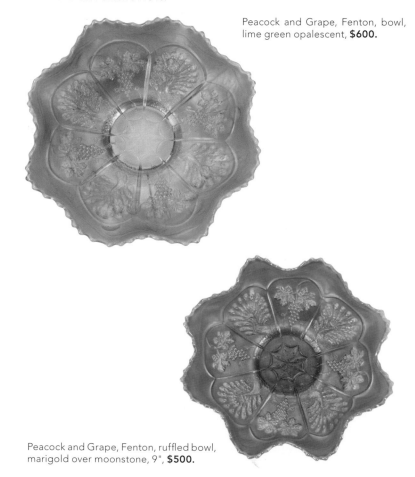

Peacock and Grape, Fenton, bowl, lime green opalescent, **$600.**

Peacock and Grape, Fenton, ruffled bowl, marigold over moonstone, 9", **$500.**

Peacock and Urn

Made by Fenton.

Colors known: amethyst, aqua, blue, green, marigold, marigold over milk glass, olive, Persian blue, purple, red, vaseline, and white.

Forms: bowls, compotes, and plates.

Identifying characteristics: This peacock pattern shows a detailed standing stiff-necked peacock with its tail extending through the floral wreath border. The background urn contains a bouquet of roses. Exterior pattern may be Bearded Berry.

Peacock and Urn

Made by Millersburg.

Colors known: amethyst, blue, green, marigold, and olive green.

Forms: berry sets, bowls, compotes, and plates.

Identifying characteristics: Like Millersburg's Peacock pattern, this pattern shows a standing peacock with a flower-filled urn behind it. This time the peacock has caught a bee and holds it in its beak. Bases have a many-rayed star. Production was centered about the 1910 to 1911 period.

Peacock and Urn, Millersburg, 3-in-1 mystery bowl, green, 9" d, **$450-$600.**

Peacock and Urn

Made by Northwood.

Colors known: amethyst, aqua opalescent, blue, clambroth, green, honey amber, horehound, ice blue, ice green, lime green, marigold, pumpkin marigold, purple, Renninger blue, and white.

Forms: berry sets, ice cream sets, and chop plates.

Identifying characteristics: The Northwood version of the popular Peacock and Urn pattern has three rows of beading on the urn and more open area surrounding the central design. Bases are smooth. Production began in 1912 and continued until 1914.

Peacock and Urn, Northwood, sauce, purple, ice-cream shape, 5-1/2" d, **$75-$125;** outstanding example, **$400.**

Peacock and Urn, Northwood, sauce, marigold, ice-cream shape, 5-1/2" d, **$75-$125;** outstanding example, **$550.**

Peacock and Urn, Northwood, master bowl, blue, ice-cream shape, 10" d, **$1,500-$2,500;** outstanding example, **$7,200.**

Peacock and Urn, Northwood, sauce, green, ice-cream shape, 5-1/2" d, **$700-$900.**

Peacock and Urn, Northwood, sauce, blue, ice-cream shape, 5-1/2" d, **$150-$250.**

Peacock and Urn, Northwood, master bowl, blue stippled, ice-cream shape, 10" d, **$1,500-$2,500;** outstanding example, **$4,200.**

Peacock and Urn, Northwood, master bowl, electric blue, ice-cream shape, **$2,500.**

Peacock and Urn, Northwood, chop plate, purple, three rows, three beads, flared, **$1,400.**

Peacock and Urn Variant

Made by Millersburg.

Colors known: amethyst.

Forms: sauce bowls.

Identifying characteristics: This variation of the peacock pattern has a strutting peacock with a bee in its beak, three rows of beads on the urn, and four rows of tail feathers.

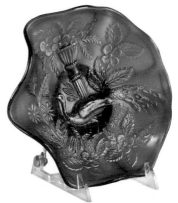

Peacock and Urn Variant, Millersburg, sauce, amethyst, six ruffles, 6" d, **$750-$1,000 (very rare).**

Peacock at the Fountain

Made by Northwood.

Colors known: amethyst, aqua opalescent, blue, blue opalescent, iridized custard, green, horehound, ice blue, ice green, lavender, lime green, marigold, purple, Renninger blue, sapphire blue, smoke, and white.

Forms: berry sets, compotes, orange bowls, punch sets, table sets, and water sets.

Identifying characteristics: This peacock pattern includes a detailed peacock, as well as a detailed fountain. Production began in 1912.

Also known as: Northwood's #637.

Peacock at the Fountain, Northwood, punch bowl, base, nine cups, aqua opalescent, very rare punch set, **$95,000.**

Peacock at the Fountain, Northwood, orange bowl, aqua opalescent, **$15,000.**

Peacock at the Fountain, Northwood, punch bowl, base, six cups, blue, **$2,500.**

Peacock at the Fountain, Northwood, berry (sauce), blue 5" d, **$25-$50;** outstanding example, **$150.**

Peacocks on the Fence

Made by Northwood.

Colors known: amethyst, aqua, aqua opalescent, blue, blue slag, electric blue, green, horehound, ice blue, ice blue opalescent, ice green, iridized custard, lavender, lime green opalescent, marigold, pastel, powder blue, purple, Renninger blue, sapphire blue, smoke, and white.

Forms: bowls and plates

Identifying characteristics: This pattern shows two peacocks, the one of the left with a fully displayed tail, the other looking back over its shoulder. The exterior pattern can be either ribbed or basketweave. Backgrounds can be plain or stippled. Production was centered around the years of 1911 to 1912.

Reproductions: Reproduction bowls are known.

Also known as: Peacocks.

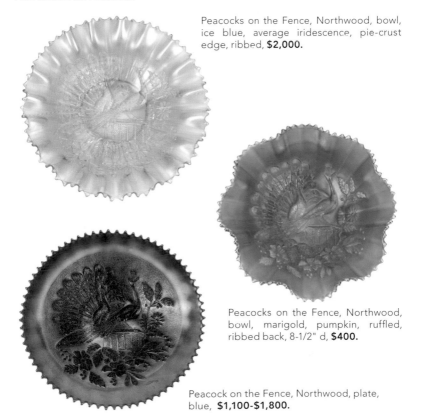

Peacocks on the Fence, Northwood, bowl, ice blue, average iridescence, pie-crust edge, ribbed, **$2,000.**

Peacocks on the Fence, Northwood, bowl, marigold, pumpkin, ruffled, ribbed back, 8-1/2" d, **$400.**

Peacock on the Fence, Northwood, plate, blue, **$1,100-$1,800.**

Peacock Tail

Made by Fenton.

Colors known: amber, amethyst, blue, green, marigold, peach opalescent, and red.

Forms: bonbons, bowls, compotes, hats, and plates.

Identifying characteristics: This pattern features peacock feathers that radiate from the center. The pattern was first advertised in 1911.

Also known as: Fenton's #409; Flowering Almonds.

Peacock Tail, Fenton, plate, marigold, has two very minute flakes on rim, 9" d, **$2,200.**

Peacock Tail, Fenton, 3-in-1 edge bowl, amethyst, 9-1/2" d, **$70.**

Pearly Dots

Made by Westmoreland.

Colors known: amethyst, aqua, blue, blue opalescent, marigold, and peach opalescent.

Forms: bowls, compotes, and rose bowls.

Identifying characteristics: The Pearly Dots pattern features rows of dots. Production began in 1910.

Pearly Dots, Westmoreland, compote, blue opalescent, 4-1/2" d, **$200-$350 (scarce).** The top view of the compote is at right.

Perfection

Made by Millersburg.
Colors known: amethyst, green, marigold, and purple.
Forms: water sets.
Identifying characteristics: This pattern has rows of beaded ovals over leaves.
Also known as: Beaded Jewel and Leaf.

Perfection, Millersburg, water pitcher and six tumblers, purple, **$8,250.**

Persian Garden

Made by Dugan/Diamond.

Colors known: amethyst, blue, green, lavender, marigold, peach opalescent, purple, and white.

Forms: berry sets, ice cream sets, and plates.

Identifying characteristics: This intricate pattern has a row of fleur-de-lis along the outward edge of the first scallop band, a row of flowers, another scallop band, more flowers, and a open flower center. Production centers around 1910-1911.

Also known as: Fan and Arch.

Persian Garden, Dugan, small plate, purple, 6-1/2" d, **$500-$800;** outstanding example, **$1,600.**

Persian Garden, Dugan, master bowl, ice cream shape, white, **$200.**

Persian Garden, Dugan, small plate, blue, 7-1/2" d, **$3,000-$4,000 (very rare).**

Persian Medallion

Made by Fenton.

Colors known: amber, amethyst, black amethyst, blue, green, lime green, marigold, red, reverse amberina, vaseline, and white.

Forms: bonbons, bowls, compotes, hair receivers, plates, and rose bowls.

Identifying characteristics: The central motif of this pattern reminds one of elements found in Middle Eastern rugs, along with scrolled borders, and stylized leaves in an outer border. Production began in 1911.

Reproductions: Fenton has issued baskets, bowls, compotes, goblets, plates, and stemmed rose bowls using original molds.

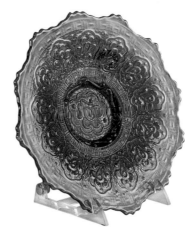

Persian Medallion, Fenton, flat plate, green, 6-3/4" d, **$400-$600;** outstanding example, **$1,700.**

Persian Medallion, Fenton, flat plate, blue, 9" d, **$400-$700;** outstanding example (rare), **$1,500.**

Persian Medallion, Fenton, sauce, blue, six ruffles, 6" d, **$50-$80.**

Persian Medallion, Fenton, flat plate, marigold, 6-1/4" d, **$50-$80.**

Persian Medallion, Fenton, flat plate, blue, 6-3/4" d, **$100-$250.**

Petal and Fan

Made by Dugan.

Colors known: amethyst, marigold, peach opalescent, purple, and white.

Forms: bowls and plates.

Identifying characteristics: The pattern is a series of alternating plain and stippled petals on a ribbed background with a fan device between each petal. Production was in 1911.

Petal and Fan, Dugan, bowl, purple, six ruffles, 10-1/2" d, **$400-$600;** outstanding example, **$1,000.**

Peter Rabbit

Made by Fenton.

Colors known: blue, green, and marigold.

Forms: bowls and plates.

Identifying characteristics: Fenton designers incorporated a fanciful border on both sides of the wreath that contains rabbits. This pattern was made in 1912.

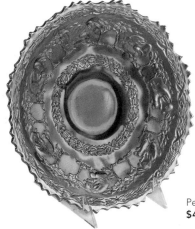

Peter Rabbit, Fenton, flat plate, green, 9" d, **$4,000-$6,000.**

Pine Cone

Made by Fenton.

Colors known: amber, amethyst, blue, green, marigold, and white.

Forms: bowls and plates.

Identifying characteristics: Detailed pinecones swirl with exaggerated pine needles and swirls in this pattern.

Also known as: Pine Cone Wreath.

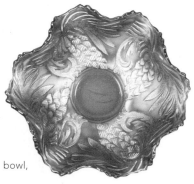

Pine Cone, Fenton, ruffled bowl, marigold, 7" d, **$20.**

Plaid

Made by Fenton.

Colors known: amethyst, blue, celeste blue, green, lavender, marigold, purple, red, and teal.

Forms: bowls and plates.

Identifying characteristics: This pattern has a very modern look to it compared to traditional carnival glass patterns. It is a series of vertical and horizontal lines, creating a plaid design. Production began in 1925.

Also known as: Granny's Gingham.

Plaid, Fenton, bowl, red, 8-1/2" d, **$2,500.**

Plaid, Fenton, plate, amethyst, **$650.**

Plaid, Fenton, 3-in-1 bowl, blue, only one known, **$1,100.**

Plume Panels

Made by Fenton.

Colors known: amethyst, blue, green, marigold, olive green, red, sapphire blue, and vaseline.

Forms: vases.

Identifying characteristics: The design is named from the panels of plumes that rise from the base to the flared top. Production began in 1912.

Plume Panels, Fenton, vase, red, 10-1/2" h, **$2,500-$4,000.**

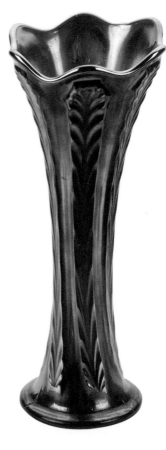

Plume Panels, Fenton, vase, green, 12" h, **$190.**

Poinsettia

Made by Imperial.

Colors known: emerald green, helios, lavender, marigold, purple, and smoke.

Forms: milk pitchers.

Identifying characteristics: A well-defined poinsettia blossom with a detailed center is linked around the top of this pattern and hovers over the beaded leaf forms. This pattern was made from 1910 until 1914.

Poinsettia, Imperial, milk pitcher, smoke, 6" h, **$250-$400.**

Poinsettia, Imperial, milk pitcher, green, 6" h, **$300-$500.**

Pony

Made by Dugan/Diamond.

Colors known: amethyst, aqua, ice green, lavender, and marigold.

Forms: bowls and plates.

Identifying characteristics: The central motif of this pattern is a detailed pony's head profile. A band of Roman Key motif surrounds the central element. Production began in 1921 and continued until 1930.

Also known as: Pony Rosette.

Reproductions: Bowls have been reproduced from original molds by L. G. Wright in the 1980s.

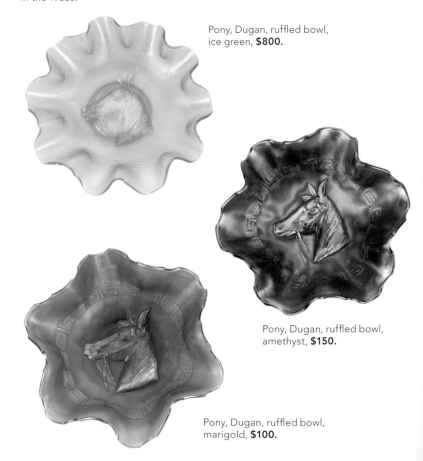

Pony, Dugan, ruffled bowl, ice green, **$800.**

Pony, Dugan, ruffled bowl, amethyst, **$150.**

Pony, Dugan, ruffled bowl, marigold, **$100.**

Poppy Show

Made by Imperial.

Colors known: amber, clambroth, helios, lavender, marigold, pastel marigold, purple, and smoke.

Forms: vases and whimsies.

Identifying characteristics: This pattern has panels filled with open poppies, foliage, and stems. Production began in 1910 and continued until 1912.

Also known as: Imperial's #488; Imperial's Poppy Show.

Reproductions: The vase has been reproduced.

Poppy Show, Imperial, vase, purple, 12" h, **$3,000-$5,500 (rare).**

Poppy Show, Imperial, vase, marigold, 12" h, **$500-$800.**

Poppy Show

Made by Northwood.

Colors known: amethyst, blue, clambroth, electric blue, green, ice blue, ice green, lime green, marigold, pastel marigold, purple, smoke, and white.

Forms: bowls and plates.

Identifying characteristics: This three-dimensional pattern features a cluster of three open poppies in the center with leaves and poppy buds for an added element. Production began in 1912 and continued until 1914.

Also known as: LaBelle Poppy.

Reproductions: Fenton has reissued vases using the original molds in contemporary colors.

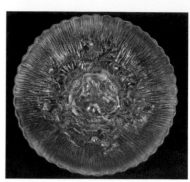

Poppy Show, Northwood, plate, white, 9" d, **$700.**

Poppy Show, Northwood, flared plate, ice blue, **$1,700.**

Poppy Show, Northwood, bowl, blue, eight ruffles, 8-1/2" d, **$700-$1,100;** outstanding condition, **$2,500.**

Poppy Show, Northwood, plate, marigold, 9" d, **$900-$1,600.**

Pulled Loop

Made by Dugan/Diamond.

Colors known: amethyst, aqua, black amethyst, blue, celeste blue, green, marigold, peach opalescent, purple, and white.

Forms: vases.

Identifying characteristics: Six loop panels separated by six wide ribs that extend over the top rim characterize this popular vase pattern. Sizes range from 6" to 16" high.

Also known as: Dugan's #1030; Loop and Column.

Pulled Loop, Dugan, vase, purple with opalescent tips, 8-1/2" h, **$550.**

Quill

Made by Dugan.

Colors known: marigold and purple.

Forms: water sets.

Identifying characteristics: This design incorporates a feather-type quill motif and elongated ovals, flourishes, and a swagged border.

Also known as: Feather and Scroll.

Quill, Dugan, water pitcher and six tumblers, marigold, **$1,000.**

Raspberry

Made by Northwood.

Colors known: amethyst, blue, green, ice blue, ice green, lavender, marigold, purple, and white.

Forms: milk pitchers, water sets, and whimsies.

Identifying characteristics: Northwood combined realistic looking raspberries and leaves over a basketweave band for this pattern. The pattern was introduced in 1911.

Also known as: Blackberry and Checkerboard.

Raspberry, Northwood, gravy boat, teal, 6" l, **$150-$250.**

Raspberry, Northwood, water pitcher and five tumblers (four shown), ice blue, **$1,400.**

Ribbon Tie

Made by Fenton.

Colors known: amethyst, black amethyst, blue, green, marigold, purple, and red.

Forms: bowls and plates.

Identifying characteristics: This pattern takes six ribbon segments and swirls them to the perimeter while other ribbons ring the bowl horizontally. Production began in 1911.

Also known as: Comet.

Ribbon Tie, Fenton, 3-in-1 low-ruffled bowl, blue, 9" d, **$100-$250;** outstanding example, **$800.**

Ribbon Tie, Fenton, 3-in-1 bowl, electric amethyst, 8-1/2" d, **$125.**

Ripple

Made by Imperial.

Colors known: amber, aqua, blue, clambroth, emerald green, helios, lavender, marigold, olive, powder blue, purple, red, smoke, teal, vaseline, violet, and white.

Forms: vases.

Identifying characteristics: This pattern resembles the ripple created when dropping a pebble into a pond. Production was centered in the 1910 until 1912 period.

Also known as: Ripple Threads.

Reproductions: Marigold, pink, and smoke vases known.

Ripple, Imperial, funeral vase, marigold, 11-1/2" h, **$200-$400**.

Ripple, Imperial, vase, purple, 8" h, 2-1/2" base, **$125-$175**.

Ripple, Imperial, squat vase, marigold, 4" h, 2-1/2" base, may be the shortest one there is, **$150-$250**.

Robin

Made by Imperial.

Colors known: marigold, marigold on light green, and smoke.

Forms: mugs and water sets.

Identifying characteristics: A whimsical bird perched on a leafy tree branch is the major design element of this pattern. Production was centered around 1910 to 1911.

Also known as: Imperial's #670; Robin Red Breast.

Reproductions: Imperial reissued the mug in pink and red. It also reissued water sets in cobalt blue, green, red, and white. These pieces are marked with the imposed IG or LIG trademarks.

Robin, Imperial, tumbler, smoke, 4-1/4" h, **$400-$600 (rare).**

Rococo

Made by Imperial.

Colors known: lavender, marigold, vaseline, and smoke.

Forms: berry sets, candy dishes, compotes, and vases.

Identifying characteristics: Swagged loops and arches create this interesting pattern. Production began in crystal in 1909 and was soon expanded to carnival colors.

Also known as: Imperial's #248-1/2.

Rococo, Imperial, vase, marigold, 4-1/4" h, **$75.**

Rococo, Imperial, vase, smoke, 4-1/4" h, **$95.**

Rose Columns

Made by Millersburg.

Colors known: amethyst, aqua, blue, green, and marigold.

Forms: vases.

Identifying characteristics: This molded vase pattern features deeply sculpted vertical roses of rose flowers, topped by leaves.

Rose Columns, Millersburg, vase, dark marigold, 10-1/2" h, **$6,500.**

Rose Columns, Millersburg, vase, blue, one of two known, 10" h, **$16,000.**

Rose Columns, Millersburg, vase, green, 10" h, **$5,000.**

Rose Columns, Millersburg, vase, amethyst, 9-1/2" h, **$5,500.**

Roses and Ruffles

Made by Consolidated Glass.

Colors known: marigold, marigold on milk glass, and red.

Forms: lamps.

Identifying characteristics: This pattern shows roses, leaves, and ruffles on the ball-shaped lamp shade and matching urn-shaped base, commonly called a "Gone With The Wind" shape.

Roses and Ruffles, lamp, Gone with the Wind, marigold, **$2,800.**

Rose Show

Made by Northwood.

Colors known: amber, amethyst, aqua, aqua opalescent, blue, emerald green, green, honey amber, horehound, ice blue, ice green, ice green opalescent, lavender, lime green, lime green opalescent, marigold, purple, Renninger blue, sapphire blue, and white.

Forms: bowls and plates.

Identifying characteristics: Northwood designers must have been inspired by beautiful roses when creating this design. The three-dimensional flowers and leaves are very life-like as they are clustered in the center of this design. Production began in 1912 and continued until 1914.

Also known as: LaBelle Rose.

Rose Show, Northwood, plate, blue, 9" d, **$1,100-$1,600.**

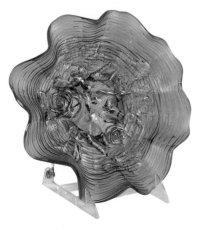

Rose Show, Northwood, bowl, purple, 8-1/2" d, **$500.**

Rose Show, Northwood, bowl, aqua, eight ruffles, 8-1/2" d, **$900-$1,600;** outstanding example, **$3,000.**

Round-up

Made by Dugan.

Colors known: amber, blue, lavender, marigold, peach opalescent, purple, and white.

Forms: bowls and plates.

Identifying characteristics: This interesting design features a swirled center flower with stippled highlighted petals, beaded borders, and an additional border with swirled beaded, plain, and floral enhanced petals. Production began in 1910 and ended by 1912.

Also known as: Egyptian Band.

Roundup, Dugan, ruffled bowl, purple, 8-1/2" d, **$400-$800.**

Rustic

Made by Fenton.

Colors known: amber, amethyst, blue, electric blue, green, lime green, lime green opalescent, marigold, peach opalescent, red, and white.

Forms: vases.

Identifying characteristics: Elongated tear-drops descend from the crown like the top of these vases in evenly spaced rows. Bases of these vases come in three sizes: 3-inch to 3-1/2-inch diameter on the standard sizes of 8 inches to 15 inches high, 4-inch to 4-1/4-inch diameter on the mid-sized 13 inches to 18 inches high vases, and 5-inch to 5-1/2-inch diameter on the tallest and funeral sized 17 inches to 24 inches high vases. Production began in 1911.

Also known as: Fenton's #507; Maryland.

Rustic, Fenton, funeral vase, plunger base, blue, 16" h, **$1,500-$2,000.**

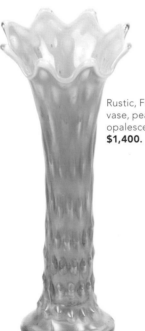

Rustic, Fenton, vase, peach opalescent, **$1,400.**

Rustic, Fenton, jardinière vase with pinched in mid section, blue, 7-1/2" h, 5-1/4" base, **$1,500.**

S-Repeat

Made by Dugan.

Color known: purple.

Forms: creamers and punch sets.

Identifying characteristics: This pattern features scrolling S forms that have a distinctive curl to the top and bottom of each form. Several forms include a beaded border.

Also known as: National.

S-Repeat, Dugan, tumbler, marigold, **$210.**

S-Repeat, Dugan, punch bowl, base, 12 cups, purple, **$8,000.**

Scales

Made by Westmoreland.

Colors known: amethyst, aqua, blue opalescent, marigold, marigold over milk glass, and teal.

Forms: bowls and plates.

Identifying characteristics: Rows of scales that diminish in size from the perimeter to the petaled center dominate this design. Production began circa 1909.

Also known as: Peacock Optic; Looped Petals.

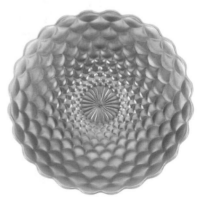

Scales, Westmoreland, plate, deep, round, marigold over milk glass, **$250.**

Scroll Embossed

Made by Imperial.

Colors known: aqua, clam-broth, emerald green, helios, lavender, marigold, purple, red, and teal.

Forms: bowls, compotes, and plates.

Identifying characteristics: Scroll Embossed has a bull's-eye center plus four additional bull's eyes that are the center of the looping scrolls that make up this interesting pattern. Production began in 1910 and continued until 1917.

Also known as: Embossed Scroll; Peacock Eye.

Scroll Embossed, Imperial, ruffled compote, marigold, 4-1/2", **$60-$90.**

Reproductions: Fenton has created a vase that resembles this pattern, perhaps because Imperial never made a vase. Imperial has reissued the 9-inch bowls in amethyst, ice blue, ice green, and pink. These have the LIG mark.

Scroll Embossed, Imperial, bowl, purple, six ruffles, 7" d, **$50-$150.**

Scroll Embossed, Imperial, flat plate, purple, 9-1/2" d, **$350-$600.**

Scroll Embossed, Imperial, ruffled compote, purple, 4-1/2", **$200-$300.**

Scroll Embossed, Imperial, miniature compote, purple, 3", **$250-$350.**

Seacoast

Made by Millersburg.

Colors known: amethyst, green, marigold, and purple.

Forms: pin trays.

Identifying characteristics: This pattern features an irregularly shaped tray with a lighthouse and other seaside motifs. The American Carnival Glass Association used this pattern as a spittoon for its convention souvenirs. These pieces are now starting to come into the secondary market so that comparable prices can be established.

Also known as: Maine Coast.

Seacoast, Millersburg, pin tray, amethyst, **$850.**

Singing Birds

Made by Northwood.

Colors known: amber, amethyst, aqua opalescent, blue, emerald green, green, horehound, ice blue, ice green, lavender, marigold, olive green, purple, Renninger blue, sapphire blue, smoke, and white.

Forms: berry sets, mugs, table sets, and water sets.

Identifying characteristics: This well-known pattern features a bird that looks like it's ready to hop off the flowering branch where it is perched. Production was centered in 1911 to 1912.

Reproductions: Tumblers have been reproduced in amethyst, blue, and vaseline.

Singing Birds, Northwood, tumbler, emerald green, 4" h, **$75-$125.**

Singing Birds, Northwood, mug, aqua opalescent, **$1,200.**

Singing Birds, Northwood, water pitcher and six tumblers, marigold, **$275.**

Six Petals

Made by Dugan.

Colors known: lavender, peach opalescent, purple, and white.

Forms: bowls and plates.

Identifying characteristics: Six Petals takes its name from the center six-petaled flower that is surrounded by leaves and a wreath border of additional flower blossoms and leaves. Production was centered between 1910 and 1912.

Also known as: Christmas Rose and Poppy.

Six Petals, Dugan, tricorner bowl, purple, 7-1/2" d, **$100-$200.**

Six Petals, Dugan, tricorner bowl, peach opalescent, **$20.**

Ski Star

Made by Dugan.

Colors known: amethyst, black amethyst, peach opalescent, and purple.

Forms: banana boats, berry sets, bowls, plates, and whimsies.

Identifying characteristics: This interior pattern features stippled rays which form an interesting eight-point star and features a delicate lacy center star design. The Compass pattern is frequently used as an exterior pattern with Ski Star, giving it further interest. Production was centered between 1910 and 1911.

Ski Star, Dugan, bowl, purple, six ruffles, 10-3/4" d, **$300-$500.**

Smooth Panels

Made by Imperial.

Colors known: amber, amethyst, clambroth, lavender, marigold, marigold over milk glass, peach opalescent, red, smoke, teal, white, and wisteria.

Forms: rose bowls and vases.

Identifying characteristics: Convex panels create this design. Many pieces, but not all, include the Imperial iron cross mark on the base. Vase sizes in this pattern range from 4 inches to 18 inches.

Smooth Panels, Imperial, funeral vase, marigold, 12" h, 10" d mouth, **$160.**

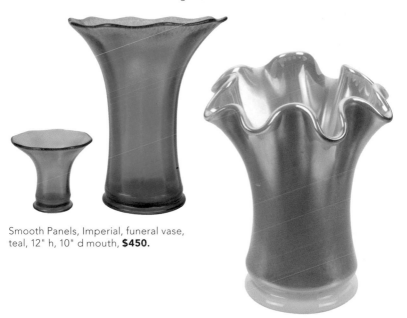

Smooth Panels, Imperial, funeral vase, teal, 12" h, 10" d mouth, **$450.**

Smooth Panels, Imperial, vase, marigold over milk glass, 4" h, **$200.**

Smooth Rays

Made by Dugan, Imperial, Northwood, and Westmoreland.

Colors known: Dugan: amethyst, marigold, peach opalescent; Imperial: amber, clambroth, marigold; Northwood: amethyst, clambroth, green, and marigold, marigold on green; Westmoreland: amber, amethyst, green, marigold, marigold over milk glass, and teal.

Forms: bonbons, bowls, compotes, plates, stemware, and water sets.

Identifying characteristics: The major manufacturers made this pattern, each giving it a slightly different treatment, in different colors, and forms. However, the basic pattern is a ribbed smooth banded type design. Values between the similar patterns are comparable.

Smooth Rays, Westmoreland, compote, 4-1/2", purple, **$100-$250**. Top view is at left.

Soda Gold

Made by Imperial.

Colors known: aqua, light blue, marigold, smoke, and vaseline.

Forms: bowls, candlesticks, chop plates, salts and peppers, and water sets.

Identifying characteristics: This pattern features pronounced random-looking veins which are raised over its stippled surface. This late production pattern first appears in a Butlers Brothers catalog in 1929.

Also known as: Spider Web.

Soda Gold, Imperial, pitcher, smoke, 8-1/4" h, **$200-$350**.

Soda Gold, Imperial, tumbler, smoke, 4" h, **$50-$75**.

Soutache

Made by Dugan.

Colors known: peach opalescent.

Forms: bowls and plates.

Identifying characteristics: This all-over pattern features a maze of squiggles that surround a flower center.

Soutache, Dugan, bowl, square, peach opalescent, **$700.**

Springtime

Made by Northwood.

Colors known: amethyst, green, marigold, and purple.

Forms: berry sets, table sets, and water sets.

Identifying characteristics: A ring of spring flowers and leaves dominates this pattern that also includes loops of basketweave, additional larger flowers and leaves. Production dates to 1910-1911. Pieces are sometimes marked.

Also known as: Butterfly and Cable.

Springtime, Northwood, water pitcher and six tumblers, dark marigold, **$1,650.**

Stag and Holly

Made by Fenton.

Colors known: amber, amberina, amethyst, aqua, black amethyst, blue, green, marigold, marigold on moonstone, pink, pumpkin marigold, red, and vaseline.

Forms: bowls, plates, and rose bowls.

Identifying characteristics: This well-known carnival glass design features a standing stag alternating with a holly tree. The center is a combination of holly berries and leaves. Production began in 1912.

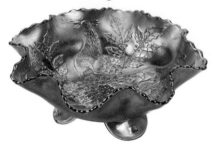

Stag and Holly, Fenton, ruffled bowl, red, spatula, 6-1/2" d, **$1,500.**

Reproductions: Reproduction bowls are known. By carefully examining details, collectors have identified period pieces as having oval-shaped eyes, while new eyes are found. Original Fenton stags have detailed tongues, an element often missing on reproductions.

Stag and Holly, Fenton, rose bowl, large, ruffled, blue, **$700.**

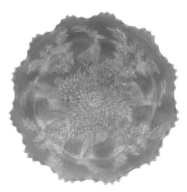

Stag and Holly, Fenton, chop plate, sawtooth, marigold, 11-1/2" d, **$1,200.**

Stag and Holly, Fenton, rose bowl, large, marigold, **$225.**

Star and File

Made by Imperial.

Colors known: amber, clambroth, helios, ice green, marigold, purple, and smoke.

Forms: bonbons, bowls, celery vases, compotes, milk pitchers, plates, stemware, tumblers, and water sets.

Identifying characteristics: An upright band of filed diamonds creates the "file" of this pattern, both hobstars and rayed stars add the "star" to the name, and areas of caning and fan fill out the rest of this busy pattern. Production began in 1916 and continued until 1929.

Also known as: Imperial's #612; Finecut and Star.

Reproductions: Imperial reissued this pattern as a wine set in marigold and smoke, while re-naming it Peacock. Look for the IG mark on reissues.

Star and File, Imperial, tumbler, marigold, **$100.**

Starfish

Made by Dugan.

Colors known: peach opalescent and purple.

Forms: bonbons and compotes.

Identifying characteristics: A large detailed starfish dominates the center of this design, each branch of the starfish end in an embossed fleur-de-lis.

Also known as: Stippled Starfish Medallion.

Starfish, Dugan, compote, purple, eight ruffles, 6" d, **$300-$500.**

Star Medallion

Made by Imperial.

Colors known: clambroth, marigold, smoke, and smoky blue.

Forms: bowls, celeries, compotes, custard cups, goblets, milk pitchers, plates, and tumblers.

Identifying characteristics: This pattern has a medallion element that is repeated on a caned-type background.

Reproductions: Imperial reissued the compote in amber, helios, ice blue, marigold, and smoke.

Star Medallion, Imperial, milk pitcher, smoke, **$75.**

Star Medallion, Imperial, tumbler, marigold, **$50.**

Star of David

Made by Imperial.

Colors known: helios, marigold, purple, smoke.

Forms: bowls.

Identifying characteristics: A stippled Star of David dominates the center of this interior pattern. The Arcs pattern is frequently used on the exterior. Production began in 1910.

Also known as: Star of David Medallion.

Star of David, Imperial, bowl, purple, eight ruffles, 9" d, **$200-$350.**

Stork and Rushes

Made by Dugan/Diamond.

Colors known: amethyst, blue, lime green, and marigold.

Forms: berry sets, mugs, punch sets, water sets, and whimsies.

Identifying characteristics: A detailed stork standing among rushes dominates this interesting pattern.

Also known as: Heron and Rushes.

Reproductions: L. G. Wright has created a butter dish, as well as changing the sugar lids. These are known in purple. They also issued water sets in marigold and purple. Reproduction berry sets are known in purple.

Stork and Rushes, Dugan, mug, blue, 4" h, **$1,000-$1,200 (rare).**

Stork and Rushes, Diamond, tumbler, lattice banded, marigold, **$20.**

Strawberry

Made by Northwood.

Colors known: amethyst, blue, green, horehound, ice green, lime green, marigold, marigold with opalescent, pastel marigold, peach opalescent, pumpkin marigold, purple, smoke, and white.

Forms: bowls and plates.

Identifying characteristics: Northwood's Strawberry has four sprigs of berries and leaves, which circle the center that features four leaves.

Strawberry, Northwood, bowl, aqua opal, stippled, ruffle edge, one of two known, **$15,000.**

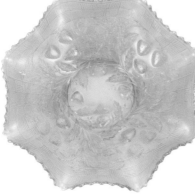

Strawberry, Northwood, bowl, lime ice green, ruffle/basketweave, **$1,200.**

Strawberry, Northwood, bowl, electric blue, stippled, ribbed, **$650.**

Strawberry Scroll

Made by Fenton.

Colors known: amethyst, blue, and marigold.

Forms: water sets.

Identifying characteristics: This pattern features strawberries and a mid band of scrolls.

Also known as: Strawberry and Scroll Band.

Strawberry Scroll, Fenton, water pitcher and six tumblers, marigold, **$2,500.**

Sunflower

Made by Millersburg.

Colors known: amethyst, green, and marigold.

Forms: pin trays.

Identifying characteristics: This pin tray is shaped as though a large sunflower blossom was just picked and flattened out, and the stem twists around with a few leaves to form the handle.

Sunflower, Millersburg, pin tray, amethyst, **$850.**

Swirl Hobnail

Made by Millersburg.

Colors known: amethyst, green, marigold, and purple.

Forms: rose bowls, spittoons, and vases.

Identifying characteristics: This pattern features horizontal rows of pointy hobnails with a background of vertical swirls. Production was centered around 1910 to 1911.

Also known as: Hobnail Swirl.

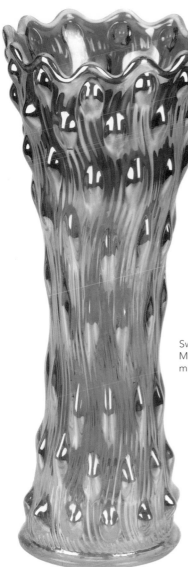

Swirl Hobnail,
Millersburg, vase,
marigold, 10" h, **$300.**

Target

Made by Dugan and Fenton.

Colors known: amethyst, blue, marigold, peach opalescent, smoky blue, and white.

Forms: vases.

Identifying characteristics: This pattern features large ribs, which separate vertical rows of raised circles, the top features crown-like points.

Also known as: Loops and Columns.

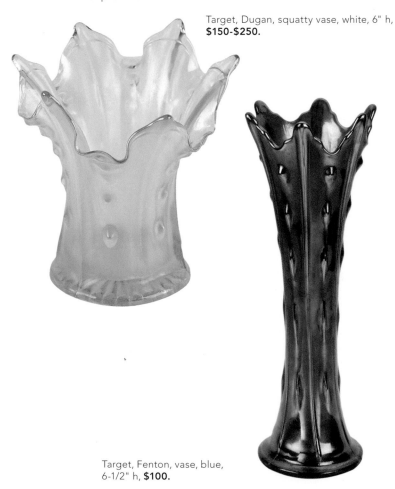

Target, Dugan, squatty vase, white, 6" h, **$150-$250.**

Target, Fenton, vase, blue, 6-1/2" h, **$100.**

Ten Mums

Made by Fenton.

Colors known: blue, green, marigold, peach opalescent, and white.

Forms: bowls, plates, and water sets.

Identifying characteristics: This interior pattern features a realistic-looking pom-pom chrysanthemum in the center with two leaves. Further leaves form a wreath with additional pom-pom chrysanthemums pointing to the exterior. Production began in 1911.

Also known as: Chrysanthemum Wreath; Double Chrysanthemum.

Ten Mums, Fenton, 3-in-1 bowl, blue, 9-1/2" d, **$350.**

Ten Mums, Fenton, water pitcher and six tumblers, tankard, marigold, **$1,550.**

Thin Rib

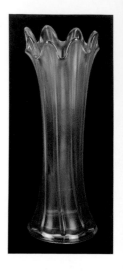

Made by Northwood.

Colors known: amber, amethyst, aqua opalescent, blue, green, emerald green, ice blue, ice green, ice green opalescent, lime green opalescent, marigold, olive, purple, sapphire blue, vaseline, and white.

Forms: vases.

Identifying characteristics: This pattern is found on the exterior and consists of thin rod-type ribs and wider smooth panels. The term "jester cap" is used to describe a style where one point is pulled higher than the rest and the other seven ribs turned outward. Both Dugan and Fenton made similar patterns, which have comparable values.

Thin Rib, Northwood, funeral vase, mid-size, white, 15" h, **$300.**

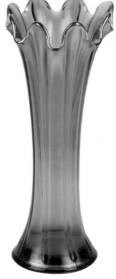

Thin Rib, Northwood, funeral vase, mid-size, ice green, **$350.**

Thin Rib, Northwood, jardinière vase, purple, signed, 8" h, 4-5/8" base, **$1,450.**

Thin Rib, Northwood, funeral vase, mid-size, sapphire with gold rim, 14-1/4" h, **$800-$1,200.**

Thistle

Made by Fenton.

Colors known: amber, amethyst, blue, green, lavender, marigold, and vaseline.

Forms: banana boats, bowls, compotes, and plates.

Identifying characteristics: This interesting pattern features four clusters of thistle foliage and flowers, each with one leaf extending to the center. Production began in 1911.

Also known as: Christmas Cactus.

Reproductions: Joe St. Clair has iridized goblets, never originally issued in carnival.

Thistle, Fenton, banana boat, amethyst, **$185.**

Thistle, Fenton, flat plate, green, 9" d, **$4,000-$5,000.**

Three Fruits

Made by Northwood.

Colors known: amethyst, aqua, aqua opalescent, black amethyst, blue, clambroth, green, honey amber, horehound, lavender, lime green, marigold, pearlized custard, pumpkin marigold, olive, purple, sapphire blue, smoke, teal, violet, and white.

Forms: bowls.

Identifying characteristics: This pattern features a wreath of peaches, cherries, and pears, leaves, and a bunch of plump cherries in the center. Production of this pattern centered between 1915 and 1916.

Three Fruits, Northwood, plate, electric blue, 9" d, **$900-$1,200.**

Three Fruits, Northwood, plate, aqua opalescent, 9" d, **$2,000-$3,000;** outstanding example, **$6,500.**

Three Fruits, Northwood, bowl, sapphire, **$2,200.**

Three Fruits, Northwood, stippled bowl, ice blue, footed, 8-1/2" d, **$1,000.**

Tiger Lily

Made by Imperial.

Colors known: amber, aqua, blue, helios, lavender, marigold, olive, purple, teal, and violet.

Forms: water sets.

Identifying characteristics: Tiger Lily is a full pattern featuring detailed open-petaled flowers on a leafy upright stalk alternating with additional buds and stalks. Production began in 1910.

Also known as: Imperial's #484; Amaryllis.

Reproductions: Imperial reissued water sets in ice blue, ice green, marigold, pink, and white. Some are marked IG, others LIG. Riihimaki, Finland, also copied the pattern, with some slight differences, including that its tumblers have a collar base.

Tiger Lily, Imperial, water pitcher, purple, 8-1/2" h, **$800-$1,200 (rare).**

Tiger Lily, Imperial, tumbler, lavender, **$100.**

Tiger Lily, Imperial, water pitcher and six tumblers, marigold, **$540.**

Tiger Lily, Imperial, tumbler, purple, 4-1/4" h, **$80-$150 (scarce).**

Tornado

Made by Northwood.

Colors known: amethyst, blue, green, ice blue, lavender, marigold, and white.

Forms: vases.

Identifying characteristics: This pattern has a swirling raised tornado-type eye that trails to the base of this vase. It is found with either a rib element on the sides or plain. Production was centered in the 1911 to 1912 period.

Also known as: Tadpole.

Tornado, Northwood, vase, amethyst, ribbed flared top, 6" h, **$1,800.**

Tornado, Northwood, small vase, purple, 6" h, **$600-$900.**

Tornado, Northwood, small vase, marigold, 6" h, **$600-$900.**

Town Pump

Made by Northwood.

Colors known: green, marigold, and purple.

Forms: vases.

Identifying characteristics: Town Pump is a pattern that features ivy on the cylindrical body, a thorn-type handle, and a naturalistic wooden-looking spigot on one side. This is one of the most widely known novelties of the carnival glass world. Production began in 1912 in carnival glass and even earlier in opalescent colors.

Town Pump, Northwood, town pump, purple, **$800-$1,100.**

Tree Trunk

Made by Northwood.

Colors known: amethyst, aqua opalescent, blue, green, ice blue, ice green, lavender, lime green, marigold, marigold on custard, purple, sapphire blue, and white.

Forms: vases.

Identifying characteristics: This pattern is so popular with collectors that they have derived five different names for the sizes: squat, standard, mid-sized funeral, funeral, and elephant foot. The pattern appears as though the designers took a piece of real tree trunk and copied it. By creating the different heights and widths, the pattern extends and expands to cause interesting variations in the design. Heights range from 5 inches to 22 inches. Most have the Northwood trademark. Production began in 1911 and continued until about 1917.

Also known as: Killarney.

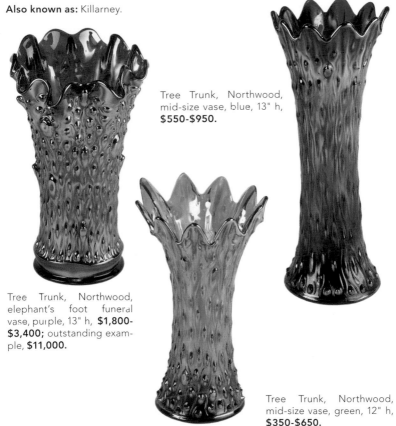

Tree Trunk, Northwood, mid-size vase, blue, 13" h, **$550-$950.**

Tree Trunk, Northwood, elephant's foot funeral vase, purple, 13" h, **$1,800-$3,400;** outstanding example, **$11,000.**

Tree Trunk, Northwood, mid-size vase, green, 12" h, **$350-$650.**

Tree Trunk, Northwood, mid-size vase, purple, 13" h, **$350-$550.**

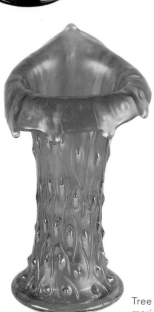

Tree Trunk, Northwood, standard vase, purple, 8" h, **$80-$150.**

Tree Trunk, Northwood, jester's cap vase, marigold, 7-1/2" h, **$3,000-$4,500 (rare).**

Two Flowers

Made by Fenton.

Colors known: amberina, amethyst, aqua, black amethyst, blue, green, lime green, marigold, powder blue, red, sapphire, and white.

Forms: bowls, plates, and rose bowls.

Identifying characteristics: A large detailed chrysanthemum dominates the center of this pattern. A wreath of open petaled flowers with oval centers and foliage is further bordered by a band of scales.

Also known as: Dogwood and Marsh Lily.

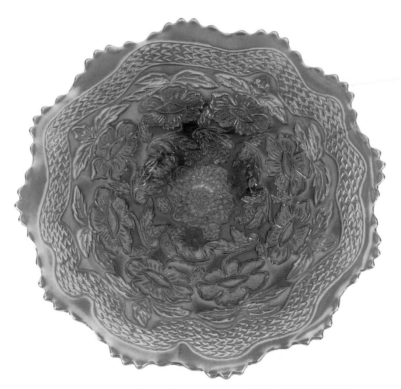

Two Flowers, Fenton, chop plate, dark marigold, 11" d, **$950-$1,200.**

Vineyard

Made by Dugan.

Colors known: marigold, peach opalescent, purple.

Forms: water sets.

Identifying characteristics: This realistic design features a tree bark background topped by grape leaves. Production began in 1910.

Also known as: Grape and Leaf; Peacock Eye and Grape.

Vineyard, Dugan, tumbler, purple, 3-3/4" h, **$50-$150.**

Vineyard, Dugan, water pitcher, peach opalescent, **$1,600.**

Vintage

Made by Fenton.

Colors known: amber, amberina, amethyst, amethyst opalescent, aqua opalescent, blue, celeste blue, green, lime green, marigold, peach opalescent, Persian blue, purple, red, vaseline.

Forms: bonbon, bowls, chop plates, compotes, ferners, pitchers, wine glass.

Identifying characteristics: Detailed grape clusters point towards the center where grape leaves are gathered. Additional grape leaves form a wreath around the grapes. Production began in 1912.

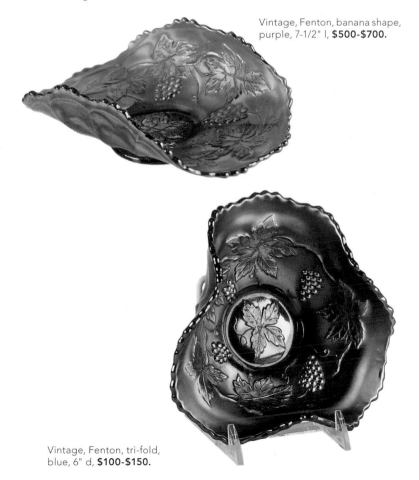

Vintage, Fenton, banana shape, purple, 7-1/2" l, **$500-$700.**

Vintage, Fenton, tri-fold, blue, 6" d, **$100-$150.**

Waffle Block

Made by Imperial.

Colors known: clambroth, marigold, purple, smoke, teal.

Forms: baskets, bowls, breakfast sets, parfaits, plates, punch sets, rose bowls, salt and pepper shakers, spittoons, vases, water sets.

Identifying characteristics: This pattern features vertical and horizontal rows of faceted blocks.

Also known as: Imperial's #698.

Waffle Block, Imperial, water pitcher and one tumbler, electric marigold, **$225.**

Water Lily

Made by Fenton.

Colors known: amber slag, amberina, amethyst, aqua, blue, green, lime green, lime green opalescent, marigold, pumpkin marigold, red, reverse amberina, reverse amberina opalescent, sapphire blue, teal, vaseline, vaseline opalescent.

Forms: berry sets, bonbons.

Identifying characteristics: This pattern combines water lily blossoms and poinsettias with a pretty water lily blossom in the center. Production began in 1915.

Also known as: Lotus & Poinsettia; Magnolia and Poinsettia.

Water Lily, Fenton, bowl, red, 5" d, **$900.**

Waterlily and Cattails

Made by Fenton.

Color known: marigold.

Forms: banana boats, bonbons, bowls, hats, plates, spittoons, table sets, water sets.

Identifying characteristics: This waterlily pattern has three blossoms that float between cattail, with a center blossom framed by an additional pair of cattails. Production began in 1911.

Also known as: Cattails and Water Lily.

Waterlily and Cattails, Fenton, vase, whimsey, marigold, 3-1/2" h, 4" mouth, **$200.**

Waterlily and Cattails, Fenton, tumbler, engraved, blue, **$1,500.**

Wide Panel

Made by Fenton, Imperial, Millersburg, and Northwood.

Colors known: amethyst, aqua, black amethyst, blue, celeste blue, clambroth, green, ice blue, ice green, marigold, olive, purple, red, russet, teal, vaseline.

Forms: baskets, bowls, breakfast sets, candlesticks, candy dish, compotes, cruets, epergnes, hats, tumblers, vases.

Identifying characteristics: This pattern was commonly used as an exterior pattern, with its wide smooth panels being easy to mold. The differences between each maker are hard to distinguish. Values are more dependent upon color and form rather than the maker.

Wide Panel, chop plate, electric red, 14-1/2" d, **$200.**

Wide Rib

Made by Dugan/Diamond.

Colors known: amethyst, blue, peach opalescent, white.

Forms: vases.

Identifying characteristics: This ribbed pattern is identified as Dugan/Diamond when the ends of each of the eight ribs have knob-like tips.

Also known as: Dugan's #1016.

Wide Rib, Dugan, vase, peach opalescent, 5" h, **$130.**

Windmill

Made by Imperial.

Colors: aqua, blue-violet, clambroth, emerald green, helios, lavender, lime green, marigold, marigold on milk glass, olive, purple, smoke.

Forms: bowls, fruit bowls, milk pitchers, pickle dishes, relish trays, water sets.

Identifying characteristics: This lively pattern shows a single windmill within a window scene of trees. Production began in 1910 and continued until 1914.

Also known as: Imperial's #514; Windmill Medallions.

Reproductions: Imperial reissued the water set in marigold, pink, and smoke, as well as marigold with frosted non-iridized panels. Bowls were reissued in marigold, pink, and smoke. Plates were reissued in blue.

Windmill, Imperial, tumbler, purple, 4-1/4" h, **$80-$150.**

Windmill, Imperial, bowl, eight ruffles, purple, 8" d, **$150-$300.**

Windmill, Imperial, water pitcher, smoke, **$500.**

Wishbone

Made by Northwood.

Colors known: amethyst, aqua opalescent, blue, green, emerald green, ice blue, ice green, marigold, pumpkin marigold, purple, white.

Forms: bowls, chop plates, epergnes, plates.

Identifying characteristics: This pattern is interesting in that wishbone shapes overlap and alternate with exotic looking orchid blossoms. A multi-petaled flower forms the center. Production began about 1911.

Also known as: Melinda.

Wishbone, Northwood, bowl, pie-crust edge, electric blue, 9-1/2" d, **$1,900-$2,400.**

Wishbone, Northwood, bowl, pie-crust edge, purple, 9-1/2" d, **$350-$500;** outstanding example, **$900.**

Wishbone, Northwood, footed plate, purple, 8" d, **$500-$700.**

Wisteria

Made by Northwood.

Colors known: ice blue, white.

Forms: water sets.

Identifying characteristics: This naturalistic pattern features wisteria flowers and foliate against a lattice background.

Also known as: Wisteria and Lattice.

Wisteria, Northwood, water pitcher and one tumbler, tankard, ice blue, **$10,000.**

Wreathed Cherries

Made by Dugan/Diamond.

Colors known: amethyst, black amethyst, blue, marigold, peach opalescent, purple, white.

Forms: berry sets, table sets, water sets.

Identifying characteristics: This pattern features a large medallion in which a wreath of leaves encircles a cluster of three hanging cherries. Some pieces exist with enameled red cherries and gilded leaves. Production began in 1911 and continued until 1914.

Also known as: Cherry Wreath; Cherry Wreathed.

Reproductions: Toothpick holders are known while none were ever made in the original production years.

Wreathed Cherries, Dugan, tumbler, white/red cherries, **$150.**

Wreathed Cherries, Dugan, water pitcher and one tumbler, tankard, white/red cherries, **$1,550.**

Wreath of Roses

Made by Fenton.

Colors known: amethyst, blue, green, and marigold.

Forms: bonbons, compotes, punch sets, rose bowls.

Identifying characteristics: This delicate pattern features a circle of open roses and leaves with a large rose in the center.

Also known as: American Beauty Roses.

Wreath of Roses, Fenton, turned-up punch bowl, base, six cups, Vintage interior, amethyst, **$650.**

Wreath of Roses, punch bowl, base, two cups, Vintage interior, square, green, **$650.**

Zig Zag

Made by Millersburg.

Colors known: amethyst, green, marigold.

Forms: bowls,

Identifying characteristics: This interior pattern is striking in that rays resembling lightning bolts start closely in the center and radiate to the edges. The exteriors are plain. Production began in 1911.

Zig Zag, Millersburg, bowl, amethyst, **$225-$450.**

Carnival Glass Price Guide

Acanthus

Bowl, 8" d to 9" d
Green	$65-$115
Marigold	$25-$75
Smoke	$35-$50

Chop plate,
9-1/2" d to 10-1/2" d
Marigold	$135-$155
Smoke	$275-$300

Acorn

Bowl, ruffled
Amber opalescent	$300-$350
Amethyst	$80-$160
Green	$40-$60
Marigold	$100-$110
Marigold over milk glass	
	$140-$150
Peach opalescent	$210-$290
Powder blue	$40-$45
Vaseline	$110-$185

Compote, ruffled
Amethyst	$2,000-$2,400
Green	$3,000-$3,100
Marigold	$1,200-$1,500
Vaseline	$3,750-$6,000

Acorn Burrs

Berry set, master bowl and six
serving bowls
Amethyst/purple	$175-$600
Green	$750-$1,000
Marigold	$275-$375

Butter dish, cov
Amethyst/purple	$165-$350
Green	$80-$200
Marigold	$150-$300

Creamer
Amethyst/purple	$75-$130
Green	$75-$150
Marigold	$165-$170

Sugar bowl, cov
Amethyst/purple	$100-$150
Green	$95-$160
Marigold	$170-$200

Advertising

Bowl, ruffled
Compliments of Central Shoe Store, amethyst, rare	$950
Geo. W. Getts Pianos, amethyst, rare	$1,100
Gevurtz Bros. Furniture and Clothing, amethyst, rare	$1,600
Horlacher, Thistle pattern, green	$125-$135
Norris N. Smith, amethyst, rare	$1,800
Sterling Furniture Co., amethyst	$600-$750

Hat, ruffled, General Furniture, 1910, Peacock Tail pattern, green | $55-$75

Mug, Hotel Vendome, Singing Birds pattern, purple $40-$55

Plate, round
Ballard, 6" d, amethyst, rare	$1,300
Birmingham Age Herald, 9" d, amethyst	$1,500-$2,600
Brazier's Candies, 6" d, amethyst, rare	$1,100
Broeker's Flour, 6" d, amethyst, rare	$3,000
Central Shoe Store, 6" d, amethyst, rare	$1,300
Dorsey & Funkenstein, 6" d, amethyst, rare	$2,600
Exchange Bank, 6" d, amethyst, rare	$1,700
Geo. W. Getts Pianos, 6" d, amethyst, rare	$1,300
Norris N. Smith, 6" d, amethyst, rare	$1,400
Spectors Department Store, Heart and Vine pattern, 9" d, marigold, rare	$1,100

Apple Blossom Twigs

Banana boat, ruffled
Amethyst/purple	$115-$325
Peach opalescent	$265-$300

Bowl, 3-in-1 edge, amethyst/purple | $200-$300

Plate, 8-1/2" d to 9-1/2" d
Amethyst/purple	$225-$325
Blue	$135-$300
Lavender	$375-$425
Marigold	$150-$200
Peach opalescent	$265-$400
White	$125-$140

April Showers

Vase, 5" h to 7-1/2" h, squatty
Amethyst	$120-$125
Blue	$75-$135
Green	$100-$195
Marigold	$45-$85
White	$150-$300

Vase, 8" h to 15" h
Amethyst	$45-$65
Blue	$35-$50
Green	$70-$75
Marigold	$30-$45
Red, rare	$2,300
Vaseline	$100-$375
White	$115-$225

Beaded Bullseye

Vase, 5-1/2" to 7-1/2" h, squatty
Green	$150-$185
Marigold	$85-$100
Purple, 6" h, 6" d mouth	$215-$300

Vase, 9" h
Green	$40-$45
Marigold	$45-$50
Purple	$165-$170

Vase, 11" h
Amber	$185-$200
Green	$50-$55

Vase, 14" h
Marigold	$55-$85
Purple	$125-$235

Beaded Shell

Bowl, ftd, 9" d
Amethyst	$45-$65
Marigold	$35-$45

Butter dish, cov
Amethyst	$60-$85
Marigold	$35-$55

Mug
Amethyst	$30-$35
Blue	$45-$115
White	$400-$450

Spooner
Amethyst	$60-$110
Marigold	$35-$55

Tumbler
Amethyst	$40-$90
Blue	$110-$120
Marigold	$25-$45

Water pitcher

Amethyst	$200-$350
Marigold	$100-$175

Beaded Spears

Lemonade tumbler, 4-1/2" h,
marigold $130-$150

Tumbler

Amethyst	$45-$60
Blue	$50-$65
Marigold	$40-$45

Water pitcher, marigold
$295-$385

Big Basketweave

Basket, large

Amethyst/purple	$135-$165
Marigold	$45-$75

Basket, small

Amethyst/purple	$40-$60
Marigold	$15-$20

Vase, 4" h to 7" h

Amethyst/purple	$300-$325
Celeste blue	$350-$475
Lavender	$200-$300
Marigold	$95-$125
Peach opalescent	$250-$300
White	$100-$150

Vase, 8" h to 14" h

Amethyst/purple	$150-$200
Blue	$225-$300
Celeste blue	$375-$425
Marigold	$25-$75
Peach opalescent	$325-$425
Sapphire blue	$400-$600

Big Fish

Banana bowl

Amethyst, rare	$1,900
Green, rare	$1,900

Bowl, ice cream shape

Amethyst, radium	$600-$750
Green, satin	$450-$475
Marigold	$800-$850

Bowl, ruffled, oval, 8-1/2"

Amethyst	$600-$675
Green	$625-$725
Marigold	$600-$625
Vaseline, rare	$6,000

Bowl, tricorn

Amethyst, rare	$1,400
Green, rare	$13,000
Marigold	$700-$800
Vaseline, rare	$2,000

Birds and Cherries

Bonbon, two handles

Amethyst	$115-$125
Green	$60-$80
Marigold	$30-$40
Vaseline	$250-$300

Bowl, 9-1/2" d

Amethyst	$200-$300
Blue	$275-$375
Marigold	$100-$200

Calling card tray, bonbon mold

Blue	$30-$35
Green	$25-$30

Plate, 10" d

Amethyst, rare	$16,000
Blue, rare	$3,000
Marigold, rare	$2,000

Blackberry

Compote, miniature

Amethyst/purple	$110-$165
Blue	$45-$70
Green	$95-$125
Marigold	$45-$90
White	$300-$450

Plate, miniature, 4-1/2" d,
blue $295-$400

Blackberry Block

Tumbler, 4" h

Amethyst	$85-$115
Blue	$30-$45
Marigold	$40-$50

Water pitcher, tankard

Amethyst	$1,000-$1,500
Blue	$1,500-$1,800
Marigold	$325-$450

Blackberry Open Edge

Basket, ruffled

Amethyst	$50-$200
Aqua	$250-$275
Blue	$55-$90
Celeste blue, rare	$1,050
Green	$60-$80
Lime green	$165-$170
Red	$275-$400

Basket, two sides up

Marigold	$30-$35
Powder blue, dark	$50-$60
White	$120-$175

Dish, rounded, whimsy, blue
$125-$150

Spittoon, whimsy

Blue, rare	$3,600
Marigold, rare	$3,000

Vase, 7" h, whimsy, blue, rare
$2,000

Blackberry Spray

Hat, jack-in-the-pulpit

Amberina	$400-$450
Aqua	$80-$100
Aqua opalescent	$700-$1,500
Cherry red, crimped edge	
	$200-$225
Green	$165-$195
Marigold	$30-$35
Red	$400-$800
Vaseline	$75-$120

Hat, ruffled

Amber	$100-$150
Amethyst	$35-$150
Aqua opalescent	$800-$850
Blue	$35-$50
Celeste blue	$525-$625
Cherry red	$300-$500
Lime green opalescent	
	$125-$150
Reverse amberina opalescent	
	$400-$450

Hat, square, four sides up

Amethyst	$75-$135
Aqua	$35-$75
Green	$65-$95
Marigold	$40-$45
Red	$215-$365
Vaseline	$40-$50

Blackberry Wreath

Bowl, ice cream shape, 6-3/4" d

Amethyst	$50-$80
Green	$65-$70
Marigold	$45-$50

Bowl, ruffled, 7" d to 9" d

Blue, rare	$1,300
Green, radium	$45-$70
Marigold	$60-$75

Bowl, 3-in-1 edge, 9" d to
10-1/2" d

Amethyst satin	$70-$75
Green, radium	$155-$175
Marigold	$60-$80

Plate, 6" d

Amethyst, rare	$2,700
Green, rare	$2,750
Marigold, rare	$2,000

Acanthus, Imperial, chop plate, marigold, pretty and flat, **$135**.

Acorn Burrs, Northwood, covered sugar, green lid with purple bottom, **$40-$60**.

Advertising, Fenton, Gevurtz handgrip plate, amethyst, has incredible mold work and electric iridescence, very small pinhead on flowers, **$1,700**.

Beaded Bullseye, Imperial, vase, electric purple, 8-3/4" h, **$250-$300**.

Blackberry Spray, Fenton, six-ruffled hat, red, 6-1/2" d, **$300-$500**.

Blossomtime
Compote, ruffled
Amethyst/purple	$170-$225
Green	$400-$700
Marigold	$175-$300

Blueberry
Tumbler
Blue	$45-$65
Marigold	$80-$100
White	$90-$175

Water pitcher
Blue	$1,000-$1,400
Marigold	$500-$825

Bouquet
Tumbler, 4" h
Blue	$55-$125
Marigold	$20-$35

Water pitcher, 9-1/4" h
Blue	$450-$600
Marigold	$150-$285

Broken Arches
Punch bowl and base
Marigold	$300-$425
Purple	$1,000-$1,300

Punch cup
Marigold	$15-$25
Purple	$40-$70

Bullseye and Beads
Vase, 7" h, flared, marigold, dark $40-$50

Vase, 12" h
Amber	$240-$260
Amethyst	$120-$180
Blue	$175-$225
Marigold	$50-$65

Bushel Basket
Basket, round, ribbed side handles
Aqua	$325-$425
Blue	$75-$165
Green	$90-$275
Horehound	$400-$600
Ice blue	$250-$450
Lavender	$185-$200
Marigold	$50-$95
Sapphire blue	$1,350-$2,000
Smoke	$300-$375

Basket, eight-sided, ribbed side handles
Aqua, rare	$1,500

Blue	$100-$160
Green	$225-$250
Horehound, rare	$650
Ice green	$200-$250
Lavender	$160-$250
Marigold	$95-$125
Renninger Blue, rare	$550
White	$95-$225

Butterfly
Bonbon, plain exterior, two handles
Blue	$30-$35
Green	$65-$185
Horehound	$120-$145
Marigold	$70-$75
Smoke	$500-$550

Bonbon, threaded exterior, two handles
Amethyst/purple	$200-$400
Blue	$500-$625
Green, rare	$1,100
Ice blue, rare	$3,000
Marigold	$550-$700

Butterfly and Berry
Bowl, 5" d, ftd
Amethyst	$65-$85
Blue	$100-$125
Green	$90-$110
White	$75-$95

Bowl, 10" d, ftd
Amethyst	$175-$225
Green	$175-$200
Marigold	$65-$85
White	$600-$725

Hatpin holder
Blue, rare	$1,200
Marigold, rare	$1,300

Sugar bowl, cov
Amethyst	$100-$150
Blue	$85-$90
Green	$175-$200
Marigold	$30-$35

Water pitcher
Blue	$325-$500
Green	$600-$750
Marigold	$175-$300
White, rare	$1,400

Butterfly and Fern
Tumbler
Blue	$35-$65
Green	$55-$95
Marigold	$20-$65

Water pitcher
Blue, radium	$750-$800
Green	$350-$375
Marigold	$175-$225

Butterfly and Tulip
Bowl, ice cream shape, 10" d, ftd, marigold $275-$285

Bowl, square or round, ftd
Amethyst/purple	$2,000-$3,500
Marigold	$275-$350
Peach opalescent, rare	$9,000

Captive Rose
Bonbon, two handles
Amethyst	$65-$95
Blue	$40-$70
Green	$90-$150

Bowl, ruffled or 3-in-1 edge
Blue	$55-$135
Green	$75-$135
Marigold	$40-$50

Calling card tray
Amethyst	$65-$95
Green	$90-$150
Marigold	$30-$45

Compote, ruffled
Amethyst	$45-$75
Blue	$200-$325
Marigold	$40-$90
White	$75-$125

Plate, 9" d
Amethyst	$700-$750
Marigold	$250-$375

Chatelaine
Tumbler, purple, rare $200-$350
Water pitcher, purple, rare $2,400-$3,000

Checkerboard
Goblet, amethyst $100-$150
Punch cup, marigold $50-$70
Tumbler, marigold, rare $800
Water pitcher
Marigold, rare	$1,100

Cherries
Banana boat, three ftd
Amethyst/purple	$250-$300
Electric blue	$250-$275
Peach opalescent	$250-$275

Bowl, flat, 5" d to 7" d
Amethyst/purple	$115-$125
Marigold	$30-$45
White	$115-$125

Bowl, ruffled, flat, 9" to 9-1/2" d
Marigold	$80-$100
Peach opalescent	$120-$125
White	$425-$525

Plate, 6" d
Amethyst/purple	$200-$350
Peach opalescent	$220-$250

Cherry Chain

Bowl, ice cream shape, ruffled, or 3-in-1 edge, 9" d to 10" d
Amethyst, ice cream shape	$300-$325
Clambroth	$50-$95
Marigold	$40-$75
Red, rare	$6,500
Vaseline, rare	$200
White, rare	$100

Plate, 6" d to 6-1/2" d
Amethyst, rare	$800
Blue	$85-$135
Lavender, rare	$800
Marigold, dark	$60-$65
White	$200-$300

Sauce, ice cream shape or ruffled
Blue	$30-$50
Marigold	$20-$35
White	$20-$35

Chrysanthemum

Bowl, ball foot, ruffled, 10" d
Amethyst	$100-$150
Green	$250-$300
Marigold	$55-$125
Vaseline	$275-$325

Bowl, flat, 9" d
Amethyst	$150-$195
Blue	$120-$175
Green	$150-$200
Red, rare	$4,500
White	$400-$500

Circle Scroll

Bowl, 10" d
Amethyst	$40-$60
Marigold	$30-$50

Butter dish, cov
Amethyst	$60-$90
Marigold	$40-$80

Compote
Amethyst	$40-$60
Marigold	$30-$50

Creamer
Amethyst	$30-$50
Marigold	$20-$40

Hat, jack-in-the-pulpit
Amethyst	$65-$95
Marigold	$40-$60

Spooner
Amethyst	$30-$50
Marigold	$20-$40

Sugar
Amethyst	$30-$50
Marigold	$20-$40

Tumbler
Amethyst	$300-$450

Water pitcher
Amethyst, rare	$2,000

Colonial Lady

Vase, 5-1/2" to 6-1/2" h
Marigold	$750-$1,400
Purple	$600-$2,300

Concave Flute

Banana dish, 9" d,
marigold	$50-$55

Jack-in-the-pulpit vase
Amethyst	$90-$135
Marigold on milk glass	$150-$200
Teal	$100-$165

Rose bowl
Amethyst	$45-$65
Marigold	$35-$55
Teal	$75-$100

Vase
Amethyst	$30-$50
Blue opalescent	$75-$250
Green	$50-$75

Concord

Bowl, ice cream shape, ruffled
Amethyst	$275-$300
Blue	$75-$150
Green	$325-$350
Marigold	$130-$200
Pumpkin marigold	$225-$250

Bowl, 3-in-1 edge
Green, silvery	$70-$75
Marigold	$50-$65

Plate, 9" d to 10" d
Amethyst, rare	$1,400
Green, rare	$3,500
Marigold, rare	$1,100

Constellation

Compote, ruffled, 5" h
Amethyst	$500-$525
Marigold	$30-$100

Coral

Bowl, ice cream shape, ruffled, or 3-in-1 edge, 9" d
Blue, rare	$650
Green	$220-$240
Marigold	$100-$300

Corinth

Banana boat, 8-1/2" d, two sides up
Amethyst	$25-$45
Marigold	$20-$35
Teal	$20-$25
White	$25-$45

Bowl, 8" or 9"
Aqua, ice cream shape	$25-$30
Marigold	$30-$45
Peach opalescent	$35-$45
Teal	$50-$75

Vase, 9" h to 10" h
Amber	$60-$95
Aqua	$40-$45
Olive green	$40-$45
Teal	$35-$40

Corn

Vase, stalk base
Amethyst/purple	$300-$650
Aqua opalescent, cracked 1" from bottom, rare	$3,750
Ice blue	$800-$900
Lime green, marigold overlay	$400-$450
Marigold, dark	$800-$900
Teal, rare	$2,400
White	$300-$350

Vase, plain base
Amethyst/purple	$365-$650
Aqua	$800-$1,000
Green	$400-$900
Ice green	$265-$425
Marigold	$325-$850
White	$225-$325

Cosmos and Cane

Basket, honey amber, rare | $1,000

Berry bowl, master, 10" d
Marigold	$55-$75
White	$200-$235

Butterfly and Berry, Fenton, vase, top flames, red, 8-1/2" h, **$800-$1,200**.

Blackberry Wreath, Millersburg, bowl with three-in-one edge, marigold, **$80**.

Captive Rose, Fenton, plate, green, **$1,200.**

Chatalaine, Imperial, watcher pitcher and six tumblers, electric purple, **$3,200-$3,500**.

Breakfast set, small creamer
and sugar
Honey amber	$150-$170
White	$400-$475

Butter dish, cov
Honey amber	$250-$300
White	$300-$450

Chop plate, 10-1/2" d
Honey amber, rare	$650
Marigold, rare	$1,200
White, rare	$1,400

Creamer
Honey amber	$60-$75
Marigold	$45-$65

Rose bowl
Amethyst, rare	$1,100
Honey amber, rare	$1,500
Marigold	$300-$350

Spittoon
Honey amber, rare	$4,500
White, rare	$3,000

Sugar bowl, cov
Honey amber	$60-$75
Marigold	$45-$65
White	$150-$195

Tray, flat, white $200-$275

Water pitcher
Honey amber, rare	$1,400
Marigold	$600-$750

Curved Star
Butter dish, cov
Blue	$175-$225
Marigold	$150-$200

Celery vase, chalice shape
Blue	$150-$275
Marigold	$50-$115

Cheese dish, cov
Blue	$195-$275
Marigold	$200-$300

Creamer
Blue	$75-$95
Marigold	$35-$60

Rose bowl
Blue	$75-$150
Marigold	$75-$125

Sugar bowl, open, ruffled,
Headdress interior, blue
$75-$125

Dahlia
Berry bowl, small, ftd, 5" d
Amethyst	$60-$65
Marigold	$30-$40
White	$55-$95

Butter dish, cov
Amethyst	$150-$185
Marigold	$100-$220
White	$200-$350

Spooner
Amethyst	$70-$95
Marigold	$60-$75
White	$95-$125

Sugar bowl, cov
Amethyst	$70-$95
Marigold	$60-$75
White	$95-$125

Tumbler
Amethyst	$60-$95
White	$75-$135

Water pitcher, ftd
Amethyst	$500-$750
White	$375-$700

Daisy and Drape
Vase, turned-in top band
Amethyst	$850-$900
Aqua	$450-$550
Aqua opalescent	$375-$625
Green, rare	$3,200
Ice blue	$1,800-$2,250
Lavender	$500-$700
Purple	$550-$600

Vase, turned-out top band
Amethyst	$750-$850
Aqua	$450-$550
Blue	$750-$900
Marigold	$400-$450
White	$175-$200

Daisy and Plume
Candy dish, ftd
Amethyst/purple	$95-$175
Green	$45-$75
Ice blue	$300-$450

Compote, stemmed
Amethyst/purple	$45-$95
Green	$75-$100
Marigold	$35-$65

Rose bowl, stemmed
Amber	$115-$195
Aqua opalescent, raspberry interior, rare	$7,000
Blue, raspberry interior	$175-$200
Green, raspberry interior	$155-$175
Horehound, raspberry interior	$175-$195

Ice green, raspberry interior
$1,000-$1,150
Marigold, raspberry interior
$55-$60
Purple, raspberry interior
$175-$200
White	$75-$80

White, raspberry interior
$500-$525

Daisy Wreath
Bowl, ice cream shape,
8-1/2" d, marigold on milk glass
$60-$110
Bowl, ruffled, 8" d to 10" d
Amethyst	$200-$250
Aqua opalescent	$200-$300
Blue opalescent	$180-$200
Marigold	$150-$175
Marigold on milk glass	$80-$90
Peach opalescent	$100-$200

Plate, blue, rare $350

Dandelion
Mug
Amethyst/purple	$155-$275
Aqua opalescent, butterscotch	$450-$600
Blue	$250-$375
Blue, electric	$575-$775
Lavender horehound	$185-$200
Ice green	$800-$950
Marigold	$210-$425

Tumbler, 4-1/4" h
Black amethyst	$70-$100
Green	$90-$110
Ice blue	$175-$300
Lavender	$175-$250
Marigold	$45-$65
White	$90-$145

Water set, tankard pitcher, six
tumblers
Amethyst/purple	$1,200-$1,300
Green	$1,200-$1,300
Ice blue	$4,000-$5,000

Diamond and Rib
Jardinière, whimsy, flared and
ruffled or straight-sided
Blue, rare	$1,300
Green, rare	$1,400

White, rare | $850

Vase, 11" h to 12" h
Amethyst	$40-$45
Blue	$80-100
Green	$40-$45
Marigold	$35-$45
Smoke	$50-$75
White	$150-$155

Diamond Lace

Berry bowl, master, 9" d to 11" d
Green	$200-$250
Marigold	$50-$85
Purple	$80-$110

Berry bowl, small, 5" d
Green	$20-$30
Marigold	$15-$25
Purple	$20-$30

Bowl, ice cream shape, clambroth | $110-$125

Rose bowl, marigold, heat check in base, rare | $1,850

Tumbler
Marigold	$275-$300
White	$200-$250

Water set, purple, five pcs | $525-$550

Diamond Points

Bushel basket
Blue	$375-$400
Marigold	$425-$450
Marigold, dark	$2,000-$2,100

Vase, 6" h to 7-1/2" h, squatty
Amethyst	$75-$125
Green	$50-$75
Ice green	$275-$325
Marigold	$100-$145
White	$175-$350

Vase, 9-1/2" h to 10" h
Aqua opalescent, butterscotch	$600-$650
Ice blue	$275-$300
Sapphire blue	$475-$500
Smoke	$250-$255

Vase, 11" h
Green	$100-$115
Ice green	$190-$300
Sapphire blue, rare	$1,700
White	$75-$135

Diamonds

Punch bowl and base
Amethyst, rare	$3,700
Green, rare	$2,600
Marigold, rare	$2,800

Spittoon, whimsy from tumbler mold, marigold, rare | $7,000

Tumbler
Aqua	$125-$175
Marigold	$45-$75

Water pitcher
Aqua	$450-$550
Marigold	$150-$275

Dogwood Sprays

Bowl, ruffled, domed, ftd, 9" d
Amethyst/purple	$85-$250
Blue	$250-$350
Blue opalescent	$275-$325
Peach opalescent	$35-$70

Bowl, tricorn, domed, ftd, peach opalescent | $40-$60

Compote, domed
Marigold	$125-$175
Peach opalescent	$200-$250

Double Star

Bowl, 9" d, green | $200-$400

Tumbler
Amethyst	$175-$225
Marigold	$150-$275

Water pitcher, marigold | $400-$600

Dozen Roses

Bowl, ftd
Marigold, edge damage, rare	$250
Purple	$900-$1,100

Dragon and Lotus

Bowl, ice cream shape
Blue	$65-$85
Cherry red	$1,400-$1,500
Cobalt blue	$175-$185
Marigold	$40-$45
Red	$650-$700
Reverse amberina	$425-$450

Bowl, ruffled, plain back
Amber	$115-$120
Amber with red slag	$200-$225
Amethyst	$145-$150
Dark blue	$90-$95

Green	$35-$55
Lime green	$300-$350
Lime green opalescent	$350-$375
Peach opalescent	$145-$175
Vaseline slag	$75-$95

Bowl, 3-in-1 edge
Amethyst, light	$220-$225
Marigold	$65-$85

Plate, 9-1/2" d
Amethyst, rare	$2,500
Blue, rare	$2,200
Marigold, rare	$1,200
Peach opalescent, rare	$2,000
Red, rare	$7,000

Dragon and Strawberry

Bowl, flat, 9" d
Amethyst, rare	$3,500
Blue, rare	$2,000
Green, rare	$2,400
Marigold	$225-$500

Bowl, ftd, 9" d to 10" d
Blue	$1,000-$1,200
Green	$1,200-$1,500
Marigold	$200-$425

Drapery

Candy dish, also known as nut dish
Amethyst/purple	$95-$255
Aqua	$160-$200
Blue	$140-$165
Green	$275-$375
Ice green	$115-$185
Marigold	$55-$135

Rose bowl
Aqua opalescent, butterscotch	$225-$250
Blue	$275-$300
Electric blue	$475-$500
Ice blue	$500-$550
Lavender	$250-$650
Renninger blue, rare	$2,500
White	$400-$425

Vase, 8-1/2" h
Green	$165-$195
Marigold	$55-$60
White	$95-$125

Vase, 9" h, lime green | $375-$400

Concord, Fenton, ruffled bowl, marigold, **$200**.

Diamond Lace, Imperial, ruffled bowl, purple, **$25**.

Dragon and Lotus, Fenton, bowl, Vaseline with marigold overlay, **$600**.

Dragon and Strawberry, Fenton, ice cream shaped bowl, blue, **$700**.

Embroidered Mums, Northwood, ruffled bowl, ice blue, beautiful pastel iridescence, **$950**.

Dragon and Strawberry, Fenton, footed ruffled bowl marigold, scarce, **$425**.

Embroidered Mums, Northwood, ruffled bowl, blue, covered with electric highlights, **$500**.

Drapery Variant
Vase, 8-1/2" h, marigold
$55-$60
Vase, 9" h
Blue $160-$165
Purple $150-$155
Vase, 9-1/2" h, sapphire blue
$275-$295

Embroidered Mums
Bonbon, stemmed, two
handles, white, rare   **$1,000**
Bowl, ruffled, ribbed back, 9" d
Amethyst $265-$275
Aqua, rare $2,500

Aqua opalescent, rare
$3,000
Ice blue $600-$950
Ice green $1,200-$1,400
Horehound, rare $2,000
Lavender $450-$695
Marigold $350-$400
Sapphire blue, rare $2,500
Plate, 9" d
Blue, rare $6,500
Ice blue $1,000-$1,300
Ice green $1,000-$1,100
White $1,000-$2,100

Enameled patterns
Bud vase, Enameled Flowers
bud vase, marigold $5-$15
Lamp shade, Enameled Castle
Scene, marigold $40-$55
Tumbler
Enameled Forget-me-knot,
marigold $10-$15
Enameled Iris, green $20-$30
Water pitcher
Enameled Cherries and Little
Flowers, blue $75-$100
Enameled Cherries and Little
Flowers, marigold $105-$150
Water set
Enameled Cherries and Little
Flowers, blue, 7 pcs, bulbous
pitcher $125-$145
Enameled Columbine, blue
$145-$165
Enameled Crocus, marigold,
7 pcs $125-$175
Enameled Dianthus, white,
7 pcs, rare $700
Enameled Iris, amethyst,
tankard pitcher, 5 pcs
$135-$300

Estate
Bud vase, 5" h
Blue $35-$50
Lime green $125-$150
Perfume bottle, smoke
$200-$375
Pin dish, cov, smoke $75-$90
Pin tray, smoke $45-$65

Fanciful
Bowl, ice cream shape, ftd
Electric blue $215-$225

Peach opalescent **$160-$175**
White   **$100-$115**
Bowl, ruffled, 8-1/2" d to 9" d
Amethyst/purple **$300-$600**
Marigold   **$60-$80**
Peach opalescent **$160-$200**
Bowl, ruffled, 3-in-1 edge
Marigold, radium   **$60-$80**
Root beer, rare   **$250**
White   **$110-$175**
Plate, 9" d
Amethyst/purple
$250-$1,300
Blue $315-$600
Green, rare $500
Lavender $700-$950
Peach opalescent $400-$550
White $300-$450

Fantail
Centerpiece bowl, flared or ice
cream shape
Blue $350-$450
Marigold $100-$200
Chop plate, ftd
Blue, rare $6,000
Marigold, rare $5,500

Farmyard
Bowl, eight ruffles, purple
$5,500
Bowl, square, ruffled
Green, rare $10,000
Peach opalescent, rare
$6,000
Purple, rare $6,000
Bowl, three-in-one edge,
purple, rare $6,000

Fashion
Bowl, ice cream shape, 9" d
to 9-1/2" d
Clambroth $80-$90
Marigold $50-$70
Smoke $155-$175
Bowl, ruffled, 9" d
Marigold $30-$40
Smoke $35-$55
**Breakfast creamer or
breakfast sugar**
Emerald green $200-$250
Helios $125-$150
Fruit bowl, ruffled, 12" d,
amber, rare $100

Punch bowl with base

Purple, rare	$1,750
Red, rare	$5,000
Smoke, rare	$1,000

Punch cup

Marigold	$20-$30
Purple	$30-$40
Red	$435-$525

Water pitcher

Marigold	$150-$200
Smoke	$400-$550

Feather and Heart

Hair receiver, whimsy made from tumbler mold, marigold, rare $1,600

Tumbler

Amethyst	$50-$80
Green	$165-$215

Water pitcher

Amethyst	$350-$425
Green	$600-$625

Feathered Serpent

Bowl, 5" d

Blue	$25-$45
Green	$25-$50
Marigold	$20-$30

Bowl, ruffled, 10" d

Amethyst	$55-$115
Blue	$40-$65
Green	$50-$90

Sauce, tricorn, 6"

Amethyst	$35-$70
Green	$115-$130
Marigold	$25-$60

Fentonia

Berry bowl, small, 5" d

Blue	$25-$45
Marigold	$15-$25

Butter dish, cov

Blue	$350-$450
Marigold	$200-$350

Creamer

Blue	$115-$245
Marigold	$60-$90

Spooner

Blue	$115-$245
Marigold	$60-$90

Tumbler, marigold $35-$75

Water pitcher, marigold $500-$685

Field Flower

Milk pitcher

Clambroth	$200-$250
Marigold	$95-$160
Purple	$200-$400

Tumbler

Cobalt blue	$275-$350
Helios	$40-$70
Olive	$75-$100
Red, rare	$1,500
Violet	$95-$200

Water pitcher

Amber	$285-$415
Aqua	$500-$550
Cobalt blue, rare	$2,000
Helios	$300-$450
Smoke	$600-$700

Field Thistle

Berry bowl, small

Ice blue	$200-$250
Marigold	$20-$35

Chop plate, marigold $500-$600

Compote, marigold	$75-$85
Creamer, marigold	$20-$35
Plate, 6" d, marigold	$115-$125
Plate, 9" d, marigold	$250-$400
Spooner, marigold	$40-$80
Tumbler, marigold	$60-$100

Water pitcher, marigold $120-$210

File

Bowl, 7" d to 9" d

Marigold	$40-$50
Purple	$40-$55

Butter dish, cov, marigold $55-$75

Chop plate, 11" d, marigold $35-$65

Creamer, marigold	$25-$45
Spooner, marigold	$25-$45

Vase, whimsy, 3-1/2" h, marigold $250-$600

Fine Rib (Fenton)

Bowl, 5" d

Amethyst	$30-$45
Green	$40-$55
Marigold	$25-$35

Bowl, 9" d to 10" d

Amethyst	$40-$60
Green	$55-$75

Marigold	$40-$60

Jack-in-the-pulpit vase, ftd, 6" h

Blue	$175-$195
Marigold	$235-$245

Plate, 9" d

Amethyst	$70-$90
Green	$100-$120
Marigold	$60-$80

Vase, 9" h

Amethyst	$225-$375
Blue	$45-$65
Marigold	$35-$55

Vase, 10" h

Amberina	$175-$185
Amethyst	$45-$50
Aqua	$75-$85
Aqua opalescent	$25-$30
Celeste blue	$400-$600
Cherry red	$325-$400
Green	$50-$55
Lavender	$85-$100
Lime green	$70-$75
Peach opalescent	$100-$150
Powder blue	$60-$70
Purple	$45-$50
Teal	$200-$250
Vaseline opalescent	$400-$550

Vase, 11-3/4" h, vaseline $65-$70

Fine Rib (Northwood)

Jack-in-the-pulpit vase, ftd, 6" h

Amethyst/purple	$215-$220
Green	$175-$185
Marigold	$80-$90

Vase

Blue	$75-$125
Ice blue	$200-$250
Ice green	$175-$450
Sapphire	$195-$315
White	$120-$135

Fisherman's Mug

Mug, 4"

Amethyst, black	$100-$250
Custard, decorated	$60-$65
Horehound	$200-$275
Lavender	$85-$185
Marigold	$200-$300

Fishscale and Beads

Banana boat, peach opalescent $35-$130

Bowl, 6" d to 7" d, candy ribbon edge or ruffled
- Amber — $55-$75
- Amethyst/purple — $95-$145
- Aqua — $35-$55
- Pastel — $135-$155
- Peach opalescent — $25-$65

Dish, tricorn, crimped edge, purple — $70-$85

Plate, 6" d to 7" d
- Marigold — $50-$185
- Peach opalescent — $85-$125
- Purple with electric highlights — $575-$1,500
- White, radium — $110-$125
- White, satin — $45-$150

Fleur De Lis

Bowl, flat, collar base, 9" d to 10" d
- Amethyst — $400-$550
- Green — $200-$250
- Marigold — $185-$225

Bowl, ftd, dome base, 9" d to 10" d
- Amethyst — $275-$525
- Green — $275-$325
- Marigold — $185-$235

Bowl, ice cream shape, marigold, radium — $200-$220

Bowl, tricorn, dome ftd
- Amethyst — $500-$650
- Green — $375-$475
- Marigold — $295-$400

Floral and Grape (Made by Dugan)

Floral and Grape Variant (Made by Fenton)

Hat, whimsy
- Horehound — $55-$75
- Marigold — $30-$45

Jack-in-the-pulpit, whimsy, horehound — $80-$100

Tumbler
- Amethyst/purple — $50-$55
- Green — $75-$100
- Marigold — $20-$35
- White — $35-$55

Water pitcher
- Blue — $300-$350
- Green — $200-$300

- Ice green — $400-$600
- Marigold — $50-$180
- White — $225-$325

Floral and Optic

Bowl, ftd, 8" d to 9" d
- Clambroth — $30-$40
- Marigold — $35-$50
- Purple — $200-$300
- Smoke — $125-$175
- Teal — $125-$175

Cake plate, ftd, 11" d
- Clambroth — $45-$65
- Marigold on milk glass — $150-$180
- Red — $400-$550
- Teal — $275-$425
- White — $65-$95

Rose bowl, ftd
- Clambroth — $55-$85
- Marigold — $65-$100
- Red — $200-$300
- Smoke — $80-$110
- Teal — $200-$245

Flowers and Frames

Bowl, ruffled, dome ftd, 9" d
- Peach opalescent — $135-$175
- Purple — $300-$450

Bowl, tricorner, crimped edge, dome ftd, peach opalescent — $45-$85

Fluffy Peacock

Hat, whimsy, amethyst, damaged base, rare — $225

Tumbler
- Blue — $110-$120
- Green — $65-$135
- Marigold — $35-$45

Water pitcher
- Blue — $700-$850
- Green — $400-$650
- Marigold — $200-$350

Flute (Imperial)

Berry bowl, master, 10" d
- Marigold — $55-$65
- Purple — $195-$225

Bowl, 7" d to 8" d
- Emerald green — $80-$100
- Marigold — $40-$60

Butter dish, cov
- Helios — $185-$210
- Marigold — $70-$180

- Purple — $210-$245

Creamer
- Helios — $80-$110
- Marigold — $60-$90
- Purple — $100-$125

Cruet, marigold — $80-$110

Fruit bowl, pedestal
- Helios — $300-$500
- Vaseline — $700-$900

Nappy, one handle
- Marigold — $40-$60
- Purple — $95-$135

Punch bowl and base
- Emerald green — $750-$850
- Helios — $300-$350
- Purple — $900-$1,100

Spooner
- Helios — $80-$100
- Marigold — $60-$90

Sugar bowl
- Blue, rare — $1,050
- Lime green — $100-$115
- Marigold — $30-$45

Toothpick holder, 2-1/2" h
- Cobalt blue, rare — $925
- Emerald green — $135-$165
- Helios — $35-$55
- Lime green — $150-$200
- Marigold — $45-$75
- Vaseline — $245-$295

Tumbler
- Aqua — $250-$300
- Clambroth — $30-$40
- Helios — $75-$150
- Red — $300-$350
- Smoke — $150-$250

Vase, 7" h, flared
- Cobalt blue — $350-$400
- Marigold — $70-$90

Vase, 11" h
- Marigold — $20-$30
- Purple — $60-$80

Flute (Northwood)

Berry set, six pcs, marigold — $75-$115

Butter dish, cov, marigold — $100-$195

Creamer
- Green — $20-$30
- Marigold — $20-$30

Nut set, seven pcs, marigold — $225-$700

Sherbet

Green	$15-$25
Lavender	$15-$25
Marigold	$12-$20

Sugar bowl

Green	$20-$30
Marigold	$20-$30

Tumbler

Green	$200-$275
Marigold	$15-$35
Purple	$15-$35

Flute and Cane

Bowl, deep, ruffled, 8-1/2" d, marigold	$25-$30
Bowl, square, marigold	$50-$70
Champagne, marigold	$100-$150
Compote, marigold	$35-$65
Cordial, marigold	$400-$500
Creamer, marigold	$50-$60
Goblet, marigold	$65-$85
Pickle dish, marigold	$20-$30
Plate, 6" d, marigold	$80-$100
Punch cup, marigold	$20-$30
Sherbet, marigold	$15-$25
Sugar bowl, marigold	$50-$60
Water pitcher, stemmed, marigold pastel	$300-$500
Wine, marigold	$40-$60

Formal

Hatpin holder

Black amethyst, rare	$1,250
Marigold	$350-$500
Purple	$350-$950

Jack-in-the-pulpit vase

Marigold	$450-$500
Purple	$500-$600

Four Flowers

Banana bowl

Amethyst	$300-$400
Peach opalescent	$250-$350

Bowl, 5" d to 7" d

Amethyst	$35-$50
Marigold	$30-$45
Peach opalescent	$60-$90

Bowl, ruffled, 8" d to 10" d

Amber	$300-$500
Green	$400-$500
Powder blue	$40-$45
Vaseline	$400-$600

Plate, 9" d to 10-1/2" d

Amethyst	$125-$800
Green	$350-$400
Marigold	$250-$350
Peach opalescent	$400-$650

Rose bowl

Amethyst	$700-$900
Marigold	$350-$500

Four Flowers Variant

Bowl, 8" d to 10" d

Black amethyst	$175-$250
Green	$150-$250
Olive green	$150-$310
Teal	$90-$175

Chop plate, 10-1/2" d, purple, rare $1,800

Plate, 9" d to 10" d

Amber	$315-$425
Amethyst/purple	$400-$750
Emerald green	$350-$550
Olive green	$200-$315

Four Pillars

Vase, 9" h

Amethyst/purple	$70-$110
Marigold	$80-$90

Vase, 10" h

Aqua opalescent	$115-$275
Blue	$135-$200
Green	$65-$110

Vase, 12" h, Howard Furniture Co. adv., green $105-$115

Four Seventy Four

Bowl, 8" d to 9" d

Helios	$65-$85
Marigold	$30-$55

Compote, 7"

Marigold	$95-$125
Purple	$225-$275

Cordial

Marigold	$65-$95
Purple	$210-$250

Goblet

Helios	$40-$65
Marigold	$55-$70
Purple	$65-$95

Milk pitcher

Emerald green	$450-$650
Lavender	$700-$800
Olive green	$300-$400

Punch bowl with base

Aqua, rare	$1,700
Emerald green, rare	$3,500

Helios	$700-$900
Purple, rare	$3,500
Smoke, rare	$2,400

Punch cup

Aqua	$30-$50
Emerald green	$100-$125
Helios	$25-$35
Purple	$30-$50
Smoke	$60-$80

Tumbler

Blue	$215-$245
Helios	$50-$70
Purple	$80-$100
Violet	$225-$275

Water pitcher

Emerald green, rare	$3,500
Helios	$300-$500
Olive green	$500-$650
Purple, rare	$2,400

Fruits and Flowers

Berry bowl, small, ruffled, amethyst/purple $8-$10

Bonbon, handle, stemmed, 8-1/2" d, 4" h

Aqua opalescent	$450-$525
Electric blue	$250-$650
Ice blue	$375-$500
Lavender	$200-$325
Lime green	$450-$900
Marigold	$45-$135
Olive green	$190-$275
Renninger blue	$250-$260
Sapphire blue, rare	$2,500

Bowl, 9" d to 10" d

Amethyst/purple	$135-$140
Blue	$200-$250
Green	$95-$125
Ice green	$700-$900
Violet	$200-$350
White	$300-$475

Plate, hand grip, 7" d

Amethyst/purple	$95-$165
Green	$165-$200
Marigold	$65-$110

Plate, 9-1/2" d

Amethyst/purple	$200-$250
Marigold	$95-$125

Garden Path

Garden Path Variant

Bowl, ice cream shape, 9" d to 10" d

Peach opalescent	$375-$850

White $150-$200
Bowl, ruffled, 9" d to 10-1/2" d
Amethyst/purple $120-$700
Marigold $25-$85
Chop plate, 11" d
Marigold $1,500-$1,750
Peach opalescent
$2,000-$2,400
Plate, 6" d
Amethyst/purple
$1,000-$1,575
Marigold $90-$150
Peach opalescent $415-$650
White $300-$600
Rose bowl, marigold $65-$120
Sauce, 6" d
Peach opalescent $40-$150
White $325-$450

Gay Nineties
Tumbler
Amethyst $300-$700
Marigold $700-$1,000
Water set, six pcs, amethyst,
rare $5,500

Good Luck
Bowl, piecrust edge, basket
weave, ribbed, or stippled
Amethyst/purple $175-$550
Aqua opalescent, rare $7,000
Dark blue $425-$450
Ice blue, rare $2,100
Marigold $275-$390
Pastel marigold $110-$125
Renninger Blue, stippled,
rare $1,500
Bowl, ruffled, basket weave,
ribbed, or stippled
Aqua opalescent, butter-
scotch $1,500-$2,600
Electric blue $450-$1,000
Green $320-$600
Horehound $400-$500
Lavender $600-$850
Lime green $825-$975
Renninger Blue, stippled,
rare $1,200
Plate, basketweave or ribbed
back, 9" d
Blue, rare $4,000
Emerald green, rare $3,000
Green $125-$750
Horehound $500-$950

Ice blue (ribbed), rare $3,400
Plate, stippled, ribbed back, 9" d
Amethyst/purple
$900-$1,200
Blue $1,400-$2000
Marigold $600-$1,200

Gothic Arches
Vase, 10" h to 12" h
Marigold $135-$350
Smoke $410-$700
Vase, 14" h to 18" h, marigold
$350-$500

Grape and Cable (Fenton)
Bowl, ball feet, 7" d to 8-1/2" d
or flat, 8" d
Amberina $325-$475
Amethyst $70-$90
Aqua $65-$85
Blue $85-$110
Blue opalescent, rare $1,750
Green $45-$85
Lime green $55-$95
Marigold $60-$75
Marigold over milk glass
$100-$200
Powder blue $85-$125
Vaseline $65-$125
Violet blue $35-$55
Bowl, flat, 8" d
Aqua opalescent $600-$850
Marigold $40-$65
Powder blue $85-$125
Red $400-$475
Bowl, spatula feet, 7" d to 8" d
Amethyst $65-$90
Blue $85-$125
Green $65-$95
Marigold $10-$65
Bride's basket, handle
Amethyst, rare $2,000
Blue, rare $2,650
Plate, spatula feet, 9" d
Amethyst $95-$125
Blue $145-$185
Green $80-$110
Marigold $60-$80
Red, rare $1,500
Spittoon, whimsy, marigold,
rare $1,250

Grape and Cable (Northwood)
Banana boat, stippled, four ftd,
12-1/2" l
Blue $400-$600
Green $300-$375
Marigold $150-$275
Pearl $250-$375
Renninger blue $500-$600
Berry bowl, master,
10" d to 11" d
Electric blue, rare $1,500
Ice green, rare $1,200
Berry bowl, sauce, 5" d to 6" d
Marigold $20-$30
Pastel $20-$40
White $90-$125
Bonbon, two handles
Amethyst/purple $60-$80
Blue $100-$190
Green $50-$115
Marigold $45-$85
White $135-$175
Bowl, 7" d to 7-1/2" d
Amethyst/purple $60-$95
Aqua opalescent, rare $4,500
Green, basket-weave exterior
$60-$80
Ice blue $450-$750
Ice green $175-$250
Marigold $35-$45
Bowl, ice cream shape, master,
collar base, 10" d to 11" d
Amethyst/purple $250-$425
Blue $600-$750
Green $100-$200
Ice blue, rare $1,200
Ice green, rare $1,400
Lavender $275-$325
Marigold $160-$200
White $145-$175
Bowl, piecrust edge,
8" d to 9" d
Amethyst/purple $65-$115
Green $60-$110
Emerald green $200-$350
Ice blue, rare $1,200
Lavender $100-$160
Marigold $45-$95
Bowl, ruffled or round, ftd or
collar base, 8" d to 9" d
Amethyst/purple $80-$250
Aqua opalescent, rare $2,500

Floral and Grape, Fenton, two tumblers, blue, **$50 and $40**.

Floral and Optic, Imperial, rose bowl, marigold over milk glass, footed, **$100**.

Fluffy Peacock, Fenton, three tumblers, amethyst, clockwise from the top: **$55, $25 and $45**.

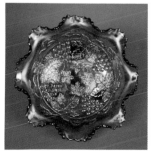

Grape and Cable, Fenton, footed bowl, smoke, rare color, **$65**.

Green	$75-$110
Ice blue, applied scrolled feet, rare	$2,100
Ice green	$200-$450
Marigold	$45-$70
Olive green	$50-$75
White	$225-$425

Bowl, stippled, 8" d to 9" d

Amethyst/purple	$200-$275
Blue	$200-$310
Green	$250-$650
Ice green, rare	$2,400
Marigold	$145-$265
Sapphire blue	$600-$1,200

Breakfast creamer or breakfast sugar

Amethyst/purple	$95-$165
Green	$70-$90
Marigold	$15-$35
Pastel	$80-$100

Butter dish, cov

Amethyst/purple	$175-$250
Green	$135-$255
Marigold	$95-$125

Calling card tray, flat

Amethyst/purple	$60-$80
Blue	$100-$190
Green	$50-$115
Marigold	$45-$85
White	$135-$175

Candle lamp

Amethyst/purple	$700-$950
Green	$625-$825
Marigold	$600-$800

Candlesticks, pr

Amethyst/purple	$285-$350
Green	$300-$450
Marigold	$185-$250

Centerpiece bowl, cupped in

Amethyst/purple	$350-$500
Blue, rare	$1,250
Ice blue, rare	$1,200
Marigold	$150-$350

Centerpiece bowl, points straight up

Green	$350-$450
Ice green	$550-$750
White	$275-$425

Cologne bottle

Green	$200-$300
Ice blue	$700-$850
Marigold	$95-$200

Compote, cov

Amethyst/purple	$325-$700
Marigold, rare	$1,300

Cracker jar, cov, two handles

Amethyst/purple	$275-$600
Blue, stippled	$700-$900
Ice green	$700-$1,100
Marigold	$200-$450
Marigold, stippled	$300-$500
Smoke	$200-$300
White	$700-$1,100

Cup and saucer

Amethyst/purple	$170-$250
Green	$130-$200
Ice blue	$500-$575
Ice green	$300-$400
Marigold	$95-$125
White	$150-$200

Dresser tray

Amethyst/purple	$155-$450
Green	$400-$650
Ice blue	$655-$1,100
Marigold	$150-$185
Marigold, stippled	$200-$300

Fernery

Green, rare	$5,000
Ice blue	$1,700-$2,000
Ice green, rare	$16,250
Marigold	$485-$900
Purple	$250-$800
White	$600-$750

Hat, made from tumbler mold

Amethyst	$35-$60
Green	$40-$70
Marigold	$35-$60

Hatpin holder

Black amethyst	$185-$325
Blue	$900-$1,200
Emerald green, rare	$3,100
Horehound	$450-$550
Ice blue, rare	$2,000
Ice green, rare	$1,500
Lavender, rare	$900
Lime green, rare	$2,000
Marigold	$160-$325
Pastel	$45-$75
White, rare	$2,000

Humidor, three-pronged sponge holder in lid

Amethyst/purple	$325-$450
Blue	$500-$600
Blue, stippled	$700-$1,000
Marigold	$200-$375
Marigold, stippled	$425-$550

Nappy, one handle

Amethyst/purple	$65-$120
Green	$65-$120
Ice blue	$500-$700

Marigold	$40-$65
Pastel	$45-$75

Perfume bottle (Dugan)

Amethyst/purple	$225-$700
Marigold	$250-$400

Pin dish, whimsy, made from punch cup

Amethyst/purple	$50-$90
Marigold	$15-$20

Pin tray

Amethyst/purple	$185-$300
Blue	$200-$400
Green	$200-$350
Ice blue	$600-$875
Marigold	$120-$250
Pearl	$300-$375

Plate, hand grip, 6" d to 8" d

Amethyst/purple	$80-$150
Green	$115-$175
Lavender	$100-$125
Marigold	$75-$100
Smoke	$100-$125

Plate, plain back, 7" d to 8" d

Amber	$75-$125
Amethyst/purple	$100-$200
Green	$125-$225
Marigold	$165-$900

Plate, ruffled, stippled, sapphire

blue, rare	$2,000

Plate, stippled, 9" d

Amethyst/purple	$375-$575
Blue	$700-$1,200
Emerald green, rare	$2,500
Green	$400-$820
Marigold	$400-$600
Sapphire blue, rare	$2,000

Powder jar, cov

Amethyst/purple	$125-$200
Blue	$650-$850
Green	$250-$450
Ice green	$750-$900
Lavender	$300-$500
Marigold	$85-$165

Punch bowl and base, master or banquet size

Amethyst/purple	$750-$900
Blue, rare	$5,500
Marigold, rare	$1,400
White, rare	$1,600

Punch bowl and base, midsize

Amethyst/purple	$750-$950
Blue, rare	$1,600
Emerald green, rare	$1,250

Punch bowl and base, small

Amethyst/purple	$450-$850

Blue	$600-$900
Marigold	$250-$500

Punch bowl set

Amethyst/purple, midsize, 14 pcs, rare	$2,100
Aqua opalescent, small size, 14 pcs, rare	$15,000
Blue, master size, 13 pcs, rare	$8,000
Blue, midsize, 8 pcs, rare	$2,800
Marigold, master size, 14 pcs	$1,700-$2,300
White, master size, 14 pcs	$3,000-$3,500

Sherbet

Amethyst/purple	$20-$40
Marigold	$15-$30

Shot glass

Amethyst/purple	$120-$135
Marigold	$125-$175

Sugar bowl, cov

Amethyst/purple	$75-$125
Green	$125-$175
Marigold	$50-$75

Sweetmeat, cov

Amethyst/purple	$150-$300
Blue, rare	$3,200
Horehound	$600-$900
Lavender	$200-$290
Marigold	$1,000-$1,750
White	$600-$900

Tumbler, water set, 4" h

Amethyst/purple	$15-$40
Green	$25-$90
Horehound	$100-$150
Ice green, rare	$700
Lime green	$125-$225
Marigold	$20-$35
Smoke	$125-$175

Water pitcher, tankard

Amethyst/purple	$550-$900
Green	$400-$475
Ice green, rare	$4,500
Marigold	$225-$500

Grape and Gothic Arches

Berry bowl, master

Electric blue	$200-$250
Marigold	$30-$50

Berry bowl, small

Aqua	$200-$225
Blue	$35-$45
Green	$35-$45
Teal	$50-$55

Butter dish, cov

Blue	$110-$160
Marigold	$85-$135
Pearl	$115-$145

Creamer

Blue	$35-$55
Green	$45-$85
Marigold	$30-$35
Pearl	$70-$75

Spooner

Blue	$35-$40
Green	$45-$85
Marigold	$30-$35
Pearl	$70-$75

Vase, 11" h

Marigold, 8" d mouth, rare	$1,200
Smoke, 7-1/2" d mouth, rare	$900

Water pitcher

Blue	$300-$900
Green	$275-$325
Marigold	$150-$350

Grape Arbor

Hat, whimsy made from tumbler mold

Blue	$70-$90
Ice green	$165-$250
Marigold	$60-$85
White	$85-$120

Tumbler

Amethyst/purple	$50-$100
Electric blue	$400-$550
Ice blue	$145-$250
Marigold	$40-$60
Sapphire blue, rare	$500
White	$50-$80

Water pitcher

Amethyst	$600-$650
Blue, damaged handle, rare	$2,000
Electric purple, rare	$3,000
Ice blue	$1,000-$2,100
Marigold	$200-$350
White	$450-$750

Grape Delight

Nut bowl, flared, ftd, 6" d, 4-1/4" h

Amethyst/purple	$50-$150
Black amethyst	$30-$90
Blue	$35-$85
Electric purple	$200-$300
Marigold	$40-$65
White	$50-$100

Rose bowl, crimped, ftd

Amethyst	$85-$165
Blue	$50-$75
Horehound	$175-$300
Marigold	$75-$135
Peach opalescent	$60-$85
Purple	$55-$80
White	$85-$100

Grape Leaves

Bowl, deep, 8" d, amethyst, rare $750

Bowl, ruffled, 9" d

Amethyst	$750-$950
Emerald green, rare	$4,600
Green, rare	$1,900

Bowl, square

Amethyst, rare	$3,500
Green, rare	$5,000

Bowl, 3-in-1 edge

Amethyst	$750-$950
Clambroth	$500-$650

Bowl, tricorn, 7" d to 8" d, green, rare $4,750

Grapevine Lattice

Bowl, ruffled, 6" d to 7" d

Amethyst/purple	$70-$110
Lavender	$40-$65
Marigold	$20-$25

Hat, jack-in-the-pulpit, whimsy made from tumbler mold

Amethyst/purple	$100-$150
Marigold	$25-$40
White	$100-$150

Plate, 6" d to 7" d

Lavender	$300-$375
Marigold	$45-$85
Peach opalescent, rare	$300
White	$65-$85

Tumbler

Amethyst/purple	$20-$65
Blue	$150-$300
Marigold	$25-$30

Water pitcher

Amethyst	$350-$650
Blue, Rare	$1,200
Marigold	$600-$825

Greek Key

Bowl, dome base, 7" d to 8" d
Amethyst/purple	$45-$85
Green	$50-$75
Marigold	$35-$50

Bowl, flat, 8" d to 9-1/2" d
Amethyst/purple	$150-$200
Blue	$300-$400
Green	$175-$225
Ice green, rare	$2,000
Marigold	$150-$475

Bowl, piecrust edge, basketweave back
Amethyst/purple	$200-$250
Blue, rare	$1,100
Green	$250-$850
Marigold	$200-$275

Bowl, ruffled, basketweave back, 9" d
Amethyst/purple	$60-$200
Blue	$450-$700
Green	$165-$215

Plate, basketweave back, 9" d
Amethyst/purple	$400-$415
Blue, rare	$2,000
Green	$625-$900
Marigold	$900-$1,250

Hanging Cherries

Bowl, ice cream shape, 7" d to 9" d
Amethyst	$195-$265
Blue, rare	$2,450
Green, satin	$75-$200
Marigold	$80-$150
Teal	$250-$350

Bowl, 9" d to 10" d
Aqua	$375-$625
Blue, rare	$2,750
Green	$300-$350
Marigold	$125-$175

Bowl, 3-in-1 edge, 9" d to 10" d
Blue, rare	$4,500
Green	$150-$300
Marigold	$125-$175

Butter dish, cov, 6" x 7"
Amethyst	$150-$250
Green	$300-$450
Marigold	$90-$200

Chop plate, 10" d
Amethyst, rare	$3,500
Green, satin, rare	$3,700
Marigold, rare	$2,500

Compote, 7" d, 6-1/4" h
Amethyst	$750-$1,200
Blue, rare	$4,500
Green	$1,400-$1,650
Marigold	$900-$1,250
Vaseline, rare	$5,000

Creamer
Amethyst	$75-$190
Aqua	$80-$125
Green	$90-$125
Marigold	$45-$75

Milk pitcher, 6-3/4" h
Amethyst	$600-$1,500
Green, rare	$1,100
Marigold	$750-$1,700

Plate, 6" d
Marigold	$1,900-$2,600
Marigold, dark, radium, rare	$3,400

Plate, 8" d
Amethyst, rare	$2,100
Green, rare	$4,250

Sauce, round, 5-1/2" d
Amethyst	$95-$125
Blue, rare	$1,500
Green	$70-$90
Marigold	$60-$80

Spooner or covered sugar bowl
Amethyst	$75-$190
Green	$115-$125
Marigold	$45-$75

Tumblers
Amethyst	$150-$175
Marigold	$220-$230

Water pitcher
Amethyst	$700-$900
Marigold	$1,700-$1,800

Hattie

Bowl, ruffled or round, 8" d to 9" d
Amber	$155-$200
Helios	$55-$75
Marigold	$35-$70
Purple	$100-$250
Smoke	$50-$75

Chop plate, 10" d to 10-1/4" d
Amber	$2,000-$3,200
Clambroth	$600-$700
Helios	$250-$350
Marigold	$1,050-$2,400

Rose bowl
Amber, rare	$1,600

Marigold	$95-$450
Purple, rare	$2,500

Hearts and Flowers

Bowl, pie crust edge, ribbed back, 9" d
Amethyst/purple	$750-$1,100
Blue	$1,200-$2,000
Electric blue, rare	$2,200
Green	$1,000-$1,500
Ice blue	$750-$1,200
Ice green	$1,000-$1,500
Lime green, rare	$2,100
Marigold	$475-$1,600
White	$350-$475

Bowl, ruffled, plain back, 9" d
Green, rare	$1,300
Ice blue	$350-$550
White	$200-$215

Bowl, ruffled, ribbed back, 9" d
Aqua	$900-$1,000
Aqua opalescent	$1,200-$1,800
Lavender	$400-$1,000
Pumpkin marigold	$700-$750
Purple	$475-$550
Renninger blue, rare	$3,000

Plate, 9" d, ribbed back
Amethyst	$800-$1,800
Green	$1,000-$3,500
Ice blue	$1,100-$1,600
Ice green, flake on base, rare	$950
Lime green	$1,900-$3,700
Marigold	$650-$1,600
Marigold, dark	$850-$1,600
Purple	$850-$940
White, rare	$2,500

Heavy Grape

Bowl, round, 5" d to 6-1/2" d
Clambroth	$30-$40
Emerald green	$40-$60
Helios	$20-$35
Lavender	$50-$65
Marigold	$15-$20
Purple or smoke	$30-$50

Bowl, round, 9" to 10" d
Amber	$40-$60
Cobalt blue	$600-$700
Emerald green	$250-$300
Helios	$80-$120
Light blue with marigold overlay	$80-$100

Marigold	$45-$85
Purple	$200-$450
Smoke	$155-$215

Bowl, ruffled, 6" d to 8" d

Lime green	$80-$100
Marigold	$10-$15

Chop plate, 10" d to 11-1/4" d

Amber	$250-$500
Emerald green	$600-$800
Helios	$155-$175
Ice green	$600-$800
Marigold	$135-$550
Smoke	$1,200-$2,500
White	$750-$1,000

Fruit bowl

Amber	$200-$400
Marigold	$175-$275

Nappy, single handle, 5" d

Aqua	$90-$120
Clambroth	$20-$40
Emerald green	$80-$100
Helios	$25-$40
Marigold	$15-$25
Olive green	$45-$75
Purple	$70-$115

Plate, 7" d to 8" d

Amber	$150-$250
Clambroth	$70-$150
Emerald green	$140-$160
Helios	$85-$125
Lime green	$200-$325
Marigold	$40-$80
Marigold, smooth edge	$90-$110
Smoke	$165-$285
Teal	$150-$200
Vaseline	$200-$300

Punch bowl and base

Amber, rare	$1,000
Emerald green, rare	$2,000
Helios	$450-$550
Marigold	$400-$800
Purple, silver base, rare	$1,100

Punch cup

Amber	$65-$85
Emerald green	$115-$135
Helios	$45-$75
Marigold	$85-$150
Purple	$50-$110

Heavy Iris

Hat, Jack-in-the-pulpit, whimsy from tumbler mold

Marigold	$400-$425
White	$250-$475

Tumbler

Amber	$60-$85
Horehound	$200-$300
Lavender	$80-$100
Marigold	$55-$120
Smoke	$70-$90

Water pitcher, tankard

Amethyst/purple	$500-$1,200
Marigold	$275-$400
White	$850-$1,200

Heron

Mug

Black amethyst	$250-$350
Marigold, rare	$3,000
Purple	$125-$135

Hobnail

Butter dish, cov

Amethyst	$300-$350
Blue, rare	$1,000
Green	$550-$650
Marigold	$350-$450

Creamer

Amethyst	$275-$375
Blue	$400-$600
Green	$350-$450
Marigold	$200-$275

Rose bowl

Amethyst	$185-$350
Green, rare	$1,200
Marigold	$125-$225

Spittoon

Green, rare	$2,000
Marigold	$500-$700
Purple	$550-$650

Sugar bowl, cov

Amethyst	$375-$475
Blue	$600-$750
Green	$450-$600
Marigold	$275-$400

Tumbler, amethyst $600-$750

Water pitcher

Amethyst, rare	$2,500
Green, rare	$4,000
Marigold, rare	$3,000

Hobstar

Biscuit jar, also known as cracker or cookie jar

Marigold	$40-$70
Purple	$100-$200

Bowl, 5" d to 7" d

Marigold	$20-$40
Purple	$40-$60

Bowl, 8" d to 10" d

Marigold	$30-$50
Purple	$80-$100

Bride's basket, silver-plated holder, marigold $100-$120

Butter dish, cov

Emerald green	$200-$250
Helios	$80-$100
Marigold	$85-$125

Compote, marigold $70-$100

Creamer

Emerald green	$90-$130
Helios	$60-$80
Marigold	$35-$45

Pickle castor, silver-plated holder, marigold $375-$575

Punch bowl with base

Emerald green	$500-$700
Marigold	$300-$500

Spooner

Emerald green	$90-$130
Helios	$80-$100
Marigold	$15-$25
Purple	$115-$135

Sugar bowl, cov

Emerald green	$90-$130
Helios	$65-$90
Marigold	$40-$60
Purple	$85-$125

Hobstar and Feather

Bowl, heart shape, marigold $450-$550

Bowl, round, 5" d

Amethyst	$350-$450
Green	$1,000-$1,350

Butter, cov

Amethyst	$1,200-$1,800
Green	$1,200-$1,800
Marigold	$1,000-$1,500

Calling card tray, white $500-$750

Compote

Amethyst, rare	$7,000
Green, rare	$8,000
Marigold, rare	$1,800

Creamer

Amethyst	$500-$700
Green	$500-$700
Marigold	$400-$600

Dish, diamond shaped, marigold, rare $1,000

Grape Leaves, Northwood, bowl with three-in-one edge, marigold, rare early edge, **$45**.

Hanging Cherries, Millersburg, milk pitcher, marigold, **$1,700**.

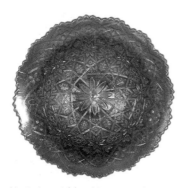

Greek Key, Northwood, ruffled bowl, electric blue, **$1,100**.

Hearts and Flowers, Northwood, compote, purple, great iridescence, **$350**.

Hattie, Imperial, bowl, ice cream shape, deep smoke, 9" d, **$65**.

Heavy Grape, Imperial, chop plate, marigold, has heavy stretch effect, **$550**.

Nappy, heart shape, marigold $150-$250

Punch bowl set, 14 pcs
  Green, Fleur-de-Lis interior, marigold base painted to look green, rare $2,400
  Purple, tulip-shaped bowl, rare $4,000

Rose bowl
  Amethyst/purple, rare $2,500
  Frosted, rare $3,200
  Green, rare $1,700

Sherbet
  Amethyst $500-$700
  Marigold $450-$650

Spittoon, whimsy, amethyst, rare $6,000

Spooner
  Amethyst $500-$700
  Green $500-$700
  Marigold $400-$600
  Vaseline, rare $4,000

Vase, whimsy
  Amethyst, rare $5,000
  Green, rare $5,000

Hobstar Flower
Compote, ruffled
  Emerald green $100-$150
  Helios $100-$150
  Lavender $150-$200
  Marigold $40-$65
  Smoke $100-$200

Holly
Bowl, candy ribbon edge, 9" d
  Amethyst $80-$90
  Marigold $135-$145
Bowl, deep, round
  Black amethyst $75-$95
  Blue $65-$85
  Lime green, marigold overlay $95-$100
  Marigold $40-$45
Bowl, ice cream shape, 9" d
  Amber $100-$120
  Amethyst $140-$150
  Aqua opalescent $150-$350
  Blue $65-$135
  Celeste blue, rare $5,250
  Green $45-$160
  Ice blue, rare $2,700
  Ice green, rare $2,000
  Lime green $145-$175

  Marigold $30-$225
  Powder blue, marigold overlay $120-$135
  Red, rare $1,200
  Vaseline $150-$275
  White $160-$175
Bowl, ruffled, 9" d
  Amber $105-$125
  Amethyst $60-$80
  Aqua $100-$115
  Black amethyst $200-$300
  Blue $70-$150
  Blue opalescent $1,200-$1,300
  Green $85-$130
  Lavender $65-$95
  Lime green $130-$150
  Marigold $115-$125
  Marigold on milk glass, rare $2,700
  Powder blue $65-$150
  Teal $115-$200
  Vaseline $115-$200
  White $85-$195
Bowl, 3-in-1 edge
  Amethyst $115-$145
  Aqua $200-$350
  Aqua opalescent $375-$395
  Blue $35-$135
  Green $75-$125
  Lime green, marigold overlay $85-$140
  Marigold $55-$250
  Olive green $70-$75
  Powder blue, marigold overlay $100-$115
  Red $1,200-$1,800
  Teal $115-$200
  Vaseline $115-$200
  White $170-$190
Compote, ruffled
  Amber, light $65-$75
  Amethyst $75-$175
  Aqua, marigold overlay $90-$215
  Aqua opalescent $75-$90
  Black amethyst $150-$175
  Blue $30-$55
  Green $85-$135
  Lime green $60-$110
  Lime green, marigold overlay $65-$175
  Marigold $25-$35
  Olive green $45-$85

  Pink $50-$60
  Powder blue $105-$125
  Red $400-$450
  Yellow-green $100-$115
Hat, candy ribbon edge, flattened
  Amber $60-$80
  Amethyst opalescent $275-$300
  Aqua $65-$90
  Aqua opalescent, rare $1,200
  Blue $25-$45
  Marigold $15-$35
  Red $300-$450
  Vaseline $50-$85
Hat, ruffled
  Amethyst opalescent $200-$235
  Aqua opalescent $300-$700
  Blue $35-$40
  Green $40-$50
  Lime green $35-$45
  Marigold on milk glass $115-$155
  Purple, dark $60-$90
  Red $200-$350
Hat, square
  Amberina $100-$125
  Aqua $35-$40
  Marigold $15-$35
  Red $125-$165
  Vaseline $115-$145
Jack-in-the-pulpit, candy ribbon edge, hat shape
  Amber $80-$95
  Amberina $200-$300
  Aqua $100-$115
  Blue $45-$115
  Lime green $120-$135
  Marigold $40-$50
  Powder blue $40-$45
  Red $200-$250
  Vaseline $65-$125
Plate, 9" d to 10" d
  Aqua opalescent, rare $2,400
  Black amethyst $600-$1,000
  Celeste blue, rare $1,750
  Clambroth $135-$195
  Pastel marigold $75-$110
  Teal, rare $1,000
  White $135-$315

Rose bowl

Aqua opalescent	**$185-$195**
Marigold	**$120-$135**
Vaseline, rare	**$650**

Holly and Berry

Bowl, ruffled, 6" d to 8" d

Marigold	**$45-$65**
Peach opalescent	**$40-$110**

Gravy boat, spout, handle

Peach opalescent	**$30-$60**
Purple	**$65-$90**

Nappy, ruffled, handle

Blue, rare	**$350**
Marigold	**$50-$70**

Nappy, ruffled or tricorn, handle

Black amethyst	**$65-$90**
Peach opalescent	**$30-$60**

Holly Sprig

Bonbon, commemorative, Issac Benesech

Marigold, radium	**$125-$150**
Marigold, satin	**$35-$75**

Bonbon or calling card tray, two handles

Amethyst	**$85-$110**
Green, radium	**$75-$80**
Green, satin	**$30-$35**
Lavender	**$60-$110**
Marigold	**$40-$55**

Bowl, ice cream or 3-in-1 shape, 5-1/2" d to 6" d

Amethyst	**$250-$350**
Green	**$275-$375**
Marigold	**$265-$345**

Bowl, round, 6" d to 7" d

Green, radium	**$45-$135**
Marigold, radium, dark	**$235-$245**

Bowl, ruffled, ice cream shape, or candy ribbon edge, 7" to 8" d

Amethyst	**$225-$275**
Green	**$225-$325**
Marigold	**$175-$250**

Bowl, square, 7" w to 8" w

Amethyst	**$300-$350**
Green	**$350-$400**
Marigold	**$275-$325**

Bowl, tricorn, 9" w to 10" w

Amethyst	**$300-$400**
Green	**$400-$500**
Marigold	**$250-$350**

Compote

Amethyst	**$1,000-$1,250**
Green, rare	**$2,000**
Marigold	**$700-$900**
Vaseline, rare	**$1,500**

Nappy, tricorn

Amethyst	**$80-$110**
Green	**$85-$150**
Marigold	**$80-$95**
Vaseline, rare	**$1,600**

Rose bowl, whimsy

Marigold	**$300-$500**
Vaseline, rare	**$2,500**

Homestead

Chop plate, 10-1/4" d to 10-1/2" d

Amber, sgd "Nuart," rare	**$2,000**
Cobalt blue, sgd "Nuart," rare	**$5,000**
Emerald green, sgd "Nuart," rare	**$4,500**
Forest green, rare	**$4,000**
Helios, not sgd	**$1,500-$2,500**
Helios, sgd "Nuart," rare	**$2,700**
Marigold	**$400-$650**
Olive green	**$900-$1,200**
Purple, not sgd	**$750-$1,250**
Purple, sgd "Nuart"	**$1,250-$3,200**
Smoke	**$325-$625**
White	**$850-$950**

Imperial Grape

Basket, handle, 10"

Clambroth	**$60-$80**
Cobalt blue	**$175-$225**
Lavender	**$160-$185**
Marigold	**$35-$55**
Smoke	**$45-$75**

Berry bowl, master, 8-1/2" d to 9-1/2" d

Amber	**$70-$90**
Clambroth	**$40-$60**
Helios	**$40-$60**
Lavender	**$100-$150**
Marigold	**$20-$25**
Marigold over milk glass	**$300-$500**
Purple	**$85-$95**
Smoke	**$130-$160**

Bowl, flared, 10" d to 11" d

Green	**$45-$75**
Smoke	**$100-$200**

Bowl, ice cream shape, 8" d to 9" d

Amethyst	**$200-$400**
Marigold	**$100-$200**

Bowl, ruffled, collar base, 4" d to 5" d

Amber	**$50-$70**
Emerald green	**$40-$60**
Lavender	**$50-$70**
Olive green	**$65-$75**
Violet	**$60-$80**

Bowl, ruffled, collar base, 10" d to 12" d

Aqua/teal	**$100-$175**
Cobalt blue	**$250-$300**
Helios	**$50-$100**
Marigold	**$35-$65**
Purple	**$80-$115**
Smoke	**$200-$245**

Compote, ruffled, threaded base

Amber	**$35-$40**
Aqua	**$100-$200**
Emerald green	**$80-$120**
Helios	**$50-$70**
Lavender	**$65-$110**
Marigold	**$20-$35**
Olive green	**$90-$90**
Purple	**$90-$195**
Smoke	**$50-$70**

Cup and saucer

Clambroth	**$35-$45**
Helios	**$45-$75**
Marigold	**$50-$75**
Purple	**$150-$175**

Decanter, matching stopper

Clambroth	**$100-$150**
Emerald green	**$300-$350**
Helios	**$95-$125**
Marigold	**$75-$95**
Purple	**$275-$325**
Smoke	**$200-$300**

Goblet

Amber	**$45-$75**
Helios	**$40-$55**
Marigold	**$30-$35**
Purple	**$115-$175**
Smoke	**$65-$95**

Milk pitcher

Helios	**$100-$200**
Marigold	**$125-$225**

Purple	$300-$350
Smoke	$125-$225
Plate, 6" d to 6-1/2" d	
Amber	$225-$325
Cobalt blue, rare	$1,800
Emerald green	$80-$100
Helios	$60-$90
Lavender	$200-$250
Lime green	$35-$115
Marigold	$75-$125
Olive green	$70-$90
Teal	$300-$400
Plate, 9" d	
Amber, rare	$1,400
Aqua	$300-$450
Clambroth	$60-$85
Emerald green, rare	$3,000
Helios	$100-$200
Lavender	$140-$170
Marigold	$100-$150
Purple, rare	$1,900
Smoke	$95-$135
Vaseline	$90-$110
Punch bowl and base	
Amber	$425-$525
Helios	$225-$275
Marigold	$300-$325
Purple	$1,800-$2,000
Smoke	$325-$375
Punch cup	
Amber	$40-$60
Helios	$20-$30
Marigold	$15-$20
Purple	$35-$50
Smoke	$25-$35
Sandwich server, 8-1/2" d	
Marigold	$25-$35
Smoke	$35-$45
Spittoon, whimsy	
Helios, rare	$2,750
Marigold, rare	$2,000
Tumbler	
Amber	$700-$900
Aqua	$60-$90
Emerald green, rare	$1,000
Helios	$40-$50
Horehound	$80-$90
Marigold	$15-$25
Olive	$50-$65
Smoke	$55-$75
Water carafe	
Aqua	$250-$300
Helios	$95-$115
Lavender	$85-$95

Marigold	$95-$115
Marigold, dark	$85-$95
Purple	$365-$400
Smoke	$400-$600
Wine	
Clambroth	$15-$20
Cobalt blue	$100-$200
Emerald green	$85-$135
Helios	$25-$35
Lavender	$25-$35
Lime green	$25-$35
Olive green	$25-$35
Purple	$30-$45
Smoke	$65-$90

Inverted Feather

Butter dish, cov	
Amethyst	$450-$550
Marigold	$350-$450
Compote, marigold	$60-$75
Cordial, marigold	$400-$500
Cracker jar, cov, amethyst, rare	
	$750
Creamer	
Amethyst	$150-$250
Marigold	$70-$100
Parfait, marigold	$60-$75
Powder jar	
Green	$250-$300
Marigold	$245-$295
Punch bowl with base	
Green, rare	$3,000
Marigold, rare	$4,500
Spooner or covered	
sugar bowl	
Amethyst	$150-$250
Marigold	$70-$100
Tumbler	
Amethyst	$500-$575
Green	$550-$650
Marigold	$350-$450
Water pitcher, amethyst, rare	
	$6,000

Inverted Strawberry

Berry bowl, master	
Amethyst	$75-$95
Marigold	$55-$75
Berry bowl, small, 5" d,	
marigold	$25-$35
Bonbon, two handles, whimsy	
from spooner mold, green,	
rare	$1,600
Bowl, 10-1/2" d, sgd "Near Cut"	

Amethyst/purple	$200-$225
Green	$125-$145
Marigold	$95-$115
Breakfast creamer and sugar	
set, pedestal, amethyst, rare	
	$750
Butter dish, cov, marigold	
	$500-$850
Candlesticks, pr	
Green	$1,000-$1,200
Marigold	$350-$450
Celery vase	
Blue	$750-$850
Green	$700-$900
Purple	$300-$350
Compote	
Amethyst	$400-$625
Blue, rare	$2,500
Marigold	$275-$400
Creamer	
Amethyst	$165-$185
Green	$400-$450
Marigold	$300-$400
Milk pitcher, purple, rare	
	$5,000
Powder jar	
Green	$175-$185
Marigold	$150-$250
Spittoon, 5-1/2" d, 3" h, sgd	
"Near Cut"	
Green	$800-$950
Marigold	$700-$750
Spooner, two handles	
Amethyst	$165-$225
Marigold	$65-$90
Sugar bowl, cov	
Green	$450-$650
Marigold	$375-$425
Purple	$450-$650
Tumbler	
Amethyst	$150-$165
Green	$115-$200
Marigold	$95-$150

Inverted Thistle

Berry bowl, master, 8" d,	
amethyst	$150-$200
Berry bowl, small, amethyst	
	$75-$90
Chop plate, 11" d, amethyst	
	$250-$450
Creamer	
Amethyst	$65-$225
Green	$95-$275

Nut bowl, collar base, green
$375-$450
Nut bowl, ftd, flared, green, rare **$1,200**
Spooner, two handles
Amethyst $125-$300
Green $150-$350
Sugar bowl, cov
Amethyst $200-$300
Green $150-$350
Tumbler
Amethyst/purple $225-$325
Marigold $500-$600

Jeweled Heart

Basket, whimsy, peach opalescent **$400-$450**
Bowl, 5" d
Amethyst $20-$40
Peach opalescent $50-$60
White $50-$60
Bowl, crimped edge, two sides up, 6" d, peach opalescent
$25-$35
Bowl, ruffled, 10" d
Amethyst $300-$350
Peach opalescent $100-$135
Purple $350-$400
White $200-$250
Plate, 6" d
Amethyst $125-$175
Marigold $115-$145
Peach opalescent $165-$195
Tumbler
Marigold $55-$95
White $400-$550

Kittens

Banana boat
Amethyst $350-$550
Blue $300-$375
Marigold $75-$185
Powder blue $250-$400
Topaz $175-$200
Bowl, ruffled, four sides up
Amethyst $175-$375
Marigold $125-$165
Pastel powder blue
$250-$475
Topaz $200-$250
Bowl, six ruffles, 4-1/2" d
Aqua $400-$500
Blue $200-$250
Pastel powder blue $140-$170

Calling card tray, two sides up
Amethyst $350-$550
Blue $300-$375
Marigold $95-$185
Pastel powder blue
$250-$400
Topaz $175-$200
Cereal bowl, 3-1/2" d
Amethyst $125-$175
Blue $295-$500
Marigold $125-$180
Cup, blue $310-$475
Plate, 4-1/2" d, two sets of kittens
Amethyst $400-$650
Marigold $135-$185
Pastel powder blue
$150-$260
Plate, 4-1/2" d, four sets of kittens, powder blue, marigold overlay $250-$265
Spittoon, marigold
$1,100-$1,200
Toothpick holder, ruffled, marigold $110-$135
Toothpick holder, two sets of kittens
Blue $240-$250
Marigold $75-$155
Vase, 3" h
Blue $200-$250
Marigold $100-$200

Knotted Beads

Vase, 8" h, crimped edge, marigold **$65-$70**
Vase, 9" h, crimped edge
Amber $500-$600
Aqua $125-$185
Blue $30-$35
Vase, 10" h, crimped edge, blue $40-$45
Vase, 13" h, marigold $30-$35

Lattice and Daisy

Bowl, 5" d
Marigold $20-$35
White $80-$100
Bowl, 9" d, marigold $80-$100
Hat, ruffled, marigold $10-$15
Tumbler
Amethyst $65-$95
Blue $150-$175
White $100-$200

Water pitcher, tankard
Amethyst, rare **$1,200**
Blue, rare **$1,500**

Lattice and Grape

Tumbler
Blue $20-$35
White $175-$200
Water pitcher, tankard
Blue $300-$600
White $300-$350

Lattice and Points

Bowl, ruffled, 7" d
Marigold $15-$30
White $50-$60
White, "Souvenir of Orwell NY" inscription $50-$60
Hat
Marigold $25-$45
Purple $50-$200
White $45-$90
Vase, 5" h, ruffled, white
$45-$50
Vase, 7" h, marigold $25-$35
Vase, 8" h
Blue $40-$45
Marigold $35-$40
Peach opalescent $140-$150
Vase, 9-1/2" h, marigold
$35-$40

Laurel Band

Tumbler, marigold $50-$80
Water pitcher, marigold
$80-$100

Leaf and Beads

Candy dish, purple $100-$110
Nut bowl, ftd
Amethyst/purple $80-$110
Blue $200-$400
Green $50-$65
Marigold $35-$65
Marigold, dark $30-$35
White $275-$350
Plate
Green $100-$115
Marigold $45-$65
Rose bowl
Electric blue $95-$250
Green $85-$125
Ice blue, rare $1,000
Ice green, rare $1,500
Lavender $500-$700

Heavy Iris, Dugan, three tumblers. marigold, **$90 for all three**.

Holly, Fenton, plate, amethyst, **$1,200**.

Hobnail Swirl, Millersburg, vase, green, 9" h, **$300-$450**.

Imperial Grape, Imperial, carafe, purple, 9" h, **$200-$400**.

Inverted Strawberry, Cambridge, milk pitcher, amethyst, supposedly one of three known, **$4,500**.

Marigold	$60-$175
Renninger blue	$300-$350
Teal	$300-$500
White	$350-$375

Rose bowl, sunflower interior

Amethyst	$85-$95
Aqua, rare	$1,200
Blue	$500-$700
Green	$200-$215
Purple	$85-$95

Leaf Chain

Bowl, ice cream shape, round, or ruffled, 7" d

Amberina, rare	$2,000
Amethyst	$75-$135
Aqua	$75-$135
Celeste blue	$800-$1,000
Clambroth	$40-$50
Ice green	$800-$1,000
Lavender	$50-$90
Red	$450-$650
Vaseline	$90-$135

Bowl, ice cream shape or ruffled, 9" d

Blue	$80-$100
Green	$40-$60
Ice green, rare	$2,400
Marigold	$40-$65
White	$70-$95

Plate, 7" d to 7-1/2" d

Blue	$150-$175
Clambroth	$135-$150
Green	$300-$350
Ice green, rare	$4,000
Marigold	$75-$100
White	$90-$100

Plate, 9" d to 9-1/4" d

Amethyst, rare	$4,000
Emerald green	$1,200-$1,300
Green	$200-$300
Marigold	$195-$375
Marigold, dark	$550-$575
White	$180-$250

Leaf Columns

Vase, 10" h to 12" h

Amethyst	$75-$125
Green	$100-$135
Horehound	$250-$300
Ice blue	$250-$450
Ice green	$300-$500
Marigold	$50-$80

Sapphire blue	$400-$700
Teal	$200-$350
White	$120-$125

Leaf Tiers

Berry bowl, master, marigold
$175-$200

Berry bowl, small, marigold
$10-$15

Butter dish, cov, marigold
$100-$150

Spooner, marigold $20-$25
Tumbler, ftd, marigold $50-$70
Water pitcher

Marigold	$450-$550
Marigold, dark	$400-$450

Lined Lattice

Vase, 5-1/2" h to 6" h

Marigold	$60-$185
Peach opalescent	$135-$195

Vase, 9" h to 9-1/2" h

Purple	$135-$145
Smoky lavender	$85-$95
White	$65-$75

Vase, 11" h

Marigold	$50-$55
Purple	$65-$75
Smoky lavender	$200-$220

Vase, 14" h, purple $220-$225

Little Fishes

Bowl, 5" d to 6" d

Amethyst	$90-$135
Aqua	$175-$200
Blue	$115-$185
Marigold	$50-$85
Marigold, dark, ftd	$185-$200

Bowl, ice cream shape or ruffled, ftd, 9" d to 10" d, blue
$225-$250

Little Flowers

Bowl, 5-1/2" d

Amethyst	$30-$40
Aqua	$80-$100
Blue	$25-$60
Green	$40-$80
Vaseline	$85-$125

Bowl, deep or ruffled, 9-1/2" to 10" d

Amethyst	$125-$145
Aqua	$95-$135
Blue	$100-$145
Green	$115-$155

Marigold	$35-$70

Bowl, ice cream shape, 6" d

Amethyst	$30-$50
Blue	$45-$65
Green	$75-$95
Marigold	$30-$40

Powder blue, marigold overlay
$45-$85

Bowl, 3-in-1 edge, 10" d, amethyst $55-$60
Bowl, tricorn, 6" w

Amethyst	$125-$175
Marigold	$100-$125

Chop plate, 10" d, marigold
$1,200-$1,400

Plate, 6" d to 7" d

Marigold	$95-$125
Powder blue	$200-$250

Little Stars

Bowl, ice cream shape or sauce, 6" d

Amethyst	$600-$700
Blue, rare	$2,500
Green	$725-$825

Bowl, ruffled, 7" d to 7-1/2" d

Amethyst, satin	$110-$115
Blue, rare	$3,000
Clambroth	$100-$135
Green, satin	$175-$185
Marigold	$100-$135

Bowl, ruffled, 8" d to 9" d

Amethyst	$350-$450
Clambroth	$300-$400
Green	$350-$450
Marigold	$250-$350
Pastel marigold	$95-$105

Bowl, 10-1/2" d

Amethyst	$600-$700
Blue, rare	$4,000
Green	$700-$900
Marigold	$500-$600

Plate, 7-1/2" d

Amethyst	$1,000-$1,400
Green	$1,200-$1,600
Marigold	$900-$1,200

Loganberry

Vase, 10" h, 3-1/4" d base

Emerald green	$775-$975
Helios	$225-$375
Marigold	$300-$350
Marigold, dark	$600-$650
Smoke	$800-$1,000

Long Thumbprint

Vase, 7" to 11" h

Amethyst	$25-$45
Aqua, 7" h	$30-$35
Blue	$85-$100
Green, 9" h	$20-$40
Marigold	$30-$45
Olive green	$45-$60

Lotus and Grape

Bonbon or calling card tray, two handles

Amethyst/purple	$80-$100
Aqua	$300-$350
Blue	$65-$85
Green	$75-$150
Lime	$80-$95
Marigold	$30-$40
Red	$350-$600
Red slag	$465-$520
Teal	$165-$200
Vaseline	$125-$175

Bowl, ruffled, 7" to 8-1/2" d

Amethyst/purple	$50-$70
Blue	$90-$100
Green	$65-$125
Marigold	$60-$65
Persian blue	$700-$800
Teal	$275-$375
Vaseline	$100-$150

Bowl, 3-in-1 edge, blue $90-$100

Plate, 9" d to 9-1/2" d

Amethyst	$1,200-$1,600
Blue	$1,500-$2,000
Green	$1,200-$1,400
Marigold	$1,000-$1,400

Sauce, ftd, 5" d to 6" d

Amethyst/purple	$50-$70
Blue	$35-$50
Green	$135-$185
Marigold	$25-$35
Vaseline	$275-$475

Lustre Rose

Berry bowl, master, ftd, 8" d to 10" d

Amber	$80-$100
Aqua	$100-$150
Clambroth	$30-$50
Cobalt blue	$300-$400
Helios	$60-$70
Marigold	$30-$50
Purple	$85-$185

Smoke	$250-$300
Vaseline	$200-$275

Berry bowl, small, ftd, 5" d

Amber	$35-$40
Aqua	$40-$60
Clambroth	$15-$20
Cobalt blue	$100-$125
Helios	$60-$80
Marigold	$15-$20
Marigold on milk glass	$90-$110
Purple	$35-$40

Bowl, ftd, 8" d to 9" d

Amber	$90-$110
Clambroth	$40-$60
Cobalt blue	$245-$290
Helios	$50-$75
Marigold	$40-$60
Olive	$125-$145
Purple	$135-$170
Smoke	$150-$200
Vaseline	$150-$225

Bowl, ice cream shape, flared, 10" d

Marigold, ftd	$200-$220
Smoke, collared base	$125-$150

Bowl, ruffled, collar base, 8" d to 8-1/2" d

Amber	$35-$45
Electric purple	$85-$100
Purple	$100-$115

Butter dish, cov, 6" x 7-1/2"

Amber	$185-$225
Helios	$70-$90
Light blue with marigold overlay	$125-$175
Marigold	$60-$100
Purple	$250-$275
Teal	$250-$300

Creamer

Amber	$60-$90
Helios	$35-$50
Light blue with marigold overlay	$80-$100
Marigold	$35-$50
Purple	$130-$150
Teal	$100-$120

Fernery, three scrolled feet

Amberina	$500-$750
Aqua	$85-$95
Clambroth	$40-$60
Cobalt blue	$150-$185
Marigold	$30-$45

Olive	$50-$90
Purple	$125-$250
Smoke	$75-$95
White	$300-$350

Fruit bowl, deep, ftd, 11" d to 12" d

Amber	$70-$90
Aqua	$185-$220
Clambroth	$45-$50
Helios	$100-$125
Marigold	$20-$40
Purple	$600-$700
Red, rare	$2,000
Smoke	$55-$90
Vaseline	$250-$300

Milk pitcher

Clambroth	$100-$125
Marigold	$80-$100

Plate, 8" d to 9" d

Amber	$100-$120
Aqua	$110-$130
Clambroth	$185-$200
Helios	$160-$185
Lime green	$200-$225
Marigold	$200-$250
Purple, rare	$2,000

Rose bowl

Amber	$40-$60
Helios	$40-$45
Lime green	$150-$200
Marigold	$30-$35
Olive	$115-$135
Purple	$600-$625
Smoke	$100-$185

Sugar bowl, cov

Amber	$80-$100
Helios	$50-$70
Light blue with marigold overlay	$80-$100
Marigold	$50-$70
Purple	$130-$150
Teal	$100-$120

Tumbler

Amber	$50-$85
Aqua	$45-$65
Clambroth	$95-$110
Marigold	$15-$20
Olive	$30-$50
Purple	$55-$90
Teal	$135-$160
White	$300-$325

Water pitcher

Amber	$300-$350
Clambroth	$95-$125

Lattice and Daisy, Dugan, tankard, marigold, **$90**.

Lattice and Points, Dugan, squatty vase, electric amethyst, **$190-$250**.

Leaf and Beads, Northwood, aqua opalescent rose bowl, butterscotch iridescence, **$325**.

Leaf Tiers, Fenton, covered sugar and creamer, marigold, **$200**.

Leaf Chain, Fenton, plate, marigold, super iridescence, 9" d, **$1,400**.

Helios $300-$350
Light blue with marigold
overlay $200-$225
Marigold $100-$125
Purple $550-$600

Many Fruits
Punch bowl with base
Blue $2,000-$2,400
Marigold $350-$400
Punch cup
Blue $95-$125
Green $20-$40
Marigold $15-$30
Purple $25-$45

Many Stars
Bowl, advertising, Bernheimer
Bros, ruffled, blue
$2,200-$3,000
Bowl, ice cream shape, 9" d
to 10" d
Amethyst $800-$1,000
Blue, rare $3,000
Green $800-$1,000
Marigold $1,000-$1,400
Bowl, ruffled, 9" d to 10" d
Blue, rare $3,700
Green $400-$600
Marigold $275-$375
Vaseline, rare $3,000
Bowl, 3-in-1 edge, marigold
$275-$300
Bowl, tricorn, amethyst, rare
$2,500
Chop plate, marigold, rare
$4,750

Maple Leaf
Berry bowl, master, stemmed,
9" d
Amethyst $80-$100
Blue $80-$100
Marigold $40-$60
Berry bowl, small, stemmed,
4-1/2" d
Amethyst $20-$35
Blue $25-$40
Green $30-$50
Marigold $15-$30
Butter dish, cov
Amethyst $100-$150
Blue $100-$150
Marigold $85-$125

Creamer
Amethyst $30-$35
Blue $45-$70
Marigold $30-$35
Spooner or sugar bowl
Amethyst $30-$35
Blue $45-$70
Tumbler
Amethyst $30-$50
Marigold $10-$40
Water pitcher
Amethyst $200-$300
Marigold $125-$175

Mary Ann
Loving cup, three handles
Marigold $350-$500
Marigold, dark $195-$225
Pink, rare $1,000
Vase, two handles, 7" h
Amethyst $175-$275
Marigold $85-$100

Memphis
Berry bowl, master
Marigold $90-$150
Purple $300-$425
Berry bowl, small
Marigold $100-$130
Purple $115-$150
Fruit bowl with stand
Amethyst $200-$325
Green $600-$900
Ice blue, rare $3,500
Marigold $200-$325
Punch bowl with stand
Ice green, rare $15,000
Purple $500-$650
Punch cup
Amethyst $15-$30
Black amethyst $25-$40
Ice blue $60-$100
Ice green $100-$200
Lime $60-$85
Purple $20-$45

Morning Glory
Funeral vase, 11" h to 22" h
Amber $200-$400
Green $200-$400
Marigold, 11" h, 9" d mouth
$185-$200
Purple, 12-1/2" h $500-$800
Purple, 16-1/2" h, 4-3/4" d
$200-$250

Smoke $200-$300
Jack-in-the-pulpit vase
Marigold, 8-1/2" h $25-$35
Marigold, 9" h $70-$75
Marigold, 10" h $35-$45
Marigold, 11" h $50-$65
Pitcher, ACGA commemorative
Marigold, 1986 $100-$120
Green, 1987 $90-$100
Purple, 1988 $80-$90
Red, 1989 $150-$155
Tumbler, amethyst
$700-$2,100
Vase, squatty
Clambroth $30-$50
Emerald green, 4-1/4" h
$145-$155
Helios, 6" h $60-$75
Helios, 7-1/2" h $35-$60
Marigold, 5" h $55-$70
Marigold, 7" h $20-$30
Marigold, light, 7" h
$30-$35
Olive green, 6-1/2" h
$45-$60
Pastel, 7" h $185-$200
Purple, 3-3/4" h $200-$220
Purple, 6" h $90-$110
Smoke, 7" h $50-$65
Vaseline, 5" h $450-$550
Vase, standard, 8" h to 15" h
Cobalt blue $200-$250
Emerald green $100-$125
Helios $80-$100
Light blue with marigold
overlay $100-$150
Smoke $65-$75
White $75-$85

Multi-Fruits and Flowers
Compote
Amethyst $650-$850
Green $350-$550
Punch cup
Amethyst $35-$50
Green $25-$35
Marigold $15-$20
Punch bowl with base
Amethyst $600-$900
Green $400-$600
Marigold $500-$700

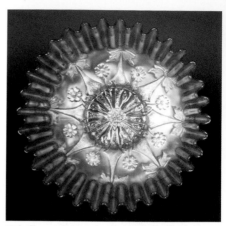

Little Flowers, Fenton, bowl with candy ribbon edge, marigold, 9" d, **$50**.

Lined Lattice, Dugan, vase, white, 11" h, **$110-$150**.

Maple Leaf, Dugan, seven tumblers marigold, **$10 each**.

Morning Glory, Imperial, funeral vase, purple, 14-1/4" h, 8-1/2" mouth, **$800-$1,200**.

Punch set, six pcs, amethyst,
  rare   **$1,800**
Tumbler
  Green   **$700-$800**
  Marigold   **$700-$950**
Water pitcher, collar base,
  amethyst, rare   **$8,000**

Nautilus
Bowl, 7-1/2" d
  Peach opalescent **$125-$175**
  Purple   **$200-$250**
Creamer
  Peach opalescent **$85-$175**
  Purple   **$65-$120**
Sugar
  Peach opalescent **$125-$150**
  Purple   **$200-$225**
Vase, 6-1/2" h
  Marigold   **$150-$165**
  Purple   **$175-$200**

Nesting Swan
Bowl, ice cream shape
  Blue, rare   **$3,200**
  Green, rare   **$2,000**
Bowl, ruffled
  Amethyst   **$200-$250**
  Amethyst, satin **$75-$195**
  Green, radium **$675-$1,000**
  Green, satin **$110-$200**
  Marigold   **$100-$300**

Nippon
Bowl, pie crust edge,
  basketweave back
  Green   **$300-$500**
  Ice blue   **$250-$450**
  Ice green   **$600-$800**
  Marigold   **$200-$300**
Bowl, pie crust edge, plain back
  Aqua, rare   **$3,300**
  Ice blue   **$235-$375**
  White   **$265-$285**
Bowl, pie crust edge,
  ribbed back
  Amethyst/purple **$250-$450**
  Aqua/teal, rare **$1,700**
  Green   **$300-$500**
  Ice blue   **$250-$450**
  Ice green   **$600-$800**
  Lime green   **$650-$850**
  Marigold   **$200-$300**
  White   **$175-$275**

Plate, 9" d
  Amethyst/purple
             $800-$1,000
  Green, rare   **$1,100**
  Ice blue, rare   **$8,500**
  Marigold   **$550-$750**
  White, rare   **$1,200**

Octagon
Berry bowl, master, 8" d to 9" d
  Helios   **$50-$70**
  Marigold   **$30-$50**
  Purple   **$25-$50**
Berry bowl, small, 4" d to 5" d
  Helios   **$25-$35**
  Marigold   **$20-$30**
  Purple   **$20-$40**
Butter dish, cov
  Aqua   **$225-$325**
  Helios   **$250-$375**
  Marigold   **$175-$200**
  Purple   **$375-$475**
Celery, two handles, marigold
                $50-$75
Compote
  Aqua   **$225-$325**
  Helios   **$60-$85**
  Marigold   **$40-$75**
  Purple   **$150-$200**
  Teal   **$40-$70**
Cordial
  Aqua   **$225-$325**
  Marigold   **$85-$100**
Creamer or covered sugar bowl
  Helios   **$80-$100**
  Marigold   **$65-$95**
  Purple   **$180-$220**
Fruit bowl, 10" d to 12" d
  Helios   **$100-$150**
  Ice blue   **$70-$95**
  Marigold   **$60-$90**
  Purple   **$200-$250**
Goblet
  Amber   **$70-$90**
  Light blue with marigold
  overlay   **$60-$95**
  Marigold   **$40-$60**
Milk pitcher
  Clambroth   **$100-$150**
  Helios   **$100-$200**
  Marigold   **$60-$65**
  Purple   **$300-$350**
Nappy, handle, marigold
             $100-$200

Salt and pepper shakers, pr
  Marigold   **$425-$500**
  Purple   **$400-$500**
Sherbet, marigold **$60-$80**
Spooner
  Aqua   **$80-$100**
  Helios   **$80-$100**
  Marigold   **$65-$95**
  Purple   **$180-$220**
Toothpick holder
  Marigold   **$90-$120**
  Purple   **$200-$300**
Tumbler, collar base
  Aqua   **$275-$375**
  Green   **$140-$165**
  Purple   **$75-$150**
  Olive green **$100-$150**
  Smoke   **$80-$200**
  Teal   **$200-$250**
Vase, pedestal foot, 8" h
  Clambroth   **$70-$90**
  Helios   **$100-$150**
  Marigold   **$75-1$00**
Wine
  Aqua   **$75-$85**
  Clambroth   **$35-$55**
  Helios   **$100-$150**
  Marigold   **$20-$25**
  White   **$400-$425**
Wine decanter
  Helios   **$550-$750**
  Marigold   **$85-$100**

Ohio Star
Compote, 4-1/2" d
  Crystal   **$30-$35**
  Marigold, rare   **$1,300**
Relish, cloverleaf shape,
  marigold, rare   **$3,000**
Vase, 10" h
  Amethyst **$2,000-$2,500**
  Clambroth **$1,500-$2,000**
  Marigold **$2,000-$3,000**

Open Edge
Basket, jack-in-the-pulpit, large
  Aqua   **$200-$225**
  Blue   **$45-$50**
  Green   **$50-$60**
  Light olive green **$135-$150**
  Red   **$135-$190**
Basket, jack-in-the-pulpit, small
  Amber   **$125-$135**
  Amberina   **$125-$135**

Nesting Swan, Millersburg, bowl, green, radium and covered with blue and pink iridescence, **$275**.

Octagon, Dugan, decanter including six cordials, **$90**.

Octet, Northwood, bowl, emerald green; tough to find, 8-1/4" d, **$175**.

Open Edge, Fenton, basket, banana-boat shape with factory applied metal base, celeste blue, 9" l, **$625**.

Open Edge, Fenton, ruffled hat, ice green, 7" d, **$250-$300**.

Amethyst	$125-$135
Aqua, marigold overlay	
	$65-$150
Blue, light	$25-$35
Lime green, marigold overlay	
	$50-$150
Marigold	$25-$30
Red slag	$175-$200
Sapphire	$200-$350
Teal	$200-$300
Vaseline	$85-$125

Basket or hat, ruffled, large

Amethyst	$45-$50
Aqua	$60-$90
Black amethyst	$60-$70
Blue	$35-$50
Celeste blue	$550-$575
Cherry red	$275-$300
Green	$35-$85
Ice green	$300-$325
Lime green with marigold overlay	
	$50-$55
Marigold	$25-$35
Red	$235-$275
White	$45-$65

Basket or hat, ruffled, small

Amethyst	$35-$50
Black amethyst	$70-$80
Blue	$35-$50
Green	$40-$45
Ice blue	$300-$350
Ice green	$350-$375
Lime green	$40-$45
Marigold	$20-$25
Powder blue	$40-$50
Red	$165-$175

Basket or hat, square, large

Celeste blue	$300-$350
Ice green	$130-$135
Powder blue	$30-$35
White	$45-$180

Bowl, ice cream shape, large

Celeste blue	$300-$350
Ice green	$150-$350
White	$175-$200

Bowl, three rows, ruffled

Celeste blue	$500-$550
Ice green	$300-$350
White, two sides up	$195-$300

Orange Tree

Berry bowl, footed, 9" to 11" d

Blue	$100-$125

Green	$150-$175
Marigold	$80-$100
White	$100-$200

Bowl, collar base, flat, 8" d to 9" d

Amber	$170-$190
Amberina, rare	$1,200
Amethyst	$200-$250
Blue	$85-$95
Celeste blue, rare	$1,750
Clambroth	$50-$70
Green	$95-$105
Ice blue, rare	$7,000
Lavender	$225-$275
Marigold	$115-$125
Marigold over milk glass	
	$500-$600
Powder blue	$100-$125
Red, rare	$3,000
Sapphire blue	$300-$350
Vaseline	$225-$275
White	$50-$110

Bowl, ice cream shape, 8-1/2" d

Blue	$65-$75
Green	$155-$350

Bowl, ice cream shape, tree trunk center, 7-3/4" d

Blue	$75-$90
Electric blue	$200-$250
White	$55-$65

Bowl, ruffled, 9" d

Blue	$85-$95
Green	$95-$105
Marigold	$115-$125
White	$50-$110

Breakfast set, two pcs

Blue, repairs	$40-$45
Marigold, damage	$70-$75

Butter dish, cov

Blue	$200-$300
Marigold	$225-$325
White	$350-$400

Centerpiece bowl, ftd, 12" d

Amethyst, rare	$4,000
Blue, rare	$1,500
Green, rare	$4,500
Marigold	$800-$900

Compote, ruffled

Amethyst	$55-$75
Aqua	$100-$150
Blue	$60-$80
Green	$70-$90
Lavender, light	$35-$65
Marigold	$40-$50

Teal	$300-$400

Creamer, whimsy, made from punch cup, added spout,

white	$150-$165

Fruit bowl, scroll feet, 10" d

Amethyst	$400-$500
Blue	$185-$200
Green	$800-$1,000
Marigold	$110-$130

Goblet

Aqua	$100-$115
Blue	$40-$80
Marigold	$80-$100
Vaseline	$100-$115

Hatpin holder

Amethyst	$500-$800
Blue	$200-$275
Chocolate, irid, rare	$2,700
Green, rare	$2,000
Marigold	$105-$195
White	$600-$700

Loving cup

Amethyst	$450-$500
Aqua opalescent, rare	
	$15,000
Blue	$155-$250
Green	$225-$1,000
Marigold	$150-$275
White	$475-$500

Mug, 2-1/2" d base, 3-1/2" h

Amber	$90-$95
Amberina	$55-$65
Aqua, dark	$130-$225
Aqua opalescent	$80-$85
Blue	$65-$185
Lime green	$25-$35
Persian blue	$45-$60
Marigold	$35-$130
Powder blue	$130-$150
Purple	$150-$165
Red, amberina base	
	$185-$215
Red	$95-$125
Vaseline	$95-$105

Plate, 8" d to 9-1/2" d

Amethyst, rare	$3,000
Clambroth	$100-$135
Electric blue	$600-$900
Green, rare	$2,600
Ice green, rare	$7,000
Marigold, pastel	$600-$700
White	$175-$250

Powder jar, cov

Amethyst	$200-$250

Orange Tree, Fenton, punch bowl and base, blue, set also includes eight cups, **$300.**

Orange Tree, Fenton, footed fruit bowl, marigold, **$60.**

Orange Tree, Fenton, loving cup, amethyst, **$500.**

Oriental Poppy, Northwood, tankard, purple, **$600-$1,100**; outstanding example, **$4,000**.

Oriental Poppy, Northwood, tankard, white, very frosty with great iridescence, **$1,400.**

Blue	$85-$115
Green	$375-$475
Marigold	$65-$85
Vaseline	$90-$115
White	$150-$190

Shaving mug, 3" d base

Amber	$85-$205
Amberina	$200-$225
Aqua	$60-$75
Aqua opalescent, rare	$1,100
Blue	$90-$150
Marigold	$35-$90
Powder blue	$90-$135
Red	$350-$400

Spooner or sugar bowl

Blue	$60-$70
Marigold	$40-$45

Syrup, made from mug, blue, rare $5,000

Tumbler

Blue	$50-$65
Marigold	$70-$95
White	$90-$110

Water pitcher, ftd

Ice green, spout damage, rare	$2,100
Marigold	$200-$300
White	$300-$400

Wine

Blue	$50-$60
Green	$95-$200
Marigold	$15-$25
Peach opalescent	$85-$100
Vaseline	$85-$100

Oriental Poppy
Tumbler, 4-1/4" h

Green	$65-$90
Ice blue, not ribbed	$85-$95
Ice blue, ribbed interior	$200-$215
Ice green	$185-$215
Lime green	$250-$900
Marigold	$30-$50
White	$95-$115

Water pitcher, tankard

Green	$1,200-$1,350
Lime green, rare	$8,000
Marigold	$400-$450
Purple	$450-$500
White	$800-$1,000

Palm Beach
Banana boat, whimsy

Amethyst, light	$150-$225
Honey amber	$150-$200
Marigold	$50-$75

Berry set, five pcs, honey amber $300-$385

Hair receiver, marigold $90-$135

Plate, 7" d

Amethyst	$200-$225
Marigold	$250-$300

Rose bowl

Amethyst	$100-$165
Honey amber	$250-$275
Lime green	$100-$115
Marigold	$100-$200
White	$55-$95

Spooner

Honey amber	$65-$95
White	$95-$185

Tumbler

Honey amber	$60-$85
Marigold	$100-$185
White	$100-$250

Vase, bulbous, 5" h, light amethyst $275-$300

Vase, whimsy, 4" h, marigold $275-$400

Vase, whimsy, 7" h, honey amber $300-$325

Water pitcher

Honey amber	$300-$500
White	$400-$600

Paneled Dandelion
Tumbler

Amethyst	$50-$55
Blue	$30-$50
Green	$50-$70
Marigold	$30-$50

Water pitcher

Amethyst	$300-$400
Blue	$500-$650
Green	$400-$500
Marigold	$200-$300

Water set, seven pcs

Amethyst	$550-$675
Blue	$500-$525
Green	$650-$750
Marigold, dark	$340-$360

Pansy
Bowl, ruffled, 8-1/2" d to 9" d

Amber	$95-$120

Clambroth	$70-$90
Cobalt blue	$250-$350
Helios	$80-$100
Lavender	$100-$185
Marigold	$35-$165
Smoke	$120-$140

Breakfast set, amber $30-$35

Creamer

Aqua	$35-$50
Clambroth	$35-$50
Helios	$40-$60
Lavender	$30-$35
Marigold	$25-$30

Dresser tray, oval

Amber	$125-$155
Clambroth	$80-$100
Helios	$50-$110
Marigold	$90-$135
Purple	$125-$170

Nappy, handle

Amber	$40-$60
Clambroth	$30-$50
Helios	$25-$40
Lavender	$60-$80
Marigold	$30-$50
Purple	$65-$95

Pickle dish

Clambroth	$25-$40
Cobalt blue	$200-$250
Helios	$40-$60
Marigold	$20-$65
Purple	$80-$100
Smoke	$50-$70

Plate, ruffled

Helios	$100-$200
Lavender	$90-$130
Marigold	$80-$100
Purple	$265-$300
Smoke	$90-$140

Sugar bowl

Amber	$30-$50
Aqua	$50-$70
Clambroth	$25-$50
Helios	$35-$40
Marigold	$25-$30
Purple	$20-$35
Smoke	$20-$25

Panther
Berry bowl, master, ftd, 10" d

Amethyst	$300-$400
Aqua	$700-$800
Blue	$135-$375
Green	$400-$500

Marigold	$80-$110
Nile green, rare	$1,200
Olive green	$250-$365

Berry bowl, small, ftd, ruffled, 5" d to 6" d

Amethyst	$175-$200
Aqua	$200-$350
Blue	$65-$85
Green	$250-$350
Lavender	$165-$190
Marigold	$25-$50
Olive green	$95-$125

Whimsy, bowl with collar base and small round feet, 5" d

Blue	$250-$350
Clambroth	$100-$200
Green	$400-$500
Marigold	$100-$200

Whimsy, bowl with collar base and small round feet, 10" d

Blue	$800-$900
Marigold	$350-$450

Peach

Berry bowl, master, 9" d, white

	$100-$150

Berry bowl, small, 5" d

Blue	$200-$225
White	$40-$50

Butter dish, cov, white

	$200-$265

Creamer, spooner or sugar bowl

Marigold	$300-$400
White	$65-$100

Tumbler

Blue	$100-$150
Marigold, rare	$2,000
White	$125-$175

Water pitcher

Blue, rare	$1,000
White	$700-$900

Peacock

Berry bowl, master, flared or ruffled, 9" d to 10" d

Green	$400-$550
Marigold	$275-$325

Berry bowl, small, 5" d to 6" d

Amethyst	$95-$115
Blue	$1,000-$1,200
Green	$200-$250
Marigold	$150-$200

Bowl, ice cream shape, 5" to 6" d

Amethyst	$200-$300

Blue, rare	$1,500
Green	$300-$400
Marigold	$200-$275

Bowl, ice cream shape, 9" d to 10" d

Amethyst, rare	$2,000
Green, radium, rare	$1,000
Marigold	$800-$900

Bowl, 3-in-1 edge, 10" d, green, radium $375-$425

Plate, 6" d

Amethyst, satin	$600-$1,100
Marigold, rare	$1,000

Rose bowl, whimsy, amethyst, rare $2,500

Peacock and Grape

Bowl, ftd, 8" d to 9" d

Amethyst	$125-$175
Blue	$80-$100
Green	$100-$150
Lime green opalescent	$500-$600
Marigold	$40-$60
Red	$700-$900

Bowl, ice cream shape, spatula foot

Amethyst	$90-$120
Blue	$50-$80
Green	$40-$60
Marigold	$20-$25
Red	$350-$400

Bowl, ruffled

Blue	$100-$175
Electric green	$300-$400
Peach opalescent	$300-$400
Pumpkin marigold	$250-$325

Bowl, 3-in-1 edge

Amethyst	$105-$165
Green	$45-$70
Marigold	$20-$25

Nut bowl, ftd

Blue	$100-$130
Marigold	$35-$55

Plate, 9" d to 9-1/2" d

Blue, rare	$1,200
Green, rare	$1,000
Lavender	$300-$500
Marigold	$450-$1,750

Plate, collar base, 9" d

Electric blue, rare	$2,500
Marigold	$750-$1,100

Peacock and Urn (made by Fenton)

Bowl, ice cream shape

Aqua, pastel, marigold overlay	$200-$225
Aqua opal, butterscotch, pink irid, rare	$22,000
Green, rare	$4,000
Marigold, dark	$400-$600
Purple	$250-$365

Bowl, ruffled, 8" d to 8-1/2" d

Amethyst	$200-$250
Aqua	$275-$300
Blue	$95-$125
Green	$195-$225
Lime green	$200-$300
Marigold	$100-$150
Marigold over milk glass, rare	$1,600
Persian blue, rare	$1,500
Vaseline	$400-$500
White	$150-$175

Bowl, 3-in-1 edge

Amethyst	$145-$220
Green	$125-$195
Marigold	$85-$145

Compote, ruffled, smooth edge

Amethyst	$250-$350
Aqua	$85-$125
Blue	$95-$150
Celeste blue	$150-$200
Green	$225-$325
Lime green, marigold overlay	$85-$125
Marigold	$30-$50
Vaseline	$125-$175
White	$95-$200

Plate, 9" d

Amethyst	$500-$575
Blue	$500-$1,150
Green	$900-$1,200
Marigold	$300-$375
Marigold, dark	$275-$375
White	$200-$400

Peacock and Urn (made by Millersburg)

Berry bowl, master, flared, 9" d to 10" d

Amethyst	$185-$300
Blue, rare	$2,100
Marigold, radium	$275-$300

Berry bowl, small, ruffled or
flared, 5" d to 6" d

Amethyst	$90-$135
Blue	$900-$1,050
Marigold	$195-$240

Bowl, ice cream shape, 9" d
to 10" d

Amethyst, radium	$175-$225
Green, satin, rare	$1,000
Marigold	$185-$325

Bowl, ruffled, 10" to 10-1/2" d

Blue	$1,200-$1,700
Green, radium	$175-$300

Bowl, 3-in-1 edge

Amethyst	$300-$450
Green	$350-$450
Marigold	$295-$365

Chop plate, 11-1/4" d,
amethyst, rare $9,500

Compote, ruffled, stemmed,
large

Amethyst	$1,400-$1,700
Green, rare	$2,000
Marigold, rare	$2,300

Mystery bowl, beads at top
of bowl and top of column,
ruffled or 3-in-1 edge, 9" d

Amethyst	$225-$350
Blue	$850-$5,500
Green, satin	$450-$600

Plate, 6" d, amethyst, rare
$1,700

Peacock and Urn
(made by Northwood)

Berry bowl, small, ruffled,
5" d to 6" d

Amethyst	$80-$100
Green	$500-$600
Ice blue	$180-$250
Ice green	$250-$300
Marigold	$65-$100
Purple	$80-$100
White	$145-$165

Bowl, ice cream shape, master,
9" d to 10" d

Amethyst/purple	$400-$600
Aqua opalescent, rare	$30,000
Clambroth	$400-$600
Green, rare	$3,000
Honey amber, rare	$1,500
Horehound	$500-$700

Ice blue	$500-$900
Ice green	$800-$1,000
Lime green, rare	$1,750
Marigold	$450-$550
Pumpkin marigold	$550-$700
Purple	$250-$350
White	$350-$600

Chop plate, 10-1/2" d to 11" d

Marigold	$1,500-$1,700
White, rare	$5,000

Peacock at the
Fountain (made by
Northwood)

Berry bowl, master, 9" d

Amethyst	$85-$125
Blue	$250-$295
Green	$285-$325
Ice blue	$550-$600
Ice green	$800-$900
Marigold	$185-$235
White	$100-$300

Berry bowl, small, 5" d

Amethyst	$40-$60
Blue	$50-$70
Green	$65-$85
Ice blue	$45-$65
Ice green	$80-$100
Marigold	$30-$45
White	$80-$100

Butter dish, cov

Amethyst	$175-$250
Blue	$250-$300
Green	$400-$600
Ice blue, rare	$1,200
Marigold	$185-$250
Purple	$175-$255
White	$200-$600

Compote, ruffled

Amethyst	$600-$750
Aqua opalescent, rare	$3,000
Blue	$850-$950
Ice blue	$500-$1,100
Ice green	$1,200-$1,600
Marigold	$550-$650
White	$300-$400

Creamer or covered sugar bowl

Amethyst	$100-$120
Blue	$85-$185
Green	$185-$285
Ice blue	$200-$250
Ice green	$250-$300

Marigold	$135-$165
White	$105-$145

Orange bowl, ftd

Amethyst	$500-$650
Green, rare	$3,500
Horehound, rare	$2,000
Marigold	$185-$300

Punch bowl with base

Amethyst	$900-$1,000
Ice blue, rare	$7,500
Ice green, rare	$8,000
Lime green, rare	$6,500
Marigold	$450-$650
Renninger blue, blue base	$900-$1,200
White, rare	$3,000

Punch cup

Amethyst	$80-$90
Ice blue	$80-$100
Ice green	$180-$300
Lime green	$200-$250
Marigold	$35-$45
Purple	$80-$90
White	$20-$60

Tumbler

Amethyst	$55-$70
Ice blue	$125-$175
Ice green	$85-$125
Lavender	$75-$100
Light blue	$125-$175
Marigold	$45-$65
Marigold, dark	$20-$25
Purple	$55-$70
White	$185-$265

Water pitcher

Amethyst	$200-$250
Blue	$400-$500
Green, rare	$3,000
Ice blue, rare	$2,000
Light blue, rare	$2,000
Marigold	$425-$475
White	$600-$800

Peacocks on the
Fence

Bowl, pie crust edge, ribbed back

Amethyst	$325-$425
Aqua opalescent, rare	$1,100
Blue	$400-$500
Green	$800-$1,000
Marigold	$155-$250
Marigold, dark	$150-$175
Marigold, stippled	$155-$250

Pansy, Imperial, ruffled bowl, electric purple, **$180**.

Peacock and Grape, Fenton, plate with collar base, marigold, **$750**.

Peacock at the Fountain, Northwood, water pitcher and six tumblers, ice blue, **$3,600**.

Peacock at Urn, Fenton, plate, blue, **$800-$1,500**; outstanding example, **$4,250**.

Peacock at Urn, Northwood, master ice cream-shaped bowl, purple, **$750**.

Purple	$325-$425
Renninger blue, rare	$1,000

Bowl, ruffled, ribbed back

Amethyst	$175-$225
Aqua, rare	$1,200
Aqua opalescent	$850-$1,450
Blue	$350-$575
Electric blue	$550-$650
Green	$400-$800
Horehound	$1,000-$1,200
Ice blue	$500-$700
Ice blue opalescent, rare	$1,600
Ice green, rare	$1,050
Iridized custard, rare	$2,500
Lavender	$400-$600
Lime green	$1,500-$1,800
Lime green opalescent, rare	$4,500
Smoke, rare	$1,750

Plate, ribbed back, 9" d

Amethyst	$500-$700
Green	$265-$1,150
Horehound, rare	$2,000
Ice blue, rare	$2,400
Ice green	$600-$775
Lavender	$500-$700
Lime green	$500-$700
Marigold	$350-$500
Pastel	$400-$475
Pumpkin marigold	$900-$1,050
Renninger blue, rare	$2,300
Smoke, rare	$2,500
White	$325-$425

Peacock Tail

Bonbon, two handles, stemmed or flat

Amethyst	$45-$65
Blue	$35-$55
Green	$60-$80
Marigold	$40-$60

Bowl, ruffled or 3-in-1 edge, 5" d to 7" d

Amethyst	$30-$40
Blue	$35-$45
Green	$40-$60
Marigold	$20-$40
Peach opalescent	$400-$600
Red, rare	$2,500

Compote

Amethyst	$35-$55
Blue	$30-$50

Green	$40-$60
Marigold	$25-$35
White	$35-$55

Hat

Amethyst	$20-$40
Blue	$35-$45
Green	$35-$45
Marigold	$20-$30

Plate, 6" d to 7" d

Amethyst	$400-$600
Blue	$600-$800
Green	$500-$700
Marigold	$600-$800

Plate, 9" d, blue $300-$500

Pearly Dots

Bowl, 8-1/2" d

Amethyst	$40-$60
Blue	$30-$45
Blue opalescent	$45-$85
Marigold	$45-$55

Compote

Marigold	$40-$65
Peach opalescent	$90-$125

Rose bowl

Amethyst	$45-$65
Aqua	$225-$275
Green	$40-$60
Marigold	$25-$45
Teal	$175-$285

Perfection

Tumbler

Amethyst/purple	$300-$475
Green	$200-$350

Water pitcher

Amethyst	$2,500-$4,000
Green	$4,000-$5,500

Persian Garden

Berry bowl, master, 10" d

Amethyst	$200-$300
Green, rare	$1,200
Marigold	$125-$225
Peach opalescent	$200-$300
White	$150-$200

Berry bowl, small 5" d

Amethyst	$40-$60
Marigold	$30-$50
Peach opalescent	$65-$85
White	$40-$60

Bowl, ice cream shape, individual, 6" d

Amethyst	$95-$120
Marigold	$40-$60

Peach opalescent	$135-$155
White	$55-$75

Bowl, ice cream shape, master, 11" d

Amethyst	$1,400-$1,600
Marigold	$325-$450
Peach opalescent	$375-$475
Purple	$1,400-$1,600

Chop plate, 13" d

Amethyst, rare	$11,000
Lavender, rare	$8,000
Peach opalescent, rare	$6,000
White, rare	$2,800

Fruit bowl with base

Amethyst	$400-$620
Lavender	$400-$500
Marigold	$565-$635
Peach opalescent	$155-$185
White	$350-$415

Plate, 6" d

Aqua	$195-$220
Lavender	$200-$275
Marigold	$40-$85
Peach opalescent	$200-$275
White	$65-$85
White, Pools of Pearls back	$105-$115

Persian Medallion

Bonbon, calling card tray

Amber	$185-$200
Amethyst	$95-$225
Aqua	$80-$200
Blue	$45-$65
Celeste blue, rare	$1,200
Green	$215-$235
Lime green	$115-$125
Marigold	$30-$65
Red	$700-$800
Reverse amberina	$800-$850
Vaseline	$120-$140

Bowl, ice cream shape

Amethyst	$150-$165
Red	$600-$675

Bowl, ruffled, 7" d

Green	$30-$35
Marigold	$65-$75

Bowl, 3-in-1 edge, 8-1/2" to 10" d

Amethyst	$55-$140
Blue	$160-$175
Green	$150-$210
Lavender	$275-$315
Marigold	$35-$45
White	$275-$315

Chop plate, 10" d, blue
$225-$750

Compote, ruffled, large
Amethyst $115-$125
Blue $55-$95
Green $250-$300
Marigold $40-$50
White $195-$225

Compote, ruffled, small
Amethyst $125-$195
Blue $65-$185
Green $300-$350
Marigold $85-$125
White $265-$365

Hair receiver, sq opening
Amethyst $80-$95
Blue $135-$150
Marigold $40-$80
White $110-$130

Orange bowl, ftd, 11" w, 6-3/4" h
Amethyst $350-$425
Blue $290-$335
Green, rare $2,400
Marigold $260-$315

Plate, 6" d
Amethyst $75-$275
Clambroth $100-$125
Lime green $100-$115
Purple $115-$125
Vaseline $600-$800

Plate, 9" d to 10" d
Amethyst, rare $3,000
Green, rare $3,000
Marigold $400-$650
White $500-$600

Rose bowl, round opening
Amethyst $300-$350
Blue $95-$115
Clambroth $65-$95
Green $175-$200
Marigold $55-$75
Marigold, light $20-$40
White $115-$125

Petal and Fan

Bowl, 5" d to 6" d
Amethyst/purple $50-$70
Marigold $60-$65
Peach opalescent $25-$75
White $65-$85

Bowl, 8" d to 9" d
Amethyst/purple $85-$165
Marigold $65-$90
Peach opalescent $115-$150

White $185-$230

Bowl, 10" d to 11" d
Amethyst/purple $250-$300
Marigold $95-$150
Peach opalescent $200-$215

Plate, crimped edge, 6" d,
peach opalescent $175-$325

Rose bowl, amethyst $250-$300

Peter Rabbit

Bowl, ice cream shape
Green, rare $2,600
Marigold, rare $1,800

Bowl, ruffled
Green, rare $2,000
Marigold, rare $1,200

Plate, 9" d to 10" d
Blue, rare $4,000
Marigold, rare $6,000

Pine Cone

Bowl, ice cream shape,
6-3/4" d to 7" d
Blue $85-$110
Emerald green $400-$450

Bowl, 7" d to 8" d
Amethyst $75-$95
Blue $50-$65
Green $35-$55
Lavender $60-$75

Plate, 6" d
Amethyst $195-$235
Blue $115-$135
Blue, silvery $85-$95
Green $185-205
Marigold $80-$200

Plate, 7" d to 8" d
Amber $425-$800
Amethyst $450-$700
Blue $165-$185
Marigold $325-$600

Sauce, round or ruffled,
5" d to 6" d
Amethyst $20-$25
Blue $25-$70
Marigold $15-$25
Sapphire blue $100-$150

Plaid

Bowl, deep, green $195-$225

Bowl, ruffled, 9" d
Amethyst/purple $250-$350
Blue $250-$300
Celeste blue $700-$850

Green $400-$450
Lavender $375-$415
Marigold $215-$300
Teal $775-$2,000

Plate, 9" d
Blue $500-$575
Marigold $300-$400
Red, rare $8,000

Plume Panels

Vase, 10" to 12" h
Amethyst $75-$110
Blue $60-$90
Marigold $30-$50
Olive green $45-$70
Sapphire $475-$600
Vaseline $500-$650

Poinsettia

Milk pitcher, 6" h
Helios $300-$425
Lavender $200-$300
Marigold $30-$80

Pony

Bowl, ruffled, 9" to 10" d
Aqua $500-$550
Lavender $200-$340

Plate, 9" d, marigold
$950-$2,000

Poppy Show
(made by Imperial)

Vase, 12" h
Amber, rare $7,500
Clambroth $900-$1,100
Helios $900-$1,500
Lavender $700-$900
Pastel marigold $800-$1,000
Smoke, rare $4,400

Whimsy, hurricane lamp
Amethyst, rare $2,500
White, rare $2,500

Whimsy, table lamp, marigold,
rare $2,500

Poppy Show
(made by Northwood)

Bowl, ruffled, 8-1/2" d to 9" d
Clambroth $450-$500
Electric blue, rare $2,300
Green, rare $2,000
Ice blue $650-$900
Ice green $750-$1,000

Persian Garden, Dugan, fruit bowl and base, electric purple, **$825**.

Persian Medallion, Fenton, plate, white, covered with pastel yellow iridescence, 9" d, **$2,000**.

Pine Cone, Fenton, plate, green, **$225**.

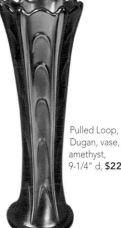

Pulled Loop, Dugan, vase, amethyst, 9-1/4" d, **$225**.

Poppy Show, Northwood, plate, electric blue, 9" d, **$5,000**.

Lime green	$700-$800
Marigold	$200-$400
Purple	$750-$800
White	$250-$400

Plate, 9" d to 9-1/2" d

Amethyst	$750-$1,150
Electric blue, rare	$5,000
Green	$3,000-$4,200
Ice green	$2,000-$2,400
Pastel marigold	$450-$1,500
Purple	$750-$1,150

Pulled Loop

Vase, 6" h, 7" d mouth

Amethyst	$70-$130
Aqua	$200-$250
Black amethyst	$120-$150
Blue	$125-$200
Celeste blue	$300-$375
Green	$150-$175
Marigold	$30-$40
Peach opalescent	$40-$60
Purple	$95-$125
White	$100-$150

Quill

Tumbler, purple	$150-$225
Water pitcher, purple, rare	$2,500

Raspberry

Candy dish, ruffled, ftd, marigold	$25-$45

Compote

Amethyst/purple	$100-$950
Green	$45-$90
Horehound	$300-$425
Marigold	$35-$60

Gravy boat

Amethyst/purple	$90-$180
Green	$140-$165
Marigold	$90-$120

Milk pitcher, 7-1/2" h

Ice blue	$600-$2,000
Lime green, rare	$4,000
Purple	$195-$225
White, rare	$1,350

Tumbler

Amethyst/purple	$35-$65
Blue, rare	$900
Emerald green	$175-$200
Green	$50-$70
Horehound	$60-$80
Ice green	$300-$400
Marigold	$30-$40

White	$500-$700

Water pitcher, 9" h

Amethyst/purple	$150-$350
Green	$175-$400
Ice green	$2,000-$6,500
Marigold	$150-$250

Ribbon Tie

Bowl, candy ribbon edge

Amethyst/purple	$90-$150
Blue	$95-$135
Marigold	$45-$65

Bowl, ruffled or 3-in-1 edge, 8" d to 9" d

Amethyst/purple	$125-$400
Black amethyst	$95-$115
Green	$45-$90
Marigold	$35-$65
Powder blue	$70-$90
Red, rare	$10,500

Plate, ruffled or 3-in-1 edge, 8" d to 9" d

Amethyst/purple	$130-$400
Blue	$200-$300

Ripple

Vase, 4" to 7", squatty

Amber, 7" h, 2-7/8" base	$70-$90
Clambroth, 5" h, 2-1/2" d base	$40-$60
Helios, 5" h, 2-1/2" d base	$185-$200
Helios, 6-1/2" h, 2-7/8" d base	$50-$70
Lavender, 5" h, 2-1/2" d base	$135-$165
Purple, 7" h, 3-1/4" d base	$45-$90

Vase, 7" h to 12" h, standard

Amber, 10-3/4" h, swung	$100-$120
Aqua, 11" h, 2-7/8" d base	$135-$160
Clambroth, 10" h, 2-7/8" d base	$40-$60
Emerald green	$200-$250
Helios, 11" h, 3-1/4" d base	$70-$90
Lavender, 9-1/2" d	$165-$200
Marigold, 9-1/2" h	$30-$50
Olive, 8-1/2" h	$145-$185
Pastel, 10-1/2" h	$150-$185
Purple, 10" h, 3-7/8" d base	$75-$95

Red	$600-$750
Smoke, 12" h, 3-3/8" d base	$75-$95
Teal, 12" h, 2-7/8" base	$70-$90
Violet, 11-1/2" h	$165-$190

Vase, 12" h to 15" h, mid-size

Amber, 12" h	$220-$225
Clambroth, 12" h	$85-$110
Lavender, 13" h	$300-$350
Marigold, 12" h, 4-5/8" base	$90-$120
Olive green, 13" h, 3-3/8" d base	$65-$90
Smoke, 12" h, 3-3/8" d base	$85-$110
Violet, 13" h	$300-$350

Vase, 15" h to 21" h, 3-7/8" d base, funeral

Helios, 16" h	$175-$195
Lime green, 16" h	$115-$135
Marigold, 16" h	$105-$120
Purple	$350-$385
Teal	$400-$425

Robin

Mug

Marigold	$60-$80
Marigold on light green	$100-$150
Smoke	$225-$275
Tumbler, marigold	$30-$50
Water pitcher, marigold	$150-$300

Rococo

Bowl, 5" d to 6" d

Marigold	$20-$40
Smoke	$40-$75
Vaseline	$35-$55
Bowl, 9" d, marigold	$20-$40
Vase, 3-1/2" h, smoke	$45-$65

Vase, 5" h to 5-1/2" h

Lavender, marigold overlay	$80-$95
Marigold	$105-$175
Smoke	$125-$225

Rose Columns

Vase, 10" h, aqua, rare | $7,000

Rose Show

Bowl, ruffled, 8-3/4" d to 9" d

Amethyst, chip	$900-$1,200

Aqua	$900-$1,600
Blue	$550-$1,000
Emerald green	$3,500-$6,000
Green	$900-$1,350
Honey amber, rare	$4,700
Horehound	$1,000-$2,800
Ice blue	$600-$900
Ice green	$950-$1,500
Lavender	$500-$1,600
Lime green opalescent	$2,000-$3,500
Marigold, dark	$400-$1,500
Renninger blue	$800-$1,000
Sapphire blue	$2,400-$3,500
White	$250-$450

Plate, 9" to 9-1/2" d

Amethyst	$700-$1,000
Blue	$1,100-$1,600
Emerald green	$3,500-$3,700
Green	$1,500-$3,500
Ice blue	$1,500-$2,100
Ice green	$750-$9,000
Lavender	$900-$3,100
Lime green/vaseline	$1,900-$2,700
Marigold	$575-$1,600
White	$325-$565

Round-up

Bowl, ice cream shape, low, ruffled, or 3-in-1 edge, 8-1/2" d to 9" d

Blue	$180-$225
Lavender	$300-$575
Marigold	$85-$105
Peach opalescent	$135-$250
White	$85-$120

Plate, 8-3/4" d to 9" d

Amber, blue irid, rare	$1,800
Amethyst	$400-$600
Blue	$150-$275
Horehound	$500-$650
Marigold	$250-$425
Purple	$225-$400
White	$175-$300

Rustic

Vase, 6" h to 7-1/2" h, 3" d to 3-1/2" d, squatty

Blue, 7" h	$30-$50
Green, 7" h	$30-$50
Lavender, light, 7" h	$45-$70

Marigold, 6" h	$80-$100
White, 6-1/2" h	$70-$150

Vase, 8" h to 13" h, 3" d to 3-1/2" d, standard

Amber	$200-$400
Amethyst, 10" h	$35-$50
Blue, 8-1/2" h	$65-$125
Green, 12" h	$80-$165
Marigold	$50-$60
Red, crimped top, rare	$4,200
White, 9" h	$45-$75

Vase, 11" h to 17" h, 4" d to 4-1/4" d, mid-size

Amethyst, 15" h	$65-$100
Blue	$150-$250
Electric blue	$200-$300
Green, 12" h	$165-$210
Marigold, 16" h	$85-$100
White, 15" h, crimped edge	$150-$250

Vase, 16" h to 23" h, 5" d to 5-1/2" d, funeral

Amethyst, 21" h	$875-$1,900
Blue, band, 18" h	$575-$1,500
Emerald green, band, rare	$3,600
Green, 17" h	$2,000-$4,000
Green, 21" h	$1,050-$1,650
Marigold, dark, 17-1/2" h	$500-$700
White, 16" h, crimped edge	$900-$1,100

S-Repeat

Creamer, made from punch cup mold, purple $50-$75

Punch cup, purple $25-$40

Scales

Banana boat, two sides up, peach opalescent $65-$120

Bowl, ice cream shape, low, or ruffled, 9" d

Amethyst	$40-$90
Blue opalescent	$150-$275
Marigold on milk glass	$95-$200
Peach opalescent	$30-$60

Plate, 6" d

Amethyst	$35-$70
Aqua	$60-$150
Marigold	$25-$45
Teal	$20-$40

Plate, 8" d to 9" d, peach opalescent $95-$175

Sauce, ruffled, peach opalescent $15-$30

Scroll Embossed

Berry bowl, master, File exterior, 7" d to 9" d

Lavender	$70-$85
Marigold	$20-$35
Purple	$65-$105
Smoke	$150-$265

Berry bowl, small, File exterior, 4" d to 5" d

Marigold	$15-$30
Purple	$35-$70
Smoke	$50-$65

Bowl, round or ruffled, 7" d to 9" d

Emerald green	$200-$250
Helios	$50-$80
Marigold	$20-$35
Teal	$90-$110

Compote, large

Amber	$95-$130
Aqua	$60-$90
Clambroth	$20-$40
Purple	$75-$150
Violet	$200-$400

Compote, mid-size or small, ruffled

Blue	$300-$350
Helios	$50-$150

Compote, miniature, 3" h

Lavender	$175-$300
Marigold	$185-$245

Nut dish, purple $185-$200

Plate, 9" d to 9-1/2" d

Aqua	$200-$245
Helios	$95-1$55
Lavender	$250-$500
Marigold	$75-$125

Sherbet, purple $95-$125

Seacoast

Pin tray

Green	$600-$1,000
Marigold	$900-$1,200

Spittoon, American Carnival Glass Association convention souvenir

1982, peach opalescent	$95-$125
1983, green	$115-$135
1984, red	$85-$100

1985, celeste blue **$95-$115**
2002, ice green opalescent
$105-$115

Singing Birds
Berry bowl, master
Green, rare	**$2,500**
Marigold, rare	**$600**
Purple	**$150-$250**

Berry bowl, small
Blue	**$125-$225**
Green	**$40-$60**
Purple	**$35-$55**

Butter dish, cov
Green	**$325-$425**
Marigold	**$145-$185**
Purple	**$150-$250**

Creamer
Green	**$125-$175**
Marigold	**$100-$150**
Purple	**$150-$250**

Mug, not stippled, 3-1/2" h
Amber	**$300-$400**
Amethyst	**$55-$100**
Blue	**$85-$100**
Emerald green	**$275-$375**
Green	**$165-$180**
Horehound	**$300-$550**
Ice blue	**$550-$580**
Lavender	**$150-$300**
Marigold	**$50-$155**
Purple	**$55-$100**
Sapphire blue, rare	**$1,500**
White	**$500-$700**

Mug, stippled, 3-1/2" h
Blue	**$400-$650**
Blue opalescent, rare	**$1,450**
Green	**$375-$475**
Marigold	**$80-$160**
Renninger blue	**$950-$1,500**
Sapphire blue	**$450-$550**

Spooner or covered sugar bowl
Green	**$200-$300**
Marigold	**$125-$225**
Purple	**$150-$250**

Tumbler
Amethyst	**$50-$90**
Emerald green	**$75-$125**
Lime green	**$150-$175**
Olive green	**$75-$135**
Purple	**$90-$135**

Water pitcher
Amethyst/purple	**$350-$550**
Green	**$450-$1,200**

Six Petals
Bowl, candy ribbon edge, ruffled, peach opalescent
$25-$45

Bowl, ruffled
Lavender	**$70-$90**
Peach opalescent	**$35-$90**
Purple	**$145-$175**
White	**$35-7$0**

Bowl, 3-in-1 edge, purple
$100-$135

Ski Star
Banana boat, crimped edge
Amethyst	**$100-$150**
Peach opalescent	**$60-$95**
Peach opalescent, pumpkin interior	**$500-$525**

Berry bowl, master, ruffled, 8" d, peach opalescent
$40-$50

Berry bowl, small, 5" d to 6" d
Black amethyst	**$40-$60**
Peach opalescent	**$30-$50**
Purple	**$50-$80**

Bowl, ruffled, 10" d to 11" d, peach opalescent **$100-$400**

Bowl, tricorn, dome ftd, 10" d, peach opalescent **$100-$125**

Bride's basket, silver plate holder, peach opalescent
$165-$200

Nut bowl, purple **$300-$350**

Plate, crimped, peach opalescent **$100-$200**

Plate, hand grip
Peach opalescent **$75-$100**
Peach opalescent, decorated
$300-$450

Smooth Panels
Rose bowl
Clambroth	**$20-$30**
Marigold	**$25-$50**
Smoke	**$35-$50**
Teal	**$115-$135**
White	**$60-$85**

Vase, 2-1/2" d to 4" d base
Amberina, stretch, 4-3/4" h	**$300-$400**
Celeste blue, stretch, 11" h, 3" d base	**$100-$150**
Clambroth, 7-1/2" h, 3-1/2" d base	**$30-$40**

Lavender, stretch, 10-1/2" d
$80-$100
Marigold, 4-1/2" h **$40-$60**
Marigold on milk glass, 7" h, 7-1/2" d mouth **$250-$275**
Purple, 10-3/4" h **$185-$210**
Red, stretch, 5" h, 2-1/2" d base **$215-$245**
Smoke on milk glass, 11" h, 3-1/2" d base **$300-$350**
White, 12" h, 3-1/2" d base
$85-$100
Wisteria/lavender, 8" h, 3-1/2" d base, 7" d mouth
$300-$350

Vase, 4-1/2" d to 5-1/2" d base
Marigold shading to clear, 11-1/2" h	**$55-$110**
Red, stretch, 12" h, 4-3/4" d base, rare	**$1,300**
Smoke, 10-1/2" h, 4-1/2" d base	**$300-$325**
White, stretch, 4-7/8" h	**$60-$80**

Smooth Rays
Berry bowl, crimped edge, ruffled, Jeweled Heart back, peach opalescent **$25-$35**

Berry bowl, small, ruffled, 6" d
Marigold	**$10-$15**
Peach opalescent	**$20-$30**
Purple	**$25-$30**

Bonbon or card tray, amethyst
$15-$20

Bowl, crimped, 9" d, peach opalescent **$35-$55**

Bowl, deep, ruffled, 9-1/2" d
Blue opalescent	**$80-$100**
Green	**$15-$35**
Vaseline	**$35-$50**

Bowl, handgrip, crimped, 8" d, peach opalescent **$35-$40**

Bowl, round, 8" d to 9" d
Amethyst opalescent	**$85-$155**
Blue opalescent	**$150-$350**
Marigold on milk glass	**$65-$110**
Teal	**$25-$50**

Bowl, ruffled, 10" d to 11" d
Green	**$15-$30**
Lime green	**$30-$35**
Marigold	**$10-$15**
Purple	**$150-$175**

Raspberry, Northwood, pitcher, purple, **$150**.

Ribbon Tie, Fenton, bowl, candy ribbon edge, amethyst, **$150**.

Rococco, Imperial, vase, smoke, **$125**.

Ripple, Imperial, squat vase, purple, 6-1/2" h, with a 3" base, **$150-$250**.

Bowl, square, 9-3/4" to 10"
Green	$30-$40
Lime green	$15-$30
Marigold	$20-$25

Bowl, tricorn, crimped, 8" d,
peach opalescent	$45-$60

Compote
Blue opalescent	$70-$160
Green	$40-$60

Plate, 6" d to 7" d
Marigold	$15-$20
Purple, crimped edge	
	$85-$90

Soda Gold

Candlesticks, pr, 3-1/2"
Marigold	$25-$35
Smoke	$40-$70

Chop plate, 11" d to 12" d,
marigold	$75-$100

Console bowl, rolled rim
Marigold	$30-$50
Smoke	$40-$60

Console set, bowl and pr candlesticks
Marigold	$55-$85
Smoke	$80-$100

Salt and pepper shakers, pr
Aqua, marigold	$110-$240
Light blue	$90-$110
Marigold	$95-$125
Smoke	$105-$135

Spittoon
Lime green	$95-$135
Marigold	$20-$35
Vaseline, rare	$1,725

Tumbler, marigold $25-$35

Water pitcher, marigold
	$50-$90

Soutache

Bowl, ruffled, dome ftd, peach
opalescent	$75-$100

Plate, crimped or plain edge,
peach opalescent	$100-$150

Springtime

Berry bowl, master
Amethyst/purple	$40-$60
Green	$35-$50
Marigold	$30-$40

Butter dish, cov
Amethyst/purple	$225-$325
Green	$400-$600
Marigold	$200-$300

Creamer or spooner
Amethyst	$90-$120
Green	$75-$100
Marigold	$65-$85

Sugar bowl
Amethyst	$110-$135
Green	$100-$125
Marigold	$95-$125

Tumbler
Amethyst	$75-$100
Green	$65-$95

Water pitcher
Amethyst	$800-$1,200
Green	$900-$1,300

Stag and Holly

Bowl, ice cream shape or round, 7" d to 8" d, ruffled
Amethyst	$35-$95
Blue	$75-$125
Green	$200-$400
Lavender	$100-$130
Marigold	$50-$75
Pumpkin marigold	$300-$350
Red	$1,000-$1,800

Bowl, ruffled, ball feet, 10" d to 11" d
Amber	$165-$200
Amberina, rare	$1,700
Aqua	$400-$450
Black amethyst	$300-$350
Blue	$250-$450
Green	$175-$275
Light blue, marigold overlay	
	$200-$400
Lime green	$100-$200
Marigold	$55-$125
Pink	$40-$60
Powder blue	$100-$200
Smoke	$400-$425
Vaseline	$250-$300

Bowl, ruffled, spatula ftd, 7-3/4" d to 10" d
Amethyst	$75-$85
Green	$65-$135
Marigold	$40-$45
Powder blue	$200-$400
Smoke	$115-$135

Nut bowl, ball feet, 7-1/2"
Blue	$115-$170
Marigold	$50-$70

Plate, 8-1/2" d to 9" d
Amethyst, rare	$5,000
Marigold	$400-$600
Smoke	$350-$550

Star and File

Bonbon, marigold $10-$15

Bowl, round, 7" d to 8" d,
marigold	$10-$15

Bowl, square, 6" w to 8" w,
marigold	$20-$25

Celery vase, two handles
Clambroth	$25-$35
Marigold	$30-$40

Champagne, marigold $85-$110

Compote, 7"
Clambroth	$25-$35
Marigold	$20-$30

Cordial, 1 oz, marigold
	$250-$295

Creamer, marigold $15-$20

Custard cup, marigold $35-$45

Goblet, marigold $40-$60

Iced tea tumbler, marigold
	$150-$175

Juice tumbler, marigold
	$165-$195

Milk pitcher, marigold $90-$110

Nut bowl, 5" d, marigold
	$15-$60

Plate, 6" d to 6-1/2" d,
marigold	$50-$150

Relish, marigold $25-$30

Rose bowl
Amber	$145-$175
Helios	$135-$150
Ice green	$275-$300
Marigold	$35-$50
Purple	$200-$250

Sherbet, marigold $30-$40

Spooner
Marigold	$15-$20
Smoke	$45-$65

Vase, marigold $30-$50

Water pitcher, marigold
	$60-$90

Wine decanter, marigold
	$155-$180

Wine glass, marigold $30-$45

Starfish

Bonbon
Peach opalescent	$75-$125
Purple	$40-$100

Compote, peach opalescent
	$85-$115

Star Medallion

Bowl, 7-1/2" d to 8" d
Clambroth	$15-$25

Marigold	$15-$25
Smoke	$20-$30
Celery vase, pedestal base	
Clambroth	$50-$65
Marigold	$60-$130
Smoke	$50-$90
Compote	
Clambroth	$25-$35
Marigold	$30-$45
Custard cup, marigold	$5-$10
Goblet	
Marigold	$25-$35
Smoky blue	$25-$35
Smoke	$100-$120
Lemonade tumbler, 4-1/2" h	
Marigold	$25-$40
Smoke	$50-$80
Milk pitcher	
Clambroth	$25-$35
Marigold	$20-$30
Nut bowl, marigold	$15-$20
Plate, 6" d to 7-1/2" d, marigold	
	$100-$125
Plate, 9-1/2" d to 10" d	
Clambroth	$20-$25
Marigold	$30-$60
Smoke	$80-$110
Tumbler, 4" h, smoke	$50-$80

Star of David
Bowl, 8" d to 9" d	
Helios	$100-$115
Marigold	$115-$135
Smoke	$300-$350

Stork and Rushes
Basket, handle	
Amethyst	$60-$115
Marigold	$55-$100
Butter dish, cov	
Amethyst	$125-$150
Marigold	$95-$125
Creamer or spooner	
Amethyst	$110-$120
Marigold	$55-$75
Hat, lattice band, two sides up	
Amethyst	$30-$50
Marigold	$30-$50
Mug, banded top, 4" h	
Amethyst	$60-$85
Marigold	$15-$35
Punch bowl	
Amethyst	$300-$400
Marigold	$100-$200

Punch cup	
Amethyst	$10-$15
Marigold	$5-$10
Sugar bowl, cov	
Amethyst	$120-$140
Marigold	$75-$95
Tumbler, beaded edge	
Amethyst	$95-$125
Blue	$50-$55
Marigold	$20-$40
Tumbler, lattice band	
Amethyst	$75-$100
Blue	$60-$90
Water pitcher, beaded or lattice	
Amethyst	$200-$400
Blue	$400-$550
Lime green	$300-$400
Marigold	$200-$400

Strawberry
Bowl, piecrust edge, plain back, 8" d	
Amethyst	$55-$90
Green	$150-$350
Lavender	$200-$800
Marigold	$100-$200
Purple	$90-$250
Smoke	$850-$900
White	$1,000-$1,300
Bowl, piecrust edge, ribbed back, stippled, 8-1/2" d	
Amethyst	$80-$375
Blue	$450-$650
Green	$600-$800
Horehound	$485-$825
Marigold	$175-$400
Purple	$500-$800
Bowl, plain back, 9" d	
Pastel marigold	$200-$300
Pumpkin marigold	$575-$675
Bowl, ruffled, basketweave back, 9" d	
Amethyst	$65-$150
Green	$80-$150
Horehound	$650-$750
Marigold	$40-$100
Marigold, opalescent tips	
	$1,950-$2,100
Peach opalescent	
	$2,100-$2,800
Purple	$50-$100
Smoke	$700-$900
Bowl, ruffled, ribbed, stippled	
Amethyst	$225-$650

Blue	$300-$900
Horehound	$750-$1,500
Ice green	$1,900-$2,500
Lavender	$225-$325
Lime green	$1,000-$1,600
Marigold	$200-$500
Purple	$225-$600
Renninger blue	$750-$1,200
Plate, basketweave back, 9" d to 9-1/4" d	
Amethyst	$145-$175
Green	$120-$235
Marigold	$95-$125
Purple	$135-$145
Plate, hand grip, 6" d to 7-1/2" d	
Amethyst/purple	$100-$200
Green	$120-$300
Marigold	$125-$225
Plate, plain back, 9" d to 9-1/4" d	
Amethyst	$170-$400
Blue	$350-$425
Green	$200-$265
Lavender	$300-$400
Marigold	$150-$300
Marigold, opalescent tips	
	$700-$1,600
Plate, ribbed back, stippled, 9" d	
Amethyst	$700-$1,400
Blue, rare	$5,000
Green	$1,100-$1,550
Ice blue	$16,250-$23,000
Marigold	$1,800-$2,500
Purple	$750-$1,100

Strawberry Scroll
Tumbler	
Amethyst	$100-$150
Blue	$140-$185
Water pitcher, blue	
	$2,000-$3,500

Sunflower
Pin tray	
Green	$500-$700
Marigold	$950-$1,300

Swirl Hobnail
Rose bowl	
Amethyst	$250-$325
Marigold	$170-$185
Purple	$225-$275

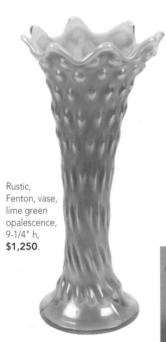

Rustic, Fenton, vase, lime green opalescence, 9-1/4" h, **$1,250**.

Scroll Embossed, Imperial, pastel lavender, with pastel color edge to edge, **$500-$850**.

Singing Birds, Northwood, mug, blue, covered with electric highlights, **$100**.

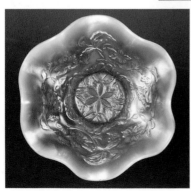

Six Petals, Dugan, ruffled bowl, marigold, **$60**.

Strawberry, Northwood, ruffled bowl with basketweave exterior, green, **$155**.

Spittoon

Amethyst	$450-$500
Marigold	$625-$925
Purple	$500-$900

Vase, 10" h to 11" h

Amethyst	$225-$250
Blue	$2,400-$3,200
Green	$400-$700

Target
Vase

Amethyst/purple	$140-$240
Green	$325-$425
Horehound	$100-$150
Marigold	$25-$50
Peach opalescent	$45-$90
Peach opalescent, squatty	$75-$125
Purple, squatty	$200-$300
White, 12" h	$45-$90

Ten Mums
Bowl, ruffled, collar base, 9" d to 10" d

Amethyst	$175-$200
Blue	$275-$375
Emerald green	$550-$650
Green	$95-$180
Marigold	$200-$300

Bowl, 3-in-1 edge, 9" to 9-1/2" d

Amethyst	$175-$300
Green	$100-$200
Marigold	$200-$300

Tumbler

Blue	$30-$60
White	$200-$350

Water pitcher, tankard

Blue	$650-$750
White	$1,900-$3,000

Thin Rib
Vase, jester's cap, eight ribs, 3-1/2" d base

Amethyst	$100-$200
Green	$170-$270
Marigold	$225-$325
Purple, 10" h	$115-$215

Vase, mid-size, eight ribs, 12" h to 15" h, 4-3/4" d base

Amber, rare	$1,700
Amethyst, 12" h	$140-$200
Aqua opalescent	$2,100-$3,200

Blue	$400-$600
Green	$150-$250
Ice blue	$650-$750
Ice green opalescent, rare	$2,500
Lime green	$1,100-$1,700
Marigold	$110-$210
Purple, 13" h	$145-$200
Sapphire blue, 13-1/2" h	$1,000-$2,000
Vaseline	$650-$750

Vase, standard size, nine ribs, 6" h to 11" h, 3-3/8" d to 3-3/4" d base

Amber	$70-$90
Amethyst, 10" h	$60-$90
Blue, 10" h	$65-$115
Emerald green	$175-$500
Green, 11" h	$45-$70
Ice blue	$150-$250
Ice green, 11" h	$195-$295
Lime green	$140-$180
Marigold, 7" h	$50-$75
Olive green, 10" h or 11" h	$25-$50
Purple, 13" h	$145-$165
Smoke	$140-$160
Vaseline	$500-$700
White	$50-$75

Thistle
Banana boat

Blue	$185-$300
Green	$325-$600
Marigold	$50-$150

Bowl, candy ribbon edge, tightly crimped, 8" d to 9" d

Amethyst	$115-$175
Blue	$75-$125
Green	$50-$150
Marigold	$45-$80

Bowl, ruffled or 3-in-1 edge, 8" d to 9" d

Amber	$140-$165
Amethyst	$45-$85
Blue	$75-$175
Green	$50-$70
Green, Horlacher adv	$135-$150
Lavender	$75-$95
Marigold	$45-$80
Vaseline	$175-$350

Plate, 9" d

Amethyst	$2,500-$4,000
Marigold, rare	$6,500

Three Fruits
Bowl, collar base, ribbed back, stippled, white $200-$250

Bowl, spatula ftd, ruffled, 9" d, 3-1/4" h

Amethyst	$65-$105
Ice green	$350-$450

Bowl, piecrust edge, basketweave back or plain back, 8" to 9" d

Amethyst	$65-$125
Green	$110-$140
Lime green	$200-$250
Purple	$200-$400
Smoke	$400-$500

Bowl, piecrust edge, stippled, 8" d to 9" d

Amethyst/purple	$250-$400
Blue	$375-$500
Green	$400-$600
Horehound	$250-$350
Ice blue, rare	$8,000
Lime green, marigold overlay	$800-$1,000
Marigold	$300-$700
Olive	$400-$600

Bowl, ruffled, basketweave, ribbed, or plain back, 8" d to 9" d

Amethyst	$60-$95
Aqua opalescent	$500-$800
Green	$150-$300
Honey amber	$350-$525
Horehound	$275-$300
Lavender	$200-$250
Lime green	$550-$800
Marigold	$80-$225
Pearlized custard	$350-$450
Pumpkin marigold	$70-$100
Purple	$60-$95
Sapphire blue	$1,700-$2,200
Smoke	$300-$500
Smoky lavender	$250-$350

Plate, basketweave back, 9" d

Amethyst	$150-$250
Black amethyst	$200-$525
Blue	$275-$450
Green	$105-$210
Horehound	$350-$500

Lavender	$200-$300
Marigold	$95-$195
Purple	$150-$250

Plate, plain back, 9" d

Apple green, rare	$650
Purple	$165-$300

Plate, stippled, ribbed back, 9" d

Amethyst	$450-$900
Aqua, rare	$2,000-$3,000
Black amethyst	$900-$1,100
Blue	$900-$1,200
Clambroth	$200-$300
Green	$2,300-$4,000
Honey amber	$2,000-$2,400
Horehound	$300-$500
Ice blue	$4,500-$6,000
Lavender	$500-$950
Marigold	$250-$350
Pumpkin marigold	$275-$375
Purple	$375-$500
Sapphire blue	$1,800-$2,800
Teal	$1,400-$1,800
Violet	$400-$1,200

Tiger Lily

Tumbler, 4-1/2" h

Amber	$190-$225
Aqua	$50-$90
Blue	$250-$350
Helios	$55-$95
Olive	$70-$95
Teal	$50-$90
Violet	$100-$200

Water pitcher

Aqua	$215-$375
Helios	$250-$300
Olive	$200-$300
Teal	$275-$375

Tornado

Vase, large, 6-1/2" h, 3" d base

Amethyst	$400-$600
Green	$400-$800
Marigold	$300-$500
Purple	$450-$650
White, rare	$6,750

Vase, ribbed

Amethyst	$1,500-$1,800
Blue	$3,100-$3,600
Ice blue	$3,600-$6,500
Lavender	$1,500-$2,000
Marigold	$1,000-$2,000
Purple	$800-$1,500

Vase, small, 6" h, 2-5/8" d base

Green	$400-$900
Lavender	$1,000-$1,300
White, rare	$5,500

Vase, whimsy

Marigold, green tornado medallions	$2,100-$4,750
Marigold, pedestal base, rare	$1,900

Town Pump

Town pump, 6-1/2" h, collar base

Green	$4,000-$4,500
Marigold	$1,600-$2,500

Tree Trunk

Vase, funeral, 15" h to 22" h, 5-1/4" d base

Amethyst	$1,500-$3,000
Blue	$2,500-$3,000
Green	$3,500-$4,000
Ice blue, rare	$26,000
Marigold	$3,500-$4,000
Purple, plunger base	$1,300-$3,000
White	$2,000-$4,000

Vase, mid-size, 11-1/2" h to 14" h, 3-3/4" d to 4-3/4" d base

Amethyst, base band	$350-$450
Aqua opalescent	$3,000-$4,000
Emerald green, base band	$4,500-$4,900
Green	$350-$650
Horehound	$400-$700
Ice blue	$1,100-$1,500
Ice green	$1,200-$1,700
Lavender	$400-$600
Lime green	$900-$1,700
Marigold	$195-$395
Marigold over custard	$10,000-$16,000
Sapphire blue	$700-$900
White	$600-$1,000

Vase, squatty, 5" h to 7" h

Amethyst	$100-$135
Blue	$200-$400
Green	$90-$175
Ice blue	$700-$1,300
Ice green	$900-$1,300
Lime green	$225-$400

Marigold	$75-$150
Purple	$100-$135
White	$125-$350

Vase, standard, 7" h to 12" h, 3-3/8" d to 3-3/4" d base

Amethyst	$100-$200
Aqua opalescent, butter-scotch overlay	$850-$950
Blue	$195-$300
Green	$50-$150
Horehound	$250-$325
Ice blue	$250-$450
Ice green	$350-$550
Lavender	$100-$150
Marigold	$50-$75
Purple	$80-$150
Sapphire blue	$400-$600
White	$95-$175

Two Flowers

Bowl, ice cream shape, ball ftd

Amethyst	$130-$160
Aqua	$150-$320
Blue	$225-$325
Lime green	$175-$215
Marigold	$50-$75
Powder blue	$175-$275
Smoke	$1,000-$1,650

Bowl, ruffled, ball ftd, 10" d to 11" d

Amethyst/purple	$100-$200
Aqua	$200-$350
Black amethyst	$125-$175
Blue	$150-$300
Green	$150-$300
Lime green	$90-$115
Marigold	$50-$100
Red, rare	$4,000
Sapphire	$375-$575
Vaseline	$200-$300

Bowl, spatula ftd, 8" d to 9" d

Amberina, rare	$900
Amethyst	$75-$100
Blue	$40-$60
Green	$60-$80
Marigold	$25-$35
Red	$1,200-$1,800
Vaseline	$135-$195

Centerpiece bowl, collar base, 9" d, 5" h, marigold $40-$60

Nut bowl, ftd, green $40-$80

Plate, spatula ftd, 9" d, marigold $250-$350

Thin Rib, Northwood, mid-size vase, marigold, 13-1/2" h with 5" base, **$270**.

Thin Rib, Northwood, squatty vase, purple, **$210**.

Thistle, Fenton, bowl with candy ribbon edge, green, **$150**.

Three Fruits, Northwood, plate with plain back, apple green, **$650**.

Tree Trunk, Northwood, funeral vase, blue, **$2,500**.

Rose bowl, giant, ball ftd
Blue	$600-$1,200
Marigold	$150-$250

Rose bowl, small, spatula ftd
Blue	$80-$100
Marigold	$30-$45
Purple	$85-$115

Sauce, collar base
Amethyst	$45-$85
Blue	$60-$80
Marigold	$85-$125

Sauce, ruffled, ftd, 5" d to 6" d
Aqua	$135-$195
Green	$35-$65
Lime green	$50-$90
Powder blue	$80-$120
Vaseline	$100-$150

Vineyard

Tumbler, marigold $25-$50
Water pitcher
Marigold	$90-$160
Purple	$300-$500

Vintage

Bonbon
Amethyst	$30-$50
Blue	$20-$40
Peach opalescent	$100-$150

Bowl, 7" d to 8" d
Amethyst	$30-$50
Aqua opalescent	$500-$900
Blue	$40-$50
Green	$30-$50
Marigold	$30-$50
Persian blue	$600-$800
Red, rare	$1,000
Vaseline	$80-$160

Bowl, 9" d to 10" d
Amber	$75-$95
Amethyst	$60-$90
Aqua opalescent	$1,600-$2,300
Blue	$60-$90
Celeste blue	$1,700-$3,000
Green	$40-$80
Lime green	$120-$160
Marigold	$30-$50
Persian blue	$450-$900
Red	$1,500-$3,000
Vaseline	$100-$150

Bowl, 3-in-1 edge, 10" d
Amethyst	$40-$70
Blue	$55-$85

Green	$50-$75
Marigold	$50-$75
Red, rare	$2,100

Compote
Amethyst	$25-$50
Blue	$40-$60
Green	$30-$50
Marigold	$25-$35
Purple	$90-$190

Epergne, two-pc, large, 6" h
Amethyst	$200-$300
Green	$250-$350

Ferners
Amber	$100-$135
Amberina	$550-$750
Amethyst	$50-$100
Blue	$90-$145
Green	$60-$80
Marigold	$30-$45
Red	$300-$500

Plate, 6" d
Amethyst	$210-$250
Green	$250-$400
Marigold	$250-$325

Plate, 9" d
Amethyst	$4,000-$4,500
Blue	$2,000-$2,750
Green, rare	$4,000
Marigold	$550-$750

Wine glass
Amethyst	$15-$25
Marigold	$10-$15
Purple	$20-$30
Vaseline	$40-$60

Waffle Block

Basket, 10" h
Clambroth	$30-$40
Marigold	$45-$65
Purple	$55-$85
Smoke	$85-$125
Teal	$200-$250
Vaseline, rare	$750

Bowl, round, 7" d to 9" d
Clambroth	$20-$30
Marigold	$20-$30

Bowl, square, 7" w to 9" w
Marigold	$30-$50
Teal	$20-$30

Breakfast set, creamer and sugar
Clambroth	$40-$60
Marigold	$60-$90

Parfait
Clambroth	$25-$50
Marigold	$40-$60

Plate, 6" d, marigold $35-$55
Punch bowl
Clambroth	$60-$80
Marigold	$50-$75
Teal	$100-$125

Punch bowl set, eight pcs
Clambroth	$150-$200
Marigold	$100-$165

Punch cup
Clambroth	$10-$15
Marigold	$35-$45

Rose bowl
Clambroth	$30-$40
Marigold	$55-$75

Salt and pepper shakers, pr,
marigold	$80-$100

Spittoon, whimsy, marigold $300-$350
Tumbler, clambroth $150-$275
Vase, 10" h, marigold $80-$100
Water pitcher, clambroth $175-$275

Water Lily

Berry bowl, master, ball ftd, 9" d to 10" d
Amethyst	$275-$375
Aqua	$225-$325
Blue	$75-$100
Green	$150-$250
Marigold	$25-$75
Pumpkin marigold	$60-$75
Teal	$185-$250
Vaseline	$225-$275

Berry bowl, small, ball ftd, ruffled
Amber slag, rare	$450
Amberina	$600-$800
Amethyst	$35-$45
Blue	$40-$85
Green	$80-$135
Lime green	$65-$195
Lime green opalescent	$800-$1,350
Marigold	$15-$30
Reverse amberina	$700-$1,000
Reverse amberina opalescent	$1,400-$2,300
Sapphire blue	$85-$125
Vaseline	$60-$120

Vaseline opalescent	$350-$750
Bonbon, two handles	
Marigold	$30-$40
White	$50-$65
Bowl, ice cream shape, blue	$850-$1,200
Chop plate, 11" d, marigold	$3,000-$3,750

Waterlily and Cattails

Banana boat	
Amethyst	$225-$350
Green	$250-$325
Marigold	$100-$150
Bonbon, marigold	$15-$30
Bowl, round, 8" d	
Blue	$150-$175
Marigold	$15-$35
Bowl, ruffled, 5" d, marigold	$5-$15
Bowl, tricorn, whimsy, marigold	$20-$30
Butter dish, cov, marigold	$300-$350
Creamer, marigold	$95-$125
Hat, rolled rim, tumbler mold, marigold	$300-$350
Match holder, 3" h, marigold	$75-$150
Plate, 6" d, marigold	$50-$75
Spittoon, 6-1/2", marigold	$800-$1,000
Spooner, marigold	$95-$125
Sugar bowl, marigold	$125-$150
Tumbler, marigold	$35-$50
Water pitcher, marigold	$300-$350

Wide Panel

Basket	
Ice green	$130-$230
Marigold	$90-$200
Bowl, 9" d	
Aqua	$35-$55
Clambroth	$15-$25
Marigold	$15-$35
Red	$145-$165
Smoke	$35-$55
Teal	$35-$55
White	$50-$75
Bowl, 12" d	
Clambroth	$35-$50

Marigold	$25-$60
Red	$225-$250
Smoke	$50-$75
Butter dish, cov, marigold	$50-$100
Candlestick	
Marigold	$20-$30
Russet	$35-$55
Candy dish, cov	
Celeste blue	$60-$75
Ice green	$45-$95
Marigold	$30-$50
Olive	$20-$45
Vaseline	$25-$50
Chop plate, 14" d, Imperial	
Clambroth	$40-$60
Marigold	$35-$70
Smoke	$65-$85
Compote, open, large	
Marigold	$30-$50
Purple, 7" h	$400-$450
Smoke	$35-$75
Creamer, red	$130-$135
Epergne, central trumpet with three jack lilies, scalloped bowl with 10 panels, 4-3/4" d base with 44-point star, Northwood	
Amethyst/purple	$1,200-$1,600
Blue	$800-$2,000
Green	$900-$1,400
Ice blue, rare	$2,000
Ice green	$1,800-$7,000
Marigold	$600-$900
White	$1,200-$1,800
Funeral vase, 16" h, 4-3/4" base with 44-point star, Northwood	
Green	$55-$115
Marigold	$70-$150
Vaseline	$90-$190
Goblet	
Marigold	$10-$15
Red	$200-$300
Hat, tricorn, crimped edge, purple	$75-$80
Mug, marigold	$20-$30
Perfume bottle, marigold	$25-$35
Plate, 6" d, Imperial, marigold	$15-$30
Plate, 11" d, Imperial	
Celeste blue	$80-$100
Clambroth	$30-$45

Marigold	$40-$50
Red	$135-$150
White	$75-$95
Powder jar, marigold	$20-$35
Sherbet	
Green	$20-$35
Russet	$20-$35
Spittoon, red	$175-$275
Tumbler, marigold	$25-$30
Vase, 10" h, red	$275-$300

Wide Rib

Vase	
Amethyst	$75-$400
Blue, 11" h	$50-$100
White	$45-$80

Windmill

Bowl, collar base, 7" d to 9" d	
Aqua	$145-$195
Clambroth	$30-$50
Emerald green	$200-$300
Helios	$65-$90
Lime green	$30-$50
Marigold	$50-$80
Marigold on milk glass	$350-$425
Olive	$30-$90
Purple	$145-$250
Smoke	$90-$125
Bowl, ftd, 7" d to 9" d	
Aqua	$45-$95
Clambroth	$30-$50
Emerald green	$200-$300
Helios	$65-$90
Lime green	$30-$50
Marigold	$50-$80
Marigold on milk glass	$350-$425
Olive	$30-$90
Purple	$150-$300
Smoke	$80-$115
Cider pitcher, 8" h, mid-size	
Marigold	$40-$60
Purple	$90-$125
Smoke	$200-$250
Dresser tray	
Aqua	$175-$200
Helios	$100-$120
Marigold	$70-$90
Purple	$375-$400
Milk pitcher, 6-1/4" h	
Clambroth	$120-$145
Helios	$75-$145

Vintage, Fenton, 3-in-1 bowl, red, 8-1/2"d **$2,000**.

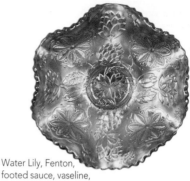

Water Lily, Fenton, footed sauce, vaseline, scarce color, **$55**.

Windmill, Imperial, bowl, ice cream shape, teal/green, covered with blue iridescence, 7"d, **$350-$500**.

Wishbone, Northwood, footed bowl, blue, has electric highlights, **$300**.

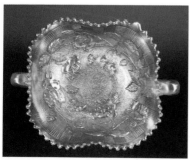

Wreath of Roses, Fenton, bonbon, amethyst, **$50**.

Zig-Zag, Millersburg, square bowl with candy ribbon edge, amethyst, **$500**.

Marigold	$40-$95
Purple	$300-$600
Smoke	$275-$300
Pickle dish, oval	
Aqua	$50-$70
Helios	$60-$90
Lavender	$150-$175
Marigold	$30-$50
Purple	$300-$365
Tumbler	
Green, marigold interior	$30-$75
Helios	$40-$60
Marigold	$25-$35
Water pitcher	
Blue-violet	$700-$725
Cobalt blue, rare	$2,000
Emerald green, rare	$1,500
Helios	$200-$250
Marigold	$125-$165
Purple	$850-$1,200

Wishbone

Bowl, collar base, piecrust edge, 9" d to 10" d	
Clambroth	$400-$450
Green	$150-$300
Lavender	$400-$500
Marigold	$200-$400
Smoke	$500-$700
White	$300-$400
Bowl, collar base, ruffled, 9" d to 10" d	
Amethyst/purple	$180-$250
Emerald green	$400-$600
Green	$200-$300
Marigold	$115-$155
Sapphire blue, rare	$3,500
Bowl, ruffled, ftd, 8" d to 9" d	
Amethyst	$110-$165
Aqua opalescent, rare	$18,000
Blue	$300-$665
Emerald green	$450-$475
Green	$120-$235
Horehound	$325-$950
Ice blue	$1,000-$1,700
Ice green	$800-$1,100
Lavender	$110-$200
Lime green	$1,200-$1,300
Marigold	$135-$210
Pumpkin marigold	$150-$175
Purple	$120-$165
White	$275-$400

Bowl, tricorn, ftd	
Amethyst	$300-$500
Green	$800-$1,000
Marigold	$350-$550
Chop plate, collar base, 10" d	
Amethyst/purple	$600-$1,600
Green	$3,000-$3,500
Marigold	$1,200-$2,000
Pumpkin marigold, rare	$4,000
Epergne, single lily and base, two pcs	
Amethyst/purple	$800-$1,000
Green	$600-$900
Ice blue	$3,750-$4,000
Ice green, rare	$6,000
Marigold	$350-$550
White	$1,000-$2,500
Plate, ftd, 8" d to 9" d	
Amethyst	$250-$400
Green	$450-$675
Marigold	$600-$1,000
Tumbler	
Amethyst	$60-$90
Green	$100-$180
Marigold	$50-$90
Purple	$700-$900
Water pitcher	
Amethyst/purple	$600-$800
Green	$650-$1,000
Marigold	$240-$245

Wisteria

Tumbler	
Lime green	$500-$800
White	$300-$500
Water pitcher, white	$2,500-$3,500

Wreathed Cherries

Berry bowl, master, ruffled, oval	
Amethyst/purple	$85-$200
Black amethyst	$85-$150
Blue	$325-$375
Marigold	$65-$100
Peach opalescent	$100-$200
White	$215-$425
White, enameled red cherries	$300-$400
Berry bowl, small, ruffled, oval	
Amethyst/purple	$35-$55
Black amethyst	$35-$55
Marigold	$20-$35
White	$45-$60

White, enameled red cherries	$55-$75
Butter dish, cov, rayed star in collared base	
Purple, sgd "D"	$275-$350
White	$250-$350
White, enameled red cherries	$350-$395
Creamer or spooner, collared base	
Marigold	$35-$55
Purple	$40-$60
White	$50-$75
White, enameled red cherries	$75-$100
Sugar bowl, collared base	
Marigold	$55-$85
Purple	$60-$90
White	$65-$110
White, enameled red cherries	$95-$120
Tumbler	
Amethyst/purple	$40-$60
Marigold	$50-$75
White	$40-$60
Water pitcher	
Amethyst/purple	$300-$350
Marigold	$400-$550
White	$300-$350

Wreath of Roses

Bonbon	
Amethyst	$35-$50
Blue	$60-$80
Green	$35-$40
Marigold	$20-$35
White	$150-$250
Compote, ruffled	
Amethyst	$30-$45
Blue	$45-$60
Green	$35-$50
Marigold	$25-$40
Punch bowl set, eight-pc, plain interior	
Amethyst	$400-$600
Blue	$300-$500
Green	$325-$525
Marigold	$200-$400
Punch bowl set, eight-pc, Persian Medallion interior	
Amethyst	$900-$1,250
Blue	$750-$800
Green	$900-$950
Marigold	$300-$500

Punch bowl set, eight-pc,
  Vintage interior
    Amethyst $600-$650
    Blue $650-$700
    Green $725-$825
    Marigold $350-$550
Punch cup, plain interior
  Amethyst $30-$40
  Blue $35-$40
  Green $35-$40
  Marigold $15-$20
Punch cup, Persian Medallion
  interior
  Amethyst $35-$50

  Blue $60-$70
  Green $45-$55
  Marigold $20-$30
Punch cup, Vintage interior
  Amethyst $30-$45
  Blue $50-$60
  Green $40-$45
  Marigold $15-$20

Zig Zag
Bowl, ice cream shape
  Amethyst $225-$450
  Marigold $225-$425
Bowl, ruffled or 3-in-1 edge
  Amethyst, radium $400-$450

  Amethyst, satin $150-$175
  Green $200-$350
  Marigold $150-$200
Bowl, square, crimped
  Amethyst $500-$1,200
  Green $850-$950
  Marigold $400-$700
Bowl, tricorn, crimped
  Amethyst $700-$1,100
  Green $400-$750

A sampling of some rare carnival glass items

Grape and Cable, Northwood, bonbon, peach opalescent, one of only three known, **$7,000**.

Imperial Grape, Imperial, deep round bowl, blue, 7" d, **$1,200-$1,500 (rare)**.

Open Rose, Imperial, six-ruffled sauce, violet blue, 5-1/2" d, **$600-$900 (rare)**.

Open Rose, Imperial, round sauce, violet blue, 5" d, **$500-$800 (rare)**.

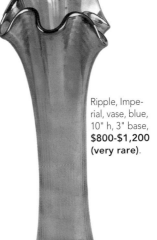

Ripple, Imperial, vase, blue, 10" h, 3" base, **$800-$1,200 (very rare)**.

Rose Show, Northwood, plate, marigold over custard, **$11,000 (extremely rare)**.

Glossary

Annealing lehr: the common name given to an annealing oven, where finished glass was placed to gradually cool down.

Ashtrays: ashtrays are rare in carnival glass.

Banana bowl, banana boat: this interesting shape is found usually on either a flat or collared base and is used to describe an oval bowl, usually with two opposing sides turned upward.

Basket: This term refers to a small bowl, usually with a handle or up-turned edge. The form could be used for candy, nuts, flowers, or as a decorative piece.

Basketweave: a design often found on the exterior of carnival glass patterns. The design consists of several rows of weaving, resembling a wicker basket.

Batch: the name given to the mixture of raw materials that are blended in a tank to make glass. The basic mixture consists of silica (sand), soda, lime, and sometimes cullet. Other ingredients are added to create colors.

Berry sets: these were a staple of carnival glass production. They consist of a large bowl to hold berries and six matching individual serving bowls. Generally they are flat, but some patterns are known with feet. Edges may be crimped, ruffled, or plain.

Bonbon, bon bon: bonbons are small, round, or shaped forms designed to hold candy or to be used as decorative pieces. Bonbons always have two handles.

Bowls: bowls are made in a number of different styles and shapes and with different kinds of edges. An ice-cream shape bowl has an upturned rim and a slightly cupped shape. A bowl with a pie-crust edge refers to a bowl with an edge finished to resemble crimping found on the edge of pie. This simple technique was usually part of the mold, which did not require any further hand finishing. Bowl, ruffled: Another popular treatment to bowls was to ruffle the edges. Bowl, tricorn: This term refers to a three-sided bowl shape.

Breakfast set: a small-sized creamer and sugar.

Bud vase: a slender vase, designed to hold one blossom. They can be footed or flat, short or tall, but always have narrow necks.

Calling card trays: usually formed by adding a foot to a bonbon shape. Some have two sides turned inward and may have handles. The form was used to receive calling cards from visitors.

Candlesticks: these are a rare form in carnival glass.

Chop plates: chop plates are large, usually 10 inches or larger, very flat plates.

Collar base: a ring of glass on the bottom of a piece that raises it very slightly.

Compote: these are an interesting carnival glass form. They can be large or small, ruffled or plain, some have straight sides or flared rims.

Contemporary: contemporary carnival glass is glass that has been made using iridized metallic surfaces in the last decade or two.

Crimped: a term used to describe an edge treatment where it looks as though the glass was pinched in regular intervals. A special tool is usually used to create this uniform effect.

CRE: Abbreviation used for candy-ribbon edge, a deeply crimped edge that resembles the ruffled candy.

Cullet: broken pieces of glass that are recycled to make a batch.

Cup and saucer: these forms are rare in carnival glass.

Decanters: also known as wine decanters, wine bottles, or bottles with stoppers, these are a lesser-known form in carnival glass.

Dope: the name given to the iridescent spray by early glassmakers. The spray consisted of a liquid solution of metallic salts applied to the hot glass form.

Dope house: a place where the mixing of chemicals for the dope metallic mixture took place.

Dresser sets: what constitutes a dresser set varies from pattern to pattern, but generally includes cologne bottles, perfume bottles, powder jars, hat pin holders, pin trays, and a larger flat dresser tray, allowing a lady to include carnival glass and it's colors into her bedroom as well as her dining room.

Electric: term used to describe shades of blue and purple that seem to have a brilliant electric quality to their iridescent finish.

Epergne: refers to an elaborate centerpiece form, usually consisting of a lily-shaped vase and a bowl or plate on a pedestal base.

Fernery, ferner, fern dish: this name refers to a footed dish that is round, with straight vertical sides. Some ferneries were made with removable liners.

Footed, ftd: Many pieces of carnival glass were made with feet, usually short and rather stubby, but they allowed a piece to be elevated off slightly.

Fruit bowls: these are highly desirable forms of carnival glass. Often they are ruffled and found on separate bases.

Gather: the name given to the glassmaker who scooped up molten glass which he used to fill a patterned mold.

Gravy boat: a rare form in any glassware is a gravy boat.

Guest sets: rare forms in carnival glass. The term is derived from the fact that a tumbler is combined with a small water pitcher. Many guest sets were designed so that the tumbler would serve as a lid when inverted over the top of the matching pitcher.

Hand finishing: when additional crimping or shaping was required, it was sometimes done by the glassmaker by using hand tools. If necessary, the piece was re-heated gently so that the metallic coatings would adhere properly.

Hat: refers to a shape found in many carnival glass patterns. The top edge may be flared, sometimes with one or two sides turned up. They have flat bases.

Hatpin: Carnival glassmakers enjoyed making unusual forms, often referred to as whimsies. One type of whimsy is a hatpin.

Hatpin holder: a slender vase-like holder was designed to hold hatpins on a lady's dressing table.

Jack in the pulpit (JIP): this name refers to a hat, bowl, or vase that has one edge turned up and pointed, creating a collar form similar to the flower of the same name.

Lamp: Carnival glass manufacturers produced fluid lamps and later electrified lamps. Some married carnival glass elements to metal lamp parts such as brass and iron.

Ice cream sets: these sets were popular in carnival glass production. They consisted of a cupped shape bowl and six individual serving bowls, often footed.

Lemonade pitcher: this form is identified as a tall tankard pitcher and may be footed or have a collared base. When accompanied by tumblers or lemonade mugs, the forms become known as a "lemonade set."

Loving cup: this term is used to describe a stemmed vase with two or three handles.

Marie: a term given to the base of carnival glass, usually the base, where the glassmaker grips the glass during the iridizing process.

Married: carnival glass elements were sometimes incorporated into other forms using metal bases or stands. An example of this technique would be a bowl that is supported on a metal stem and base, creating an interesting compote form.

Milk pitcher: a pitcher, usually bulbous, that is larger than a creamer but smaller than a water pitcher.

Mold: this term refers to the metal or wooden form used to shape glass into specific patterns. Molds could be one piece or hinged to allow easier access to the finished piece.

Mugs: mugs are straight-sided drinking vessels with a handle. Many were used with punch bowls or designed as children's feeding vessels.

Nappy: a candy dish or small bowl form with one handle.

Nut bowl: a small round bowl, sometimes footed, with a fluted or smooth upper edge that rises straight up.

Orange bowl: this form is a large round, footed bowl, with a large opening that easily accommodates the display of oranges.

Piecrust edge (PCE): this term is used to describe an edge that has a crimped edge on a bowl or plate that resembles the kind of crimps made in a pie crust. When Northwood used this edge, it was part of the mold, requiring no further shaping.

Pickle dish: a small oval dish, usually flat with slightly curved up or ruffled sides.

Picture frame: picture frames in vintage glassware production are extremely rare. Researchers have questioned whether this design was intended as a picture frame as there is no way to secure a photo or hang the heavy piece. Few 8-inch square examples exist, some do have the circular device in the center removed and the edges neatly trimmed.

Pin tray: several carnival glass manufacturers made interesting small trays which were used to hold hair pins on a lady's dressing table.

Plate, hand grip: the term "hand grip" is used to describe a plate that has one side turned down.

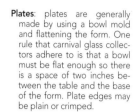

Plates: plates are generally made by using a bowl mold and flattening the form. One rule that carnival glass collectors adhere to is that a bowl must be flat enough so there is a space of two inches between the table and the base of the form. Plate edges may be plain or crimped.

Punch bowl: punch bowls are a highly desirable form in carnival glass collecting. Most are two pieces, with a separate base. Sometimes the bases were designed so they could be used as open compotes when not supporting a punch bowl. Punch bowls range in size from small to quite large.

Punch bowl set: these sets consist of a punch bowl, base, and six or more cups.

Punch cups: these are found in a variety of styles.

Radium: a term used to describe a mirror-like shiny surface, created when iridescent materials were applied to slightly cooler glassware.

Re-issue: one of the names used to describe carnival glass that has been made using original molds, sometimes by the original company, but after 1960, not during primary production years.

Reproductions: these mean carnival glass that has been made in colors or forms other than those that were created by the original glass manufacturer.

Ribbed back: many forms have ribbed backs with vertical ribbing that usually radiates from the center.

Rose bowls: these small bowls are identified by their cupped-in tops, often with additional crimping. They are usually round forms with an upper edge that is turned in toward the center or deeply ruffled.

Ruffled: this term refers to when edges are slightly undulating.

Satin: the name given to a matte finish. It was created by applying metallic salts to very hot glassware.

Snap: the name of a glass-making tool that was attached to the marie to release the piece from its mold.

Spatula feet: these are small curved shapes, resembling spatulas, which flare out to act as feet.

Sweet pea vase: this term is used to describe a short vase with a wide mouth, usually found 10 to 12 inches high, but occasionally found from 16 to 18 inches high.

Swung vase: this term is used when a vase is made using some molding processes. As it is being hand finished, the glass blower actually swings the hot molten glass to lengthen the vase.

Table set: a covered butter dish, a creamer and sugar bowl, and spooner make up a table set.

Tankard pitcher: this term is used to describe a slender straight-sided cylinder-shaped water pitcher. This form usually has an applied handle.

Toothpick holder: this term is used to describe a small container that was designed to hold toothpicks on a table. Several patterns in carnival glass include this form.

3-in-1: this term refers to a deep ruffle edge that has a repeated effect with three ridges and a space.

Tumbler: tumblers are a common form in carnival glass.

Vase: vases are one of the most popular forms in carnival glass. They can be pressed into molds and then finished either totally by machine or with hand finishing. (Also see swung vase.)

Water pitcher: carnival glass water pitchers were made in several styles. One form is known as bulbous because the base is usually quite round. Tops may be ruffled, crimped, or plain with a pinched pouring spout. Handles can be applied or mold pressed.

Water sets: water sets, consisting of a water pitcher and tumblers, are one of the most popular forms of vintage carnival glass. The pitchers may be either bulbous or tankard styles. The number of matching tumblers can vary, with the most desirable being six matching tumblers.

Wine set: wine sets contain a stoppered wine decanter and serving glasses, usually stemmed wine glasses, cordial glasses, or small-sized tumblers.

Collectors Clubs

Carnival glass collectors are able to join with other collectors to further their education, research, read and contribute to newsletters as they enjoy their collecting hobby. Information about these clubs follows, but please note that often club members move, dues may change, etc.

Air Capital Carnival Glass Club
15201 E. 47th St.
Derby, KS 67037
Annual dues: **$15**

American Carnival Glass Association
3951 Fredericksburg Road
Wooster, OH 44691.
Web site: www.woodsland.com/acga
Annual dues: **$19**

Australian Carnival Enthusiasts Association (SA) Inc.
P.O. Box 1028
New Haven, SA, 5018
Annual dues: **$12, $15 overseas.**

Australian Carnival Enthusiasts Association (Victoria) Inc.
RSD Fryerstown
Victoria, Australia 3451
Annual dues: **$15**

Canadian Carnival Glass Association
12 Dalhouse Crescent
London, Ontario N6G 2H7 Canada
Annual dues: **$20**

Carnival Club of Western Australia
179 Edgewater Drive, Edgewater
Western Australia 6027

Carnival Glass Collectors Association of Australia, Inc.
4 Scarborough Chase
NARELLAN NSW 2567
Web site: www.austarmetro.com.au/~wdelahoy/cgcaa

Collectible Carnival Glass Association
2001 Fairway Drive
Joplin, MO 64804
Annual dues: **$12**

Gateway Carnival Glass Club
108 Riverwoods Cove
East Alton, IL 62024
Annual dues: **$5**

Great Lakes Carnival Glass Club
612 White Pine Blvd.
Lansing, MI 48917
Annual dues: **$10**

Heart of America Carnival Glass Association
4305 W. 78th St.
Prairie Village, KS 66208
Annual dues: **$25**

Hoosier Carnival Glass Club
944 W. Pine St.
Griffith, IN 46319
Annual dues: **$18**

International Carnival Glass Association
P.O. Box 306
Mentone, IN 46539
Web site: www.inernationalcarnivalglass.com
Annual dues: **$20**

Keystone Carnival Glass Club
719 W Brubaker Valley Road
Lititz, PA 17543
Annual dues: **$10**

L'Association du Verra Carnaval du Quebec
3250 rue Leon Brisbois
Ile Bizard, QC, H9C IT6 Canada
Annual dues: **$20 (Canadian)**

Lincoln-Land Carnival Glass Club
P.O. Box 320
Tremont, IL 61568
Web site: www.cgc.homestead.com
Annual dues: **$20**

National Cambridge Collectors, Inc.
P.O. Box 416
Cambridge, OH 43725
Web site: www.cambridgeglass.org.

National Duncan Glass Society
P.O. Box 965
Washington, PA 15301

National Imperial Glass Collectors
P.O. Box 534
Bellaire, OH 43906
Web site: www.imperialglass.com

New England Carnival Glass Club
P.O. Box 100
Limerick, ME 04048-0100
Web site: necga.com
Annual dues: **$15**

Northern California Carnival Glass Club
1205 Clifton Ave.
Modesto, CA 95355
Web site: home.pacbell.net/doris-qlevents.htm
Annual dues: **$10**

Pacific Northwest Carnival Glass Club
22424 94th Avenue South
Kent, WA 98031
Web site: carnival.ksnews.com/pacific/
Annual dues: **$15**

San Diego County Carnival Glass Club
9500 Harritt Road, #226
Lakeside, CA 92040-3544
Web site: aol.com/sdccgcc/sandiego.htm
Annual dues: **$18**

San Joaquin Carnival Glass Club
3906 E. Acacia Ave.
Fresno, CA 93726
Annual dues: **$5**

Southern California Carnival Glass Club
1430 Kendall Ave.
Camarillo, CA 93010-3606
Web site: geocities.com/sccgcl.
Annual dues: **$18**

Sunshine State Carnival Glass Association
9087 Baywood Park Drive
Seminole, FL 33777
Web site: www.carnivalglass.net/sscga
Annual dues: **$25**

Tampa Bay Carnival Glass Club
5501 101st Ave. N
Pinellas Park, FL 34666
Annual dues: **$7.50**

Texas Carnival Glass Club
P.O. Box 7332
Round Rock, TX 78683-7332
Web site: www.texascarnivalglass.com
Annual dues: **$20**

The Carnival Glass Society (UK)
P.O. Box 14
Hayes, Middlesex, England UB3 3NU
Annual dues: 15 pounds

www.cga
210 W Market St.
Hartford, NC 27844
Web site: www.cga.com
Annual dues: **$18**

Auctions

Much of the carnival glass collectors seek is sold through specialized carnival glass auctions. Some of these interesting auctions are held in conjunction with carnival glass collector club conventions, but are usually open to the general public as well. Do check often with local auctioneers for small carnival collections that they may offer from time to time.

Here is a list of auctioneers who have the largest specialized auctions. Those interested in learning more about carnival glass and the rainbow of colors that are so enchanting are encouraged to contact these auctioneers to obtain their catalogs or flyers, as well as visit their Web sites.

Ayers Auction Service
P.O. Box 320
Tremont, IL 61566-0520
(309) 925-3115
Web site: www.ayerauction.com

Burns Auction Service
P.O. Box 608
Bath, NY 14810
(607) 776-7932
Web site: www.tomburnsauction.com

Dotta Auction Company, Inc.
330 W Moorestown Rd.
Nazareth, PA 18064
(610) 759-7389
Web site: www.dottauction.com

Mickey Reichel Auction Company
18350 Hunters Ridge
Boonville, MO 65233
(660) 882-5292
Web site: www.awk-shn.com

Remmen Auctions & Appraisal Services
P.O. Box 301398
Portland, OH 97294
(503) 256-1226
Web site: www.remmenauction.com

Seeck Auctions
P.O. Box 377
Mason City, IA 50402
(641) 424-1116
Web site: www.seeckauction.com

Woody Auction Company
Douglas, KS 67039
(316) 747-2694
Web site: www.woodyauction.com

Jim Wroda Auction Services
5239 St. Rt. 49 South
Greenville, OH 45351
(937) 548-2640
Web site: www.jimwrodaauction.com